A Fan's Guide to
WORLD RUGBY

The essential rugby travel guide

ACKNOWLEDGEMENTS

Additional research by Bekah West and David Chapman. Thanks to Richard Prescott and Lucie Bonsey at the RFU, Nick Blofeld and Kate Oram at Bath Rugby, Duncan Wood at Gloucester Rugby, Dave Swanton and Lisa Robinson at Sale Sharks, Steve Hayes, Chris Paull and Laura Brown at London Wasps, Chris Wearmouth at Northampton Saints, Mark Evans and Sarah Butler at Harlequins, Paddy Lennon at London Irish, Mark Smith at Newcastle Falcons, Mike Hartwell at Saracens, Georgina Hughes and Gwydion Griffiths at Cardiff Blues, Phil James at Rodney Parade, Charlotte Moriaty at the Dragons, Barny Harper at the Ospreys, Gary Baker for Newport hostelry advice, Alex Luff at Millennium Stadium, Nerys Henry at the Scarlets, Peter Breen and Karen Murray at Leinster, Lyndsey Irvine and Christine McNally at Ulster Rugby, Roisin Walsh, Alison MacDonald and Roddy Guiney at Aviva Stadium, Claire Hickey at Thomond Park, Paolo Pacitti for help with Italian clubs, Matteo Pia at Aironi Rugby, Pete Simm and Andy Tremlett for Treviso, Andrea Gardina at Benetton Treviso, Alejandro Canale at Rovigo Rugby, Mike O'Reilly and Andrew Robson at the Scottish Rugby Union, Stuart Martin at Glasgow Warriors, Celine Hercelin at Stade de France, Stéphanie Lieppe and Simon Gillham at CA Brive, Aurelie Bernat and his team at Toulouse, Fanny Riere at USA Perpignan, Benjamin Larrue at Toulon, Lionel Rossigneux at Federation Francaise de Rugby, Alexandre Rosee at Olympique de Marseille, Marseille Tourism Office, Mark White at Western Force, Sarah Brown at nib Stadium, Kate Miller and Amelia Farrington at Subiaco Oval, Hannah Evans at ANZ Stadium, Brett Moore and Paris Jecklin at New South Wales Rugby Union, Paul Reid at Queensland Rugby Union, Wani Wall at the Melbourne Rebels, Jeff Dowsing at Melbourne Olympic Park, Jodie Fogarty at the Brumbies, Andy Colquhoun at South African Rugby Union, Susan Odendaal at Ellis Park, Michael Marnewick at the Sharks, Lindsey Rayner and Gavin Lewis at Western Province, Tracy-Lee Lombard at the Blue Bulls, Hugo Kemp at Loftus Versfeld, Walter Language at www.lionsweb.co.za, Ronel Pienaar at Free State Rugby Union, Frankie Deges for Argentina help, Sam Rossiter-Stead at the Hurricanes, Kate Shirtcliff at the Highlanders, Doug McSweeney at Otago Rugby Football Union, Mata on reception at Wellington Rugby, Ashley Sutton at the Chiefs, Tim Calder of Our Stadium, Dunedin, Marie Jones at Carisbrook Stadium Trust, Justine Jarden at Waikato Stadium, Steven Thompson and Annette Miller at Westpac Stadium, James Rigby at Eden Park, Robert Brooke at Auckland Rugby, Val Sisson at AMI Stadium, Alice Kerr, Kirsty Brown and Simon Carter at Vbase, Vilikesa Rinavuaka at the Fiji Rugby Union, Lúcás Ó'Ceallacháin for Georgia help, Hiroshi Gamo of the Japan Rugby Football Union, Topou Pone of Tonga Rugby Union, Sakkie Mouton at Namibia Rugby Union, Lawrence S. Acanufa Jr at Papua New Guinea Rugby Football Union Inc, Jarrod Beckstrom at USA Rugby, Joanita Colaco at Dubai Sevens, Paul Morgan at *Rugby World* and Stephen Jones of *The Sunday Times* for advice, Edwin Wollacott at the Marquis N16, for French translations, Steve Bale of *The Daily Express* for non-judgemental and typically meticulous proof-reading, Brendan Gallagher of *The Daily Telegraph* for remembering what happened in Toulouse, Funda Senturk for clearing up, Hugh Godwin of *The Independent on Sunday* for Clermont reminders.

PICTURE CREDITS

Cover and back cover: PA. Pg 8: PA. Pg 9: Wikipedia, Diliff. Pg 10: Wikipedia, Arpingstone. Pg 11: Stephen D Gibson. Sat Singh/www.sxc.hu (1), Atif Gulzar Miriam Kato (2), Paul Duffett/www.flamephotos.co.uk (3). Pg 12: Courtesy of club/union. Pg 13: Gartmor. Pg 14: Courtesy of club/union. Pg 15: Fat dad. Pg 16: jj glos. Pg 17: Courtesy of club/union. Pg 18: kassy humphreys (top), Dave Roberts3 (below), mcq73 (1), Revup67 (2), Green @pples (3). Pg 19: loadermw. Pg 20: Courtesy of club/union. Pg 21: Wikipedia, Patrick Khachfe. Pg 22: Courtesy of club/union. Pg 23: Swiv. Pg 24: Steve _C. Pg 25: Marc Bertrand/www.photos.parisinfo.com. Pg 26: traveldealstoparis.com. Pg 27: David Lefranc/Paris Tourist Board. bodaestilo.com (1), Amelie Dupont/Paris Tourist Board (2), Marc Bertrand/Paris Tourist Board (3). Pg 28: publichot.com. Pg 29: N@th. Pg 30: Wikipedia, Jddmano (top), inabjs (below), KnowYourOnions (1), pili_stage(2), BicheyreJean-Paul (3). Pg 31: Dominique Pipet. Pg 32: Agurno. Pg 33: rogerfv. Pg 34: Paul 'Tuna' Turner (top), neovain (below). 4F Cooking Home(1), *_* (2), Laurent Jégou (3). Pg 35: M+MD. Pg 36: lewishamdreamer, PheyZiJie82 (1), jean-louis zimmermann (2), paradisechamber.com (3). Pg 37: rugbyduo.blogspot.com. Pg 38: lambertwm (top), M.Angeles y Manuel (below), Adrien L. (Photographer) (1), Wikipedia, André Karwath aka (2), 803 (3). Pg 39: info-stades.fr. Pg 40: fat dad. Pg 41: flacombat. Pg 42: sliderdeo. Pg 43: Courtesy of club/union. Pg 44: OrliPix. Pg 45: Kelly Ry. NP1X (1), Jojinu (2), charlesdeland (3). Pg 46: Courtesy of club/union. Pg 47: TG4 *. Pg 48: Iker merodio (top), sjdunphy (below). Peter Visontay (1), boldorak2208 (2), TheContrays (3). Pg 49: 97 not out. Pg 50: travelbestphoto.com (top), Maciej Dakowicz (below). CupCaketheBold (1), Limerick racecourse (2), Jolphin (3). Pg 51: climberhunt (Dave Hunt). Pg 52: Gino Cianci/Foto-teca ENIT. Pg 53: Sander Klaver/www.sxc.hu. Pg 54: Victor Iglesias/ www.sxc.hu. Pg 55: Alex Fittipaldi/www.sxc.hu. Jim Goodrich/www.sxc.hu (1), Wojtec Kutyla/www.sxc.hu (2), Sorina Bindea/www.sxc.hu (3). Pg 56: Courtesy of

club/union. Pg 57: matteopinti. Pg 58: Riccardo Trianni. Pg 59: Gli Scudieri (Cavalieri Rugby Supporters). Pg 60: Armin Hanish/www.sxc.hu. Pg 61: iancowe. Pg 62: Kathy. Pg 63: Wikipedia, James Gillespie Graham. Mark Levin (1), Pierre Lesage (2), Harwood Photographic (3). Pg 64: Carol & Wayne. Pg 65: gartmor. Pg 66: _skynet (top), My Scotland (below). www.seeglasgow.com/ Glasgow City Marketing Bureau (1, 2, 3). Pg 67: Danny Lawson/PA Wire. Pg 68: Visit Britain. Pg 69: PhillipC. Pg 70: david.bank. Pg 71: VisitBritain. Andrew Hazard (1), Peter Morgan (2), Pete Birkenshaw (3). Pg 72: Wikipedia, TFDuesing / Thomas Duesing. Pg 73: gartmor. Pg 74: 1woodcutter@1 (top), fullflow.com (below). Frontlineblogger (1), Ace Apida (2), subcityphotos (3). Pg 75: Chris P Jobling. Pg 76: davebswansea. Pg 77: Welsh_Si. Pg 78: PA. Pg 79: shieldsaroundtheworld.com. Pg 80: zengomb.com. Pg 81: wliw21, torpesco (1), Stuck in Customs (2), quiquemen-dizabal (3). P82 taringa.net. Pg 83: taringa.net. Pg 84: ol' snappa. Pg 85: Hai Linh Truong. Pg 86: les.butcher (top), scottsavage.net (below), John489 (1), betta design (2), DigitalCHET (3). Pg 87: bartosik.org. Pg 88: lagartijotrav-elworld. Pg 89: martindb. Adam JWC (1), Winterdove (2), Nev Stokes (3). Pg 90: aus16. Pg 91: rosswebsdale. Pg 92: Endre Krossbakken. Pg 93: Brisbane marketing. www.thenormanbyhotel.com.au (1), Allan Henderson (2), M Maddo (3). Pg 94: swin5. Pg 95: 97 not out. Pg 96: Tourism Australia copyright. Pg 97: jon.tosa. Spearmint Rhino (1), Crown (2), Visual Density (3). Pg 98: J.C.K. Pg 99: Courtesy of club/union. Pg 100: Down Ampney Album. Pg 101: Vaughan James, Jeremiah Struppy (1), Stewart But-terfield (2), Pascal Subtil (3). Pg 102: xskyscrapercity.com. Pg 103: Chen and Becki. Pg 104: rugbymeansdiamond. blogspot.com. Pg 105: Andy Radka. Pg 106: Wikipedia, Philip Capper. Pg 107: Sefton Blinkhorne. Wikipedia (1), Khirol (2), Wikimedia (3). Pg 108: Dee Art. Pg 109: Dave Lintott/SPARC NZ. Pg 110: Wikipedia, Stephen Witherden (1), Mark Carter (3). Pg 112: Kim Christensen. Pg

113: adzuan aziz. Pg 114: Ralph Talmont. Pg 115: Kieran Scott. Claudio Gennari (1), Conor Ogle (2), Corey Leopold (3). Pg 116: Courtesy of club/union. Pg 117: SPARC NZ. Pg 118: Benjamin Earwicker. Pg 119: Antoine Hubert. Morgan (1), Phillipe Casablanca (2), Ville Miettinen (3). Pg 120: Darcy Schack, Imagine Photographics Limited. Pg 121: richseow. Pg 122: makenewzealandhome.com. Pg 123: Wikimedia 'Justaddlight'. Ricardo Carreon (1), Basil Black (2), Sara K (3). Pg 124: Wikipedia, Hamilton City Council. Pg 125: PA. Pg 126: Greatstock/SA Tourism. Pg 127: Irene. Pg 128: SA Tourism. Pg 129: James Lourens. Brian Snelson (1), William Warby (2), Alberto Botton (3). Pg 130: Wikipedia, legio09. Pg 131: closebtasmanie. Pg 132: slack12. Pg 133: Mark Skinner/SA Tourism, Gaz n Nic(1), Damien de Toit (2), Josep M Rosel (3). Pg 134: Dion Foster. Pg 135: D300@Hobbitsville. Pg 136: SA Tourism. Pg 137: Greatstock/SA Tourism. Kevin King (1), Greenacre (2), Javier Lastras (3). Pg 138: Greatstock/SA Tourism. Pg 139: noelmcmullen. Pg 140: Roger de la Harper/SA Tourism. Pg 141: Media Club. Charles Edwin Fripp (1), Vividy (2), David Berkowitz (3). Pg 142: YattaCat. Pg 143: PA. Pg 144: Chris Kirchhoff. Pg145: Graeme Williams, Collin J (1), Cradle of Humankind (2), Robin (3). Pg 146: Vark1. Pg 147: PA. Pg 148: world of jan. Pg 149: msdstefan. Pg 151: wallpapers.free-review.net. Pg152: Isaac Julien. Pg 153: Conor and Kellee Brennan. Pg 154: jiuguangw. Pg 155: msdstefan. Pg 156: lipjin. Pg 160: Courtesy of club/union.

A Fan's Guide to
WORLD RUGBY
The essential rugby travel guide

by **DANIEL FORD** and **ADAM HATHAWAY**

First published in 2011 by
New Holland Publishers (UK) Ltd
London • Cape Town • Sydney • Auckland
www.newhollandpublishers.com

Garfield House	80 McKenzie Street	Unit 1, 66 Gibbes Street,	218 Lake Road
86–88 Edgware Road	Cape Town 8001	Chatswood	Northcote
London W2 2EA	South Africa	NSW 2067	Auckland
United Kingdom		Australia	New Zealand

A catalogue record for this book is available from the British Library.

ISBN 978 1 84773 813 4
This book has been produced for New Holland Publishers by
Chase My Snail Ltd
www.chasemysnail.com
London • Cape Town

Project Manager: Daniel Ford
Art Director: Darren Exell
Photo Editor: Ana Lalinde
Publisher: Guy Hobbs
Production: Marion Storz

The author and publishers have made every ⟨...⟩ but they cannot accept liability for any
resulting injury or loss or dam⟨...⟩ and howsoever arising.

INTRODUCTION

Glenn Webbe, the former Wales wing, got it about right when he said 'When I die, I don't want to go to heaven, I want to go on tour'.

Anyone who has been on any sort of rugby trip – as a fan or a player for their third XV – knows exactly what Webbe meant. The rugby is great but it is not all about the rugby.

It is about going to different places, making friends for life, finding the barman who stays open late because he is a rugby fan and having banter with the opposition. It is about persuading the restaurant owner who normally shuts on Saturdays to open up on match day and it is about seeing things you wouldn't see on a normal run-of-the-mill holiday. But the best thing about rugby is that, like cricket, you get treated like a human being when you are abroad and you can happily mingle with other supporters.

Everyone has a top touring story. Personal favourites include missing the last Eurostar after the 2001 Heineken Cup final in Paris and staying with a colleague in the Gare du Nord in one of the most down-at-heel hotels you could ever (not) wish to find. When we asked what time breakfast was, the proprietor looked at us like we had just got off a spaceship.

Then there was chatting rugby with Dan Carter in a bar in Christchurch, and bumping into the legendary Wallaby fly-half Mark Ella in a pub in Townsville, Australia, called the Mad Cow, that was crammed with kilted Scotland fans. Seeing more than 28,000 people turn up for a match between Georgia and Uruguay in Sydney and trying to teach a bunch of French supporters how to play spoof in Marseille are other highlights.

That same night in Marseille, during the 2007 Rugby World Cup, thousands of French, Australian and English fans gathered in the city's old port to watch France beat the All Blacks on a giant screen. The Aussies had forgotten their quarter-final defeat to England earlier that day and everyone seemed to be behind the French. It was one of the best rugby nights ever. Talking of the All Blacks, I once had the cleaner in my hotel in Auckland lecture me for half an hour on what the make-up of the New Zealand back row should be. Everyone in New Zealand has an opinion on the game.

The Six Nations has always provided great weekends in Dublin, Rome, Edinburgh, Paris, Cardiff and London and since the mid-1990s the Heineken Cup and the Challenge Cup have offered the chance for fans to go to places that would never previously have been on their radar.

Hands up, before the European competitions started, how many people would have booked a weekend in Treviso, Perpignan, Newport or Limerick?

With Super Rugby now comprising 15 teams and Argentina at last being allowed to join the SANZAR countries in their annual tournament, there are even more opportunities for the touring brigade to enjoy new venues.

Add in summer tours, the autumn international trips made by South Africa, New Zealand, Australia and the South Sea Islands, massive Lions journeys, a vibrant Sevens circuit and World Cups and the travelling fan has never had it so good.

We hope this book helps you plan your trips all over the rugby globe.

Enjoy.

Adam Hathaway

Statistics correct to October 2010. The Heineken Cup was called the European Cup in 1999. Although Europe's second-tier club competition has had many names over the years it is always referred to here as the Challenge Cup. References to the Lions refer to the touring team variously known as the British Isles, the British Lions and the British & Irish Lions. If clarity is needed the Lions of Super Rugby have been referred to as Lions (South Africa).

CONTENTS

ENGLAND

THE 3 MINUTE GUIDE

Capital: *London.* **Language:** *English.* **Beers:** *Spitfire, Newcastle Brown Ale.* **Food:** *Pork pie, bangers (sausages) and mash, English breakfast (sausages, bacon, eggs, beans, mushrooms, toast and tea).* **National Anthem:** *God Save the Queen.* **Population:** *51 million.* **Time zone:** *GMT.* **Emergency number:** *999.* **Did you know?** *England is 74 times smaller than the USA.* **Rugby body:** *Rugby Football Union, Rugby House, Rugby Road, Twickenham, Middlesex TW1 1DZ. Tel: +44 208 892 2000. Web: www.rfu.com*

Below: Jonny Wilkinson will always be remembered as the man whose drop goal won the World Cup.

The power in the north

England's World Cup winners of 2003 were the epitome of a professional sporting outfit but it was very different when the Rugby Football Union was formed in 1871 at the Pall Mall Restaurant in London. Twenty-two clubs were to have been present but the Wasps representative went to the wrong hostelry and his club missed the boat. Since then English rugby has gone through the 1895 split (which led to the rise of rugby league), club v country rows, Will Carling's '57 old farts' jibe (referring to the union's big wigs), a player strike and reached three World Cup finals, winning one.

The game was invented in England with the first rules laid down at Rugby School in the 1840s – although the legend that pupil William Webb Ellis 'picked up the ball and ran' has never been completely confirmed by historians.

England has the biggest playing base in the world, with over 2.1 million registered players in 2010 according to the International Rugby Board, but its fortunes have fluctuated.

Coach Clive Woodward soon left after the 2003 World Cup win, slamming the RFU for not supporting him, and the national side sank. After Andy Robinson's dismal tenure, Brian Ashton did get them to the 2007 World Cup final, where, captained by Phil Vickery, they lost to South Africa, and to second place in the Six Nations. His reward was to be sacked and replaced by former captain Martin Johnson who quickly realized managing was harder than playing.

Domestically the game flourishes with attendances at an all-time peak and five Heineken Cup wins in the 2000s.

Above: *London, the heart of the country that invented the game of rugby.*

TEST RECORD (capped internationals only)

Versus	First Test	Played	Won	Lost	Drawn
Argentina	May 1991	15	10	4	1
Australia	Jan 1909	39	15	23	1
France	Mar 1906	93	50	36	7
Ireland	Feb 1875	123	70	45	8
Italy	Oct 1991	16	16	0	0
New Zealand	Dec 1905	33	6	26	1
Scotland	Mar 1871	127	67	42	18
South Africa	Dec 1906	31	12	18	1
Wales	Feb 1881	119	54	53	12

Most international caps: Jason Leonard (1990–2004) 114 Tests
Most international points: Jonny Wilkinson (1998–) 1,111 points, 80 Tests, (6t, 149c, 228p, 33d)
Most international tries: Rory Underwood (1984–1996) 49 tries, 85 Tests

WORLD CUP RECORD

Year	Venue	Finished
1987	Australia & NZ	Quarter-finals
1991	England	Runners-up
1995	South Africa	Semi-finals
1999	Wales	Quarter-finals
2003	Australia	Winners
2007	France	Runners-up

Most World Cup appearances: Jason Leonard, 22 matches (1991, 1995, 1999, 2003)
Most World Cup points: Jonny Wilkinson, 249 points, 15 matches (1999, 2003, 2007)
Most World Cup tries: Rory Underwood, 11 tries, 15 matches (1987, 1991, 1995)
Record World Cup win: 111-13 v Uruguay, Brisbane, 2003
World Cup coaches: 1987: Martin Green; 1991: Geoff Cooke; 1995: Jack Rowell; 1999: Clive Woodward; 2003: Clive Woodward; 2007: Brian Ashton

LONDON

Above: Around 600 people work at City Hall, home of the Mayor of London and the London Assembly. The glass globe is built at an incline of 31 degrees.

Choices, choices

With more tourist books on London than other cities have attractions, if you struggle for something to do while you are here then you are probably walking about with your eyes closed.

Pubs? On every street corner. History? Buckingham Palace, the Houses of Parliament, the whole city. Theatre? Head to the West End for some of the world's best shows. Museums to match any city's, clubs, fashion, royalty, parks and sport, this is a city that can offer it all. You want a chat with a Londoner? Get in a taxi. Drivers are paid to take you where you are going and give you their views on everything from politics to the national obsession, the weather.

For a bit of sun (yes, it does come out sometimes) head to one of London's famous Royal Parks such as Hyde Park, Regent's Park, St James's Park or Greenwich Park. These and other green areas have an important part to play in the city and in the summer in particular this is where Londoners blossom.

Watch for the famous moment when the sun appears for the first time of the year and people start shedding clothes to get a bit of colour.

People have lived along this part of the River Thames, where London is situated, for thousands of years, and today more than 7.5 million people call it home. Famously the city grew as a collection of villages that simply merged together, which is why you will find pockets of neighbourhood life like other great old cities such as New York and Paris.

The national stadium, Twickenham, is about 18 km (11 miles) southwest of the city centre, as is Twickenham Stoop, home of Harlequins. Some 32 km (20 miles) northwest is Vicarage Road Stadium in Watford, home to Saracens, while Wembley, also used for big matches, is 15 km (9 miles) in the same direction. Reading's Madejski Stadium, where London Irish play, is 66 km (41 miles) west of London. The 2012 Olympic Stadium is to the east.

3 THINGS YOU MUST DO...

1 WEMBLEY STADIUM

The new 90,000 seater Wembley Stadium (No 1 Olympic Way, Wembley, tel: +44 844 800 2755) is England's football home. When: tours daily 09.30–16.30. Price: adults £15, children £8. To get there: tube to Wembley Park Station or Wembley Central, or rail to Wembley Stadium or Wembley Central.

2 INDIAN FOOD

Hot, spicy, mild, expensive, cheap, smart, down-at-heel – the country's favourite food comes in all guises, with over 2,000 Indian restaurants in the city. Try Brick Lane, which has a concentration of them that will astound. To get there: tube to Aldgate East.

3 GREYHOUND RACING

Not as glorious as it was in its heyday, but dog racing is still a great night out. Wimbledon Greyhound Stadium (Plough Lane, tel: +44 870 840 8905). When: Tues, Fri, Sat, racing from 19.30. Price: adults £5, child 12–17 £2.50. To get there: rail to Haydons Road or tube to Wimbledon or Tooting Broadway.

Above: Big Ben, the capital's iconic clock, first ticked into action on 31 May 1859. Bong!

Weather	Low (°C)	High (°C)	Rain (mm)	Sunset
January	2	6	54	16.02
February	3	7	40	16.50
March	3	9	37	17.39
April	6	13	37	19.33
May	8	17	48	20.22
June	12	20	45	21.08
July	15	23	57	21.21
August	13	21	60	20.50
September	11	20	49	19.47
October	9	14	57	18.39
November	5	10	64	16.33
December	4	7	48	15.55

TWICKENHAM

Home of English rugby

When RFU committee member Billy Williams was charged with finding a permanent home for English rugby he would not have forecast that 3.6 hectares (8.9 acres) of market garden in southwest London, bought for £5,572, 12s and 6d, would become one of the greatest sporting venues around.

Twickenham staged its first England international in 1910, in front of King George V, when the hosts beat Wales 11-6 with Fred Chapman scoring the first Test try at Twickenham.

The recently renovated ground features a hotel and health club in the new South Stand plus 26 bars. The Council Room, for RFU officials, the ERIC, for former players, and the President's Suite are plush areas behind the scenes that most of the Twickenham crowd will never get to see.

The Scrum Bar, at the northeast corner of the ground, is the biggest bar at any sporting venue in Britain and stretches for 47.5 metres (156 feet), with 96 pumps and 44 very busy staff, although many fans simply picnic in the car parks before games.

Twickenham was the venue for the 1991 Rugby World Cup final, stages rock concerts and hosts an annual Jehovah's Witnesses convention.

Below: Twickenham first hosted an international in 1910. It has since staged over 250 Test matches.

MATTER OF FACT
Stadium: Twickenham Stadium
Located: London, England
Address: Twickenham Stadium, Rugby Road, Twickenham TW1 1DZ
Tel: +44 870 222 2120 (reception), +44 208 831 6733 (Rugby Store)
Email: stadiumqueries@therfu.com
Website: www.rfu.com/TwickenhamStadium
Capacity: 82,000
To get there: 10-minute walk from Twickenham Station (train) or bus 267/281/H22 or free shuttle from Richmond (match days)
Stands: West, North, South, East

Stadium tours
Open: Tues–Sat 10.30, 12.00, 13.30, 15.00, Sun 13.00, 15.00; closed Mon. £14 adults, £8 concessions, £40 family ticket. Museum only £6 adults, £4 concessions (open Tues–Sat 10.00–17.00); Sundays 11.00–17.00; public holidays 10.00–17.00.
Tel: +44 208 892 8877
Email: museum@rfu.com

First match: Harlequins 14 Richmond 10, 1909
First Test: England 11 Wales 6, 1910
Tests hosted: 259
England record: P 257, W 163, L 71, D 23

Bars in ground: Scrum, Line Out, Ruck and Maul, West Car Park
Bars nearby: The Orange Tree (45 Kew Road, Richmond TW9 2SA, +44 208 894 0944, www.orangetreerichmond.co.uk); **The Bear** (26–28 York Street, Twickenham TW1 3LJ, +44 208 843 7281, www.thebeartwickenham.co.uk); **The Albany** (1 Queens Road, Twickenham TW1 4EZ, +44 208 891 1777, www.thealbanyintwickenham.co.uk); **The Barmy Arms**, Riverside, Twickenham TW1 3DU, +44 208 892 0863

Finally . . . Prince Alexander Obolensky, an exiled Russian, who scored two tries against the All Blacks in 1936, then died during World War II at 24, is one of 100 players whose careers are commemorated by blue plaques at Twickenham. Others include Martin Johnson, Cliff Morgan, Jonah Lomu and Mark Ella.

HARLEQUINS

They Stoop to conquer

Founded in 1866, Harlequins have a history as colourful as their quartered shirts which have attracted sneers from opposing fans for more than 140 years. Widely derided as city slickers, during the amateur era many of their players worked in London's financial district.

But Quins were given a dose of reality when they were relegated from the Premiership in 2005. Enter Dean Richards, the former Leicester coach and Lions legend, who refused to renege on his deal to join the club even though they had been demoted. Richards insisted his players stood their round at the bar in their season in National Division One at places such as Sedgley Park, Doncaster and Otley and rid the club of at least some of the snobby reputation.

Quins lost just once in 26 games that season, were duly promoted, and by the end of the 2007–08 season they had qualified for the following campaign's Heineken Cup where they reached the quarter-finals. Then the fun began as the club were embroiled in the 'Bloodgate' saga during the last-eight match against Leinster. Richards lost his job over the fake injuries, was banned from the sport for three years and the guts were temporarily ripped out of the club.

Off the field Harlequins are as well-run a rugby club as you could visit. For starters they play home games on a Saturday – the only of the four so-called 'London' sides to do so – and the redevelopment of their ground, the Twickenham Stoop, has turned it into an extremely spectator-friendly venue. The ground is named after Adrian Stoop, reputedly the father of modern back-play, who won 15 caps for England before serving as president of the club. It stands in the shadows of Twickenham and was the venue for the 2010 Women's Rugby World Cup final when New Zealand beat England 13-10 in front of 13,252 supporters. It is also home to the Harlequins rugby league side.

Below: Mike Brown (with ball) and Danny Care both won England caps under boss Dean Richards at Harlequins.

MATTER OF FACT
Club: Harlequins
Formed: 1866
Located: London, England
Administrative address: Twickenham Stoop Stadium, Langhorn Drive, Twickenham TW2 7SX
Tel: +44 208 410 6000 (main),
+44 871 527 1315 (tickets)
Email: info@quins.co.uk
Website: www.quins.co.uk
Honours: Domestic Cup 1988, 1991
Euro honours: Challenge Cup 2001, 2004

Heineken Cup records
Best finish: Quarter-finals 1998, 1999, 2009
Record: P 49, W 15, L 31, D 3
Most appearances: 24 Ceri Jones (2005–)
Most points: 91 Thierry Lacroix (1997–2000)
Biggest win: 45-7 v Bourgoin, 1997
Biggest defeat: 13-58 v Castres Olympique, 2005

Ground: Twickenham Stoop Stadium
Address: Langhorn Drive, Twickenham TW2 7SX
Capacity: 14,282
To get there: 10-minute walk from Twickenham station (train) or bus 267/281/H22
Stands: Etihad, LV, North, South

Bars in ground: East Stand Bar, Quins Head, Etihad, Kings, Players'
Bars nearby: The Scrummery (105 Whitton Road TW1 1BZ, +44 208 892 9797); **The Cabbage Patch** (67 London Road TW1 3SZ, +44 208 892 3874 www. cabbagepatch.co.uk); **The Up 'n' Under** (33 York Street, +44 208 9034); **The William Webb Ellis** (24 London Road TW1 3RR, +44 208 744 4300, www. jdwetherspoon.co.uk)

Legends
Wavell Wakefield: He played 136 games for Quins as a flanker and was also MP for Swindon. Alternatively known as the 1st Baron of Kendal, he won 31 England caps before becoming president of the RFU.
Jason Leonard: 'The Fun Bus', who propped 114 times for England, could play on both sides of the scrum and went on three Lions tours. A feared opponent in the scrum and in the bar after the match where he espoused the old-fashioned values of the game.

Need to know: Diamond Geezers are the Harlequins fans who you will see at games wearing faintly ridiculous diamond patterned trousers. Usually found in the East Stand Bar before, during and after games.

SARACENS

Men in black

Nigel Wray has pumped millions of pounds into Saracens since taking the reins in 1995 and was entitled to expect more than one domestic trophy in his first 15 years at the helm. Galacticos such as François Pienaar, Michael Lynagh, Philippe Sella and Thomas Castaignède all graced the unlikely surroundings of Vicarage Road without Wray getting much return on his investment.

Ironically, Saracens reached the Premiership final in 2010 only after they had reined in their habit of signing massive international names. Brendan Venter became the latest big-name director of rugby in 2009 – Wayne Shelford, Alan Gaffney and Pienaar had preceded him – but the South African succeeded where the others failed and moulded a team with genuine title aspirations. He also succeeded in rubbing up the RFU the wrong way, and he missed his side's appearance in the Premiership final because of a suspension after a fracas at Leicester.

Saracens started their ground-sharing agreement with Watford FC at the start of the 1997–98 season, a campaign which saw them narrowly miss out on the Premiership title but win the Domestic Cup.

Vicarage Road has looked like a building site for several years and is no place for a top rugby club to be playing. Saracens have successfully staged games at Wembley, including one against South Africa in 2009 when a fan, Stuart Tinner, won £250,000 (€275,000) in a half-time kicking competition. In the 2010–11 season they hosted Leinster at Wembley in the Heineken Cup and a Boxing Day match against Wasps.

In November 2010 Saracens unveiled plans to move to Barnet Copthall Stadium, an athletics venue they hoped to double in capacity to 12,000. There was even talk of an artificial surface.

Below: Vicarage Road became the home of Saracens in the 1997-98 season.

MATTER OF FACT
Club: Saracens
Formed: 1876
Located: Watford, England (ground), St Albans, England (office)
Administrative address: Unit 3, Kingsley House, Sandridge Park, Porters Wood, St Albans, AL3 6PH
Tel: +44 1727 792800
Email: feedback@saracens.net
Website: www.saracens.com
Honours: Domestic Cup 1998
Euro honours: None

Heineken Cup records
Best finish: Semi-finals 2008
Record: P 26, W 17, L 9, D 0
Most appearances: 24 Kevin Sorrell (1996–2010)
Most points: 193 Glen Jackson (2004–2010)
Biggest win: 71-7 v Viadana, 2007
Biggest defeat: 43-13 v Biarritz, 2006

Ground: Vicarage Road Stadium
Address: Watford, Hertfordshire WD18 0EP
Capacity: 18,214
To get there: 15-minute walk from Watford Junction Station (train), 10-minute walk from Watford High Street Station (train), 10-minute walk from Watford Station (tube)
Stands: Rookery, Rover South, Rous, Main

Bars in ground: V Bar, Members'
Bars nearby: The Flag (Station Road, Watford WD17 1ET, +44 1923 218413); **Odd Fellows** (14 Fearnley Street, Watford WD18 0RD, +44 1923 225766); **Moon Under Water** (44 High Street, Watford WD17 2BS, +44 1923 223559, www.jdwetherspoon.co.uk); **Bar Bodega** (151 The Parade, Watford WD17 1NA, +44 1923 229651, www.barbodega.co.uk)

Legends
Michael Lynagh: Australian 1991 World Cup-winning fly-half joined Sarries in 1996 and attracted other big names to the club. Steered Saracens to a 48-18 win over Wasps in the 1998 domestic Cup final – his last competitive game of rugby.
Richard Hill: One-club man, dubbed 'the Silent Assassin', and best back rower produced by England. The only player never dropped by Clive Woodward, he was central to England's domination up to, and during, the 2003 World Cup.

Need to know: The 'Fez Heads' are Saracens fans who wear hats normally associated with Tommy Cooper.

WASPS

Sting in the tail

Wasps were formed in a pub, the Eton and Middlesex Tavern in north London, in 1867 but when they were invited to become founder members of the RFU, who were meeting in the Pall Mall Restaurant, in 1871, their representative, according to which version you believe, turned up at the wrong pub, on the wrong day, and at the wrong time…

It has gone a bit better since as Wasps, along with Leicester, dominated the English rugby scene in the decade from 2000, and did their bit on the European front by winning the Heineken Cup twice, the first thanks to Rob Howley's last-ditch try against Toulouse in 2004, the second when they outsmarted, of all teams, Leicester in the final thanks to the tactical insight of then-coach Ian McGeechan.

Lawrence Dallaglio was a constant presence in their successes from the start of professionalism until his retirement in 2008 and he inspired youngsters such as Tom Rees, James Haskell and Danny Cipriani as they made their way through the Wasps ranks and into the white shirt of England. Former rugby league star Shaun Edwards who joined as a coach in 2001 has also been a mammoth figure in the club's history.

Wasps play matches at Adams Park, home of Wycombe Wanderers FC, and were previously tenants of QPR FC in west London although their spiritual home is Sudbury. Adams Park is set in an industrial estate in High Wycombe and is an unlikely venue for a team that has conquered Europe and are officially called 'London' Wasps. Their training base is a very basic facility in Acton, west London, where Edwards conducts his famous tough defence sessions.

Below: Phil Vickery won the Heineken Cup in 2007 with the club but was forced to retire in October 2010.

MATTER OF FACT
Club: London Wasps
Formed. 1867
Located: High Wycombe, England
Administrative address: Adams Park, Hillbottom Road, High Wycombe HP12 4HJ
Tel: +44 1494 472100
Email: contact via website
Website: www.wasps.co.uk
Honours: English champions 1990, 1997, 2003, 2004, 2005, 2008; Domestic Cup 1999, 2000, 2006
Euro honours: Heineken Cup 2004, 2007, Challenge Cup 2003

Heineken Cup records
Best finish: Winners 2004, 2007
Record: P 72, W 47, L 24, D 1
Most appearances: 58 Simon Shaw (1997–)
Most points: 294 Alex King (1996–2007)
Biggest win: 71-5 v Benetton Treviso, 2006
Biggest defeat: 31-0 v Stade Français, 2002

Ground: Adams Park
Address: Hillbottom Road, High Wycombe HP12 4HJ
Capacity: 10,516
To get there: High Wycombe Station (train) then free match day shuttle bus
Stands: Bucks New University, Dreams, Family, Frank Adams, Greene King IPA

Bars in ground: Match Day, Scores, Vere Suite, Woodlands Suite
Bars nearby: The Bootlegger (3 Amersham Hill, High Wycombe HP 13 6NQ, +44 1494 525457, www.thebootleggerpub.co.uk); **The Hour Glass** (144 Chapel Lane, High Wycombe HP12 4BY, +44 1494 511125); **O'Neill's** (Pauls Row, High Wycombe HP11 2HQ, +44 1494 532499, www.oneills.co.uk/oneillshighwycombe)

Legends
Lawrence Dallaglio: Held Wasps together when Rob Andrew and co defected to Newcastle, leading them to their first professional title in 1997. Was part of England's 'Holy Trinity' back row with Neil Back and Richard Hill.
Richard Sharp: Enrolled as a Wasp when five weeks old as his father and uncle played for the club in the 1920s. Talented fly-half who won 14 England caps.

Need to know: Loyal Neville Compton was a member of the unbeaten Wasps team in 1930–31 (points scored 530 points, conceded 76). He then served as fixture secretary and president.

LONDON IRISH

Having the craic

Another club with London in their name who play outside the capital, London Irish share the Madejski Stadium with Reading FC and now have many fewer Irish players in their squad than was historically the case. However the club still trades on its Irish heritage and the annual St Patrick's Day match, usually a Premiership fixture, packs out the ground.

Formed in 1898, Irish were the third London side for young exiles after London Scottish and London Welsh and played at The Avenue, Sunbury, until switching to the Madejski in 2000 after a season at the Stoop, sharing with Harlequins. Sunbury is still used as a training ground, is the home of the London Irish amateur team and is regarded as the spiritual heart of the club.

Clive Woodward helped the club stay viable on the pitch at the start of professionalism, Dick Best – another England coach – was there for three seasons and Brendan Venter, recruited by Best as a player had a powerful influence on the pitch and as director of rugby. World Cup-winner Venter led Irish to their first silverware when they beat Northampton 38-7 in the final of the Powergen Cup at Twickenham in 2002. Toby Booth, appointed head coach in 2008, then took the Exiles to the Premiership final in his first season in charge where they were beaten by a single point by Leicester.

Spectators at the Madejski are entertained, or irritated, depending on your point of view, by drummers and a man with a microphone who constantly screams 'Come on you Oirish!' Irish have made a real effort to attract fans to the out-of-town ground, with shuttle buses running from Reading Station as well as pre- and post-match entertainment and they have been rewarded with reasonable attendances.

Below: London Irish have been encouraged to spread the ball by boss Toby Booth. Chris Malone follows orders.

MATTER OF FACT
Club: London Irish
Formed: 1898
Located: Reading, England
Administrative address: The Avenue, Sunbury-on-Thames, Middlesex TW16 5EQ
Tel: +44 1932 750 100
Email: info@london-irish.com
Website: www.london-irish.com
Honours: Domestic Cup 2002
Euro honours: None

Heineken Cup records
Best finish: Semi-finals 2008
Record: P 26, W 13, L 12, D 1
Most appearances: 39 Justin Bishop (1994–2007)
Most points: 268 Barry Everitt (2000–2007)
Biggest win: 78-3 v Rugby Rovigo, 2008
Biggest defeat: 32-6 v Bordeaux-Begles, 1996

Ground: Madejski Stadium
Address: Junction 11, M4, Reading RG2 0FL
Capacity: 24,250
To get there: Reading Station (train) then match day shuttle bus
Stands: North, South, East, West

Bars in ground: Not named
Bars nearby: (These bars are near the station as there is nothing near the ground). **Three Guineas** (Station Approach, Reading, RG1 1LY, +44 1189 572743, www.three-guineas.co.uk); **Yates's**, (The Former Post Office, Friar Street, Reading RG1 1DB, +44 118 959 7090, www.weareyates.co.uk); **Pitcher & Piano** (18 Friar Street, Reading, RG1 1DB, +44 118 958 8964, www.pitcherandpiano.com)

Legends
Conor O'Shea: Full-back for London Irish for five years before injury struck in 2000. With 35 Ireland caps he went on to become director of rugby and managing director at Irish before joining the RFU, then the English Institute of Sport and Harlequins in 2010.
Justin Bishop: Long-serving winger who scored 58 tries in 279 appearances for Irish up to 2007. Won 25 Irish caps and went on to work at the London Irish academy helping the likes of Delon Armitage and Topsy Ojo develop into international players.

Need to know: With pubs in short supply around the ground the best place for a post-match beer if you don't fancy going straight into town is at the post-match party 'The Craic in the Valley' in the North Stand.

NORTHAMPTON

Saints go marching in

Opponents of relegation must have been choking on their beers when Northampton, European Champions in 2000, were demoted to National League One in 2007 but like Harlequins before them they emerged stronger after a year in the muck and nettles of lower league rugby. Coming straight back up after 30 straight wins, under a new management team of Jim Mallinder and Dorian West, they won the Challenge Cup in 2009 and the LV= Cup in 2010 while finishing second in the Premiership regular season table. In that summer three young Northampton players, Ben Foden, Courtney Lawes and Chris Ashton, helped England to only their third win over Australia on Wallaby soil.

Northampton is a rugby town, and Franklin's Gardens is a rugby stadium and a lesson to other Premiership teams who act as second-class tenants to lower-grade football clubs. Although a modern stadium, it is in danger of outgrowing its capacity which reached a shade over 13,500 when the new South Stand (now Burrda) was opened in 2005. At the beginning of 2010 owner Keith Barwell said the club would have to consider moving if plans to increase capacity to over 17,000, financed by sale of some of their land to a supermarket chain, were blocked by the local council.

A short stroll from Northampton, past a couple of decent pubs (there is a cracking fish and chip shop opposite), Franklin's Gardens has just about everything a fan needs on match days. For the players it is reckoned to be one of the best playing surfaces in the country, thanks to the efforts of groundsman and former England prop David 'Piggy' Powell.

Below: '*They Tackled the Job'. This bronze statue was a gift to supporters from owner Keith Barwell and family.*

MATTER OF FACT
Club: Northampton Saints
Formed: 1880
Located: Northampton, England
Administrative address: Franklin's Gardens, Weedon Road, Northampton NN5 5BG
Tel: +44 1604 751543
Email: ticketoffice@northamptonsaints.co.uk
Website: www.northamptonsaints.co.uk
Honours: Domestic Cup 2010
Euro honours: Heineken Cup 2000, Challenge Cup 2009

Heineken Cup records
Best finish: Winners 2000
Record: P 56, W 33, L 23, D 0
Most appearances: 46 Ben Cohen (1996–2007)
Most points: 272 Paul Grayson (1997–2005)
Biggest win: 68-21 v Overmach Parma, 2006
Biggest defeat: 50-17 v Montferrand, 2001

Ground: Franklin's Gardens
Address: Weedon Road, Northampton NN5 5BG
Capacity: 13,591
To get there: 15-minute walk, or number 22 bus, from Northampton Station (train)
Stands: Tetley's, Church's, Burrda, Sturtridge Pavilion

Bars in ground: Crooked Hooker, Rodber Suite
Bars nearby: Thomas A Beckett (52 St James Road, Northampton NN5 5HY, +44 1604 751177, www.mcmanuspub.co.uk); **Foundryman Arms** (135 St James Rd, Northampton NN5 5LE, +44 1604 751830, www.mcmanuspub.co.uk); **The Rover** (157 Weedon Road, St. James's End, Northampton NN5 5BS, +44 1604 751664); **St James WMC** (2 Weedon Road, Northampton NN5 5BE, +44 1604 751686)

Legends
Dickie Jeeps: Saints scrum-half who was capped for the 1955 Lions in South Africa before making his England debut. Captained England 13 times in 24 internationals before becoming president of the RFU and chairman of the Sports Council.
Tim Rodber: Army captain who played back or second row for Saints and England. The hard man was a huge figure in the Lions 1997 win in South Africa.

Need to know: The Saints have been playing at Franklin's Gardens since 1880. It was named after John Franklin, who bought the site in the 1886 and owned the hotel which is now the club's administration offices and superstore. The area was formerly a pleasure garden that included a zoo and a lake.

BATH

Where the Romans roamed

The Romans loved Bath and today thousands of visitors love it too. The town was established 2,000 years ago as the civilization spread its reach and those missing the warmer climes of southern Europe were no doubt delighted to discover the hot natural springs – the only ones which occur naturally in the country. In later years a temple was built and the bathing complex developed.

Today the historic city, with a population of just over 80,000, continues to be an attraction for people from all over the world. The baths themselves are the central attraction, of course, but there is also the impressive Bath Abbey, a Gothic structure from the 16th century, the Royal Crescent, a sweeping semi-circular of houses which was finished in 1744, as well as a good range of parks, museums and tours.

For those looking for a beer after all the culture, the small size of the town means it is easy enough to find a decent pub by simply strolling around, although the area around George Street and Broad Street has a good collection for those looking to save on shoe leather.

Above: Music in Bath Abbey. Below: Lazy down the Avon River.

Weather	Low (°C)	High (°C)	Rain (mm)	Sunset
January	1	7	70	16.12
February	2	8	55	16.59
March	3	10	56	17.50
April	5	13	47	19.42
May	8	17	48	20.33
June	11	20	57	21.16
July	13	22	48	21.29
August	12	21	56	20.56
September	10	19	64	19.56
October	9	14	67	18.48
November	4	11	65	16.42
December	3	9	83	16.05

3 THINGS YOU MUST DO...

1 ROMAN BATHS MUSEUM
Everything you need to know about the water of the city (Abbey Church Yard, tel: +44 1225 477 785). When: Nov–Feb 09.30–16.30, Mar–Jun, Sept–Oct 09.00–17.00, Jul–Aug 09.00–21.00. Price: from £11.25 adult, £10 concessions, £7.50 child six-16. To get there: a short walk from the bus station.

2 LADY LENA BOAT TRIP
Enjoy a trip down the river in an electric launch that was built in 1890 (Tel: +44 1225 834 250) with champagne and lunch if required. Trips take from two hours upwards. Price: private charter of the boat from £200–£400.

3 THE RAVEN PUB
The city's pub of the year in 2010 according to CAMRA (6-7 Queen Street, tel: +44 1225 425 045) is a traditional pub specializing in real ales and pies. When: Mon–Thur 11.30–23.00, Fri–Sat 11.30–midnight, Sun midday–22.30.

BATH

Out of the Rec age

The city has long been a stronghold of English rugby but its golden period was during the 1980s and 1990s culminating in the Heineken Cup triumph of 1998. That win was masterminded by Andy Robinson but Jack Rowell, who went on to coach England, as Robinson would eventually do, presided over their best period in the domestic game. Rowell's time in charge, from 1978 to 1994, realized eight domestic cups and five league championships but, with players such as Jerry Guscott, Richard Hill, Stuart Barnes and John Hall in the squad, he was entitled to expect a few trophies. Brian Ashton is another former Bath head coach to go on to the England job after a distinguished career at 'the Rec'.

The Rec, in the centre of Bath, on the banks of the River Avon, has been the subject of speculation in recent years. A team of Bath's stature need a better and bigger ground, but plans for movement and expansion were unclear to the start of the 2010–11 season. Encouraging for the supporters was the sale of the club, by Andrew Brownsword, to Bruce Craig, a West Country-born multi-millionaire in April 2010. Craig, a pharmaceutical tycoon and decent scrum-half who played for Racing Metro in Paris, announced the creation of a new training complex at Farleigh House and a commitment to a 20,000-plus stadium. It was a relief after 2009, a season that saw five Bath players sacked for drug offences.

The Rec remains an anachronism in the professional era, with its ramshackle press box and temporary stands but it is a hive of activity on match days. The ground is surrounded by pubs that get packed on match days, while the clubhouse bar is a decent place for a few pints and a pie before the game.

Below: The blue, white and black hoops of Bath were England's first Heineken Cup winners in 1998.

MATTER OF FACT
Club. Bath Rugby
Formed: 1865
Located: Bath, England
Administrative address: Farleigh House, Farleigh Hungerford, Bath BA2 7RW
Tel: +44 1225 325 200
Email: info@bathrugby.com
Website: www.bathrugby.com

Heineken Cup records
Best finish: Winners 1998
Record: P 60, W 39, L 20, D 1
Most appearances: 31 Steve Borthwick (1998–2008)
Most points: 216 Jon Callard (1989–1999)
Biggest Cup win: 56-15 v Petrarca Rugby, 1999
Biggest defeat: 31-9 v Munster, 2000
Stands: IPL, Wadworth 6X

Ground: The Recreation Ground
Address: The Recreation Ground, Spring Gardens, Bath BA2 6PW
Capacity: 12,300
To get there: 10-minute walk from Bath Spa station (train)
Honours: English champions 1989, 1991, 1992, 1993, 1994, 1996, Domestic Cup 1984, 1985, 1986, 1987, 1989, 1990, 1992, 1994, 1995, 1996
Euro honours: Heineken Cup 1998, Challenge Cup 2008

Bars in ground: Clubhouse, IPL, Blackthorn Rig, Bath Rugby Rig, Heineken
Bars nearby: Coeur de Lion (17 Northumberland Place, Bath BA1 5AR, +44 1225 463 568, www.coeur-de-lion.co.uk); **The Huntsman** (1 Terrace Walk, North Parade, Bath BA1 1LY, +44 1225 482900, www.marstonstaverns.co.uk); **The Boater** (9 Argyle Street, Bath BA2 4BQ, +44 1225 464211)

Legends
Jerry Guscott: Three-time Lion, known as 'Prince of Centres', was pivotal figure in the 1989 triumph in Australia and his dropped goal clinched the 1997 series in South Africa. Scored over 700 points for Bath.
Roger Spurrell: Uncapped ex-paratrooper revered by locals as hard-man flanker and captain of first cup-winning side in 1984. Owned a local nightclub known as 'Bog Island' (a former public toilet) and employed Jerry Guscott and Gareth Chilcott as doormen.

Need to know: Since 1921 whenever Bath has played Llanelli the winner of the contest gains possession of a rag doll which is hung on the crossbar before play.

GLOUCESTER

Heroes of the Shed

Kingsholm may lie in the shadows of Gloucester Cathedral but the ground is one of the most raucous in England with fanatical fans, particularly in the stand known as The Shed, letting opposition players know exactly what they think of them. A real rugby ground, as opposed to some of the soccer grounds used by certain teams in the Premiership, Kingsholm is surrounded by pubs, chip shops and an excellent café, Mangoes, directly opposite to line the stomach pre-match.

The club have not quite delivered the silverware their supporters demand since the advent of professionalism. In the Premiership they finished top of the table in the regular season in 2003, 2007 and 2008 only to be denied the trophy in the play-offs by a system that claims that winning a couple of extra games at the end of the campaign is more important than the nine-month slog.

Gloucester have a fierce rivalry with Bath so those failures to land trophies stuck in the throat of their fans frustrated by their rival's successes of the 1980s and early 1990s. Gloucester have had their fair share of talented backs over the years – with James Simpson-Daniel and Anthony Allen among the more recent vintages – but the locals love their forwards. Hard men such as Mike Teague, Phil Blakeway, Phil Vickery, Trevor Woodman and Olivier Azam are the real heroes of The Shed Heads and the crowd like nothing more than cheering on a dominant scrum from the 'Cherry and Whites'. If you visit Kingsholm you will see a proper rugby town and have a proper rugby day out fit for anyone who knows the game.

Below: Welcome to Castle Grim. The name given to Gloucester's stadium comes from the estate it was built on.

MATTER OF FACT
Club: Gloucester Rugby
Formed: 1873
Located: Gloucester, England
Administrative address: Kingsholm Stadium, Kingsholm Road, Kingsholm, Gloucester GL1 3AX
Tel: +44 871 871 8781 (switchboard), +44 1452 302187 (office)
Email: admin@gloucesterrugby.co.uk
Website: www.gloucesterrugby.co.uk
Honours: English champions 2002, Domestic Cup 1972, 1978, 1982, 2003
Euro honours: Challenge Cup winners 2006

Heineken Cup records
Best finish: Semi-finals 2001
Record: P 52, W 32, L 19, D 1
Most appearances: 38 Peter Buxton (2000–)
Most points: 181 Henry Paul (2002–2005)
Biggest win: 80-28 v Viadana, 2002
Biggest defeat: 34-3 v Wasps, 2004

Ground: Kingsholm Stadium
Address: Kingsholm Road, Kingsholm, Gloucester GL1 3AX
Capacity: 16,500
To get there: Gloucester Station (train) 10-minute walk
Stands: The Shed, C&G, JS Facilities, West Terrace

Bars in ground: Shogun Bar, Lion's Den
Bars nearby: Teague's (48 Kingsholm Road, Gloucester GL1 3BH, +44 1452 421733); **Coach and Horses** (2–4 St Catherine Street, Gloucester GL1 2BX, +44 1452 416015); **Kingsholm Inn** (8 Kingsholm Square, Gloucester GL1 3AT, +44 1452 530 222); **Dean's Walk Inn** (Deans Walk, Gloucester GL1 2PX, +44 1452 415 762)

Legends:
Mike Teague: The real 'Iron Mike' – forget Tyson – was a legendary back rower who starred for the Lions on the 1989 tour to Australia. A former builder who is talked of in hushed tones at Kingsholm, he went on to own a pub opposite the ground.
Mike Burton: Hard-man prop who became first player sent off for England in a Test when he was dismissed in Brisbane in 1975. Became a successful businessman specializing in rugby hospitality and tours.

Need to know: Kingsholm is known as Castle Grim after the estate on which the ground was built. The club bought the estate for £4,000 in 1891. Some locals maintain the name is also a reference to the effect the stadium has on visiting teams.

LEICESTER

Tigers earn their stripes

L oved by their fans, hated but respected by everyone else, Leicester are the Manchester United of English rugby with their bulging trophy cabinet and long list of legendary players. With the likes of Martin Johnson, Austin Healey, Neil Back and Martin Corry, Leicester won two European Cups at the start of the 2000s with the 2001 final, a 34-30 win over Stade Français in Paris, considered one of the finest club matches ever played.

Chalkie White, who took over as coach in 1968, is credited with revolutionizing the club and membership grew before they reached their first cup final in 1978. They lost to Gloucester in the-then John Player Cup but three decades of almost constant finals and trophies followed. The Johnson-Dean Richards, captain-coach combination, yielded huge success but Leicester, who had seven players in England's World Cup-winning squad in 2003, unsurprisingly slipped down the table in their absence. That led to the acrimonious sacking of Richards and by the time they reached the EDF Energy Cup final in 2007, they had not won a trophy for five years. Success over the Ospreys galvanized them and they added successive Premiership titles in 2009 and 2010.

The Tigers' lair is Welford Road Stadium, a short walk out of the town centre which is a shrine to their past achievements with bars, stands and lounges commemorating old players. It is also the highest capacity club ground in the country used primarily for rugby after recent redevelopments.

The Caterpillar Stand, opened at the start of 2009–10 season, is a 10,000 seater award-winning structure that took the capacity of the stadium to 24,000. It houses the Final Whistle Bar, a popular meeting place before and after matches. Leicester run tours of the stadium for groups of 10 or more.

Below: Martin Johnson (left) and Graham Rowntree. Johnson made over 300 appearances for the Tigers.

MATTER OF FACT

Club: Leicester Tigers
Formed: 1880
Located: Leicester, England
Administrative address: Aylestone Road, Leicester LE2 7TR
Tel: +44 844 856 1880
Email: tigers@tigers.co.uk (enquiries), tickets@tigers.co.uk (tickets), conferenceandevents@tigers.co.uk (tours)
Website: www.leicestertigers.com
Honours: English champions 1988, 1995, 1999, 2000, 2001, 2002, 2007, 2009, 2010, Domestic Cup 1979, 1980, 1981, 1993, 1997, 2007
Euro honours: Heineken Cup 2001, 2002

Heineken Cup records
Best finish: Winners 2001, 2002
Record: P 97, W 65, L 29, D 3
Most appearances: 69 Martin Corry (1997–2009)
Most points: 406 Andy Goode (1998–2008)
Biggest win: 90-19 v Glasgow, 1997
Biggest defeat: 33-0 v Ulster, 2004

Ground: Welford Road Stadium
Address: Aylestone Road, Leicester LE2 7TR
Capacity: 24,000
To get there: 10-minute walk from Leicester Station (train) along Waterloo Way and Tigers Way
Stands: Caterpillar, Goldsmiths, H&B Crumbie, Clubhouse

Bars in ground: Captains', Tiger, Droglites, ABC, Lions, Final Whistle
Bars nearby: The Counting House (40 Almond Road, Leicester, Leicestershire LE2 7LH, +44 1162 755527); **The Polar Bear** (44 Oxford Street, Leicester LE1 5XW, +44 116 254 1164); **The Barley Mow** (149 Granby Street, Leicester LE1 6FE, +44 116 254 4663, www.everards.co.uk)

Legends
Martin Johnson: Possibly England's greatest player. A lock who captained Tigers to two Heineken Cups and England to the World Cup in 2003. Two-time Lions captain, Johnson went on to manage England.
Dean Richards: Legendary number eight who was in charge of Leicester when they won two Heineken Cups and four consecutive English Premierships.

Need to know: The ABC Bar in the Crumbie Stand is named after the Leicester front row of Graham Rowntree, Richard Cockerill and Darren Garforth who played when the Tigers wore letters not numbers on their shirts. Open to the public on match days, it also serves a mean curry.

SALE

Sharks bite

Promoted to the top flight in 1994, Sale were barely pulling 1,000 fans a game when professionalism arrived but their move from Heywood Road to Edgeley Park, the home of Stockport County FC, in 2003 has seen a reasonable increase in attendances. In a soccer-mad area, they play most home games on a Friday night and the attractions of watching the likes of Jason Robinson, Charlie Hodgson and Mark Cueto kept up local interest. By 1999 however, Sale were in serious trouble. Then in stepped Brian Kennedy, a millionaire businessman, who recruited Peter Deakin from Warrington Wolves rugby league team as chief executive to promote the club.

Under the guidance of Jim Mallinder – a former Sale player himself – they won the European Challenge Cup in 2002 and 2005. Then in 2006 they took the Premiership by beating perennial champions Leicester 45-20 in the final, by which time the legendary Frenchman Philippe Saint-André was director of rugby. That should have been the signal for the club to kick on but it never quite materialized and they flirted with relegation in 2010. That should not however detract from Sale's achievement in luring some outstanding overseas talent – such as Graeme Bond, Luke McAlister, Sebastien Chabal and the Fernandez Lobbe brothers, Ignacio and Juan Martin – to the outskirts of Manchester. Sale have also produced their fair share of home-grown stars like Hodgson, Cueto, Chris Jones and Steve Hanley, who all represented England.

For a side with aspirations towards the top of the English game however, Edgeley Park is not up to scratch compared with stadia such as Welford Road and Franklin's Gardens and a ground share with the Salford rugby league outfit was mooted at one point.

Below: An aerial view of Edgeley Park and surrounds.

MATTER OF FACT
Club: Sale Sharks
Formed: 1861
Located: Stockport, England
Administrative address: Edgeley Park, Hardcastle Road, Stockport, Cheshire SK3 9DD
Tel: +44 161 286 8915
Email: dave.swanton@salesharks.com
Website: www.salesharks.com
Honours: English champions 2006
Euro honours: Challenge Cup 2002, 2005

Heineken Cup records
Best finish: Quarter-finals 2006
Record: P 37, W 17, L 20, D 0
Most appearances: 32 Chris Jones (2001–)
Most points: 245 Charlie Hodgson (2000–)
Biggest win: 67-11 v Calvisano, 2006
Biggest defeat: 43-15 v Bourgoin, 2003

Ground: Edgeley Park
Address: Hardcastle Road, Stockport, Cheshire SK3 9DD
Capacity: 10,641
To get there: Stockport Station (train) 10-minute walk
Stands: MBNA, Printerland, Vernon, Railway End

Bars in ground: Shark Tank Marquee Bar
Bars nearby: Sir Robert Peel (83 Castle Street, Stockport SK3 9AR, +44 161 477 3424); **Armoury Inn** (31 Shaw Heath, Stockport SK3 83D, +44 161 477 3711); **The Jolly Crofter** (15 Castle Street, Stockport SK3 9AB, +44 161 476 1308); **Ye Olde Vic** (1 Chatham Street, Stockport SK3 9ED, +44 161 480 2410, www. yeoldevic.com)

Legends
Jason Robinson: Rugby league legend who turned to union and won a World Cup with England in 2003, scoring their only try in the final against Australia. Known as Billy Whizz he had an unsuccessful stint coaching at Sale and played for Fylde aged 36.
Fran Cotton: Stalwart prop who could play both sides of the scrum and was a star on the 1974 Lions tour of South Africa. Won a Grand Slam with England in 1980, managed the 1997 Lions and became a multi-millionaire through his clothing business.

Need to know: There are more than a dozen pubs within staggering distance of Edgeley Park – most serving good northern ales. If you can't find one around here that takes your fancy you might as well give up.

NEWCASTLE

Falcons' nest

When property tycoon Sir John Hall bought the-then Newcastle Gosforth, and soon to be Falcons, on 5 September 1995, in the first year of overt professionalism, the ripples spread right through the English game. Hall persuaded Rob Andrew, then of Wasps, to revitalize the club, as director of rugby and player, on an unheard salary of £150,000 (€165,000) especially for a side languishing in Division Two. Dean Ryan, Nick Popplewell and the legendary Va'aiga Tuigamala followed Andrew from Wasps, while he also attracted, among others, Tony Underwood, Tim Stimpson and Alan Tait. Andrew was in the last throes of his playing career but they did not need to sign a new fly-half as they had an adolescent one, and he went by the name of Jonny Wilkinson. Wonder what happened to him? By 1998, with Wilkinson and Andrew in partnership in midfield, they had won the Premiership.

But the expected domestic dominance did not materialize and bar a couple of cup wins the Newcastle trophy cabinet has hardly been overflowing. Hall gave way to Dave Thompson in 1999 and rugby in the North East, despite the presence of Wilkinson until his move to France in 2009, remains a hard sell. Home matches are mostly staged on Friday nights and Sunday afternoons to prevent a clash with the city's soccer side.

For those who do turn up, Kingston Park is a decent enough ground. For pre-match beers many travelling fans concentrate on the pubs around Newcastle Station before heading to the stadium on the metro. Once there they can enjoy the Hiding Place bar at the ground, which also serves good pub food, shows all the sport and is open every day of the week so you can have a pint even if there is no rugby on.

Below: The Falcons take on London Irish at Kingston Park.

MATTER OF FACT
Club: Newcastle Falcons
Formed: 1877
Located: Newcastle, England
Administrative address: Kingston Park, Brunton Road, Kenton Bank Foot, Newcastle-upon-Tyne NE13 8AF
Tel: +44 191 214 5588
Email: info@newcastle-falcons.co.uk
Website: www.newcastle-falcons.co.uk
Honours: English champions 1998, Domestic Cup 1976, 1977, 2001, 2004
Euro honours: None

Heineken Cup records
Best finish: Quarter-finals 2005
Record: P 13, W 6, L 7, D 0
Most appearances: 13 Michael Stephenson (2001–2005)
Most points: 80 Jonny Wilkinson (1997–2009)
Biggest win: 42-9 v Toulouse, 2001
Biggest defeat: 48-8 v Stade Français, 2005

Ground: Kingston Park
Address: Brunton Road, Kenton Bank Foot, Newcastle-upon-Tyne NE13 8AF
Capacity: 10,200
To get there: Kingston Park Station, Bank Foot Station (Metro), five-minute walk
Stands: North, West, East, John Smith's

Bars in ground: The Hiding Place, West Stand, South Stand
Bars nearby: Twin Farms (22 Main Road, Kenton Bank Foot, Newcastle-upon-Tyne, NE13 8AB, +44 191 2861263, www.sjf.co.uk). **Near Newcastle station: The Centurion** (Newcastle Central Station, Neville Street, Newcastle-upon-Tyne, +44 191 261 6611, www.centurion-newcastle.com); **The Dog & Parrot** (52 Clayton Street West, Newcastle-upon-Tyne NE1 4EX, +44 191 261 6998)

Legends
Va'aiga Tuigamala: Huge Samoan known as 'Inga the Winger' joined Newcastle from Wasps in a £1 million (€1.1 million) deal after successful rugby league career. Crucial part of title-winning side in 1998.
Dean Ryan: Former soldier regarded as one of the hardest back rowers around. Part of the Rob Andrew revolution and captained the side to the Premiership title in 1998. Capped four times by England.

Need to know: Gosforth, the original name of the club, can be traced back to 1877. Players like Roger Uttley, Peter Dixon and Malcolm Young all wore green and white as Newcastle didn't wear black and white until 1996.

FRANCE

Capital: *Paris.* **Language:** *French.* **Currency:** *Euro.* **Beers:** *Kronenbourg 1664, Desperados (tequila flavoured).* **Food:** *Baguettes, truffles, foie gras (fattened duck or goose liver), cassoulet (bean stew with meat), cheese (with wine).* **National Anthem:** *La Marseillaise (The Song of Marseille).* **Population:** *65 million.* **Time zone:** *GMT +1.* **Emergency numbers:** *Police 17, medical 15/18, fire 18.* **Did you know?** *The bikini was invented by French designers Jacques Heim and Louis Réard. Fine idea boys.* **Rugby body:** *Fédération Française de Rugby, 3-5 Rue Jean de Montaigu, Marcoussis, 91460, France. Tel: +33 1 5321 1515. Web: www.ffr.fr*

Below: The iconic French forward Sebastien Chabal (pictured here playing for Sale).

Brilliant but brutal

If you haven't been to an international in Paris or Marseille, or a European club tie in Toulouse, Castres, Brive, Biarritz or Perpignan it is a box you must tick. French fans, especially in the south, are fanatical and treat players with the same reverence the rest of the world reserves for soccer stars. William Webb Ellis is even buried in Menton, Provence.

In England rugby is considered, wrongly, the game of the upper classes – in France it is considered the game of the farmers and the labourers and is encapsulated by the phrase '*l'esprit de clocher*' (the spirit of the bell tower), meaning any man born within hearing distance of the bells must defend the honour of the town.

The English introduced rugby to France in the 1870s. By 1906 they were playing internationals and were admitted to the Five Nations tournament in 1910, although they did not win the title outright until 1959. Since then they have consistently been among the top nations in Europe, supplying glorious players such as Jean-Pierre Rives, Serge Blanco, the Boniface brothers and the magnificent prop Robert Paparemborde, known as the 'Bear of the Pyrenees'.

Former England hooker Brian Moore hit the nail on the head when he described the French team of 1995 as '15 Eric Cantonas, brilliant but brutal'. They are hard but they can play as well.

The Grand Slam in 2010, under Marc Lièveremont, was the ninth by the French national side and they have reached two World Cup finals, in 1987 and 1999.

Above: When it comes to cuisine, nobody does it better than the French.

TEST RECORD (capped internationals only)

Versus	First Test	Played	Won	Lost	Drawn
Argentina	Aug 1949	43	31	11	1
Australia	Jan 1928	40	16	22	2
England	Mar 1906	93	36	50	7
Ireland	Mar 1909	86	52	31	5
Italy	Oct 1937	31	30	1	0
New Zealand	Jan 1906	49	12	36	1
Scotland	Jan 1910	83	46	34	3
South Africa	Jan 1913	38	11	21	6
Wales	Mar 1908	87	41	43	3

Most international caps: Fabien Pelous (1995–2007) 118 Tests
Most international points: Christophe Lamaison (1996–2001) 380 points, 37 Tests (2t, 59c, 78p, 6d)
Most international tries: Serge Blanco (1980–1991) 38 tries, 93 Tests

WORLD CUP RECORD

Year	Venue	Finished
1987	Australia and NZ	Runners-up
1991	England	Quarter-finals
1995	South Africa	Semi-finals
1999	Wales	Runners-up
2003	Australia	Semi-finals
2007	France	Semi-finals

Most World Cup appearances: Raphael Ibanez, 18 matches (1999, 2003, 2007)
Most World Cup points: Thierry Lacroix, 124 points, 9 matches (1991, 1995)
Most World Cup tries: Christophe Dominici, 8 tries, 15 matches (1999, 2003, 2007)
Record World Cup win: 87-10 v Namibia, Toulouse, 2007
World Cup coaches: 1987: Jacques Fouroux; 1991: Daniel Dubroca; 1995 Pierre Berbizier; 1999: Jean-Claude Skréla; 2003: Bernard Laporte; 2007: Bernard Laporte

PARIS

Above: *Notre Dame de Paris (Our Lady of Paris), scene of Victor Hugo's famous novel 1831 novel* The Hunchback of Notre Dame. *The largest bell weighs 13 tonnes.*

For the love of food and romance

As soon as you arrive in Paris for the first time you naturally crane your neck to see the famous Eiffel Tower. Keep your eyes looking towards the west part of the central area and you'll see it peeping through soon enough, even if it's not so huge that it dominates the skyline by its size alone.

Not too far away is the historic Arc de Triomphe looking down along the famous boulevard, the Champs-Elysées. Like other major world cities such as London and New York, it's impossible to wander around Paris without stumbling across film-set-favourite landmarks.

There are two big reasons to come to Paris: romance and food. Which one costs you more is up to you, but combine the two to the maximum and it'll cost you a fortune. French food, is of course, renowned and if you disappear to the nearest international fast-food joint you are missing a major part of this city (not to mention upsetting the romance part).

Even a mid-range restaurant, or a cheaper one tucked away down a side street, if you can get advice from someone with local knowledge, will give you a taste of what all the fuss is about, whether or not it's truffles and caviar on your plate. Whatever happens you certainly won't have a problem finding a decent glass of wine or Champagne to wash down whatever you do choose. The French certainly know how to eat well and a meal out in Paris is an experience you should savour, never rush.

The international Stade de France is about 9 km (5.5 miles) north of city centre, while Stade Jean-Bouin, home to the city's club Stade Français, is 8 km (5 miles) southwest by the Boulevard Périphérique, the freeway that rings the city centre.

3 THINGS YOU MUST DO...

1 MOULIN ROUGE

Legendary cabaret club (82 boulevard de Clichy, tel: +33 1 5309 8282), which opened in 1889. When: lunch and show from 13.00. Dinner and show from 19.00. Price: dinner and show from €150. To get there: métro white (line 2).

2 KNICKERS

Girls treat yourself, and boys get them for your girlfriend. The French do women's underwear better than anyone. Try Alice Cadolle (4 Rue Cambon, tel: +33 1 4260 2807). To get there: subway M1 to Tuileries.

3 LOUVRE

If you love art, head for the Louvre (99 Rue de Rivoli, tel: +33 1 4020 5050) for one of the world's most celebrated collections. When: Mon, Thur, Sat, Sun 09.00–18.00, Wed, Fri 09.00–21.45. Price: €9 for full day entry to permanent collections. To get there: subway M1 or M7 to Palais Royal – Musée du Louvre.

Above: The area around the Eiffel Tower attracts tourists with cameras and locals with fun on their minds.

Weather	Low (°C)	High (°C)	Rain (mm)	Sunset
January	2	7	54	17.04
February	3	8	44	17.48
March	5	12	49	18.34
April	7	15	53	20.21
May	11	19	65	21.06
June	13	23	55	21.46
July	16	25	63	21.58
August	15	25	43	21.29
September	13	21	55	20.33
October	9	16	60	19.30
November	5	10	52	17.31
December	4	8	59	16.57

STADE DE FRANCE

Rugby's flying saucer

Resembling a flying saucer and found 9 km (5.5 miles) north of Paris in Saint-Denis, Stade de France was built for football's 1998 World Cup, staging the final which France won. In 2007 it hosted the Rugby World Cup final, with South Africa beating England 15-6. It is renowned as one of the best grounds in the world.

With its space-age appearance, it is the fifth largest stadium in Europe, holding nearly 82,000 people, although it lacks the bear-pit atmosphere of Parc des Princes where the French national team played most of their matches in Paris from the mid-1970s until 1997.

The distance fans are from the action on the pitch – the stadium was also the venue for the 2003 World Athletics Championship – probably does not help in this respect. (The stadium has a movable stand that is shifted to uncover part of the athletics track). The Stade de France hosted the 2010 Heineken Cup final, when Toulouse edged out Biarritz 21-19, it hosts the French annual Championship final and has staged occasional Stade Français regular season home games where dancing girls and reduced price tickets see mammoth crowds flock to the matches.

There are some established bars around the ground, mostly to the north, and many temporary ones as you walk up from the stations but many fans prefer to drink at Gare du Nord in bars such as the popular Le Falstaff and then make the short 10-minute train journey to the match.

There are plenty of big chain hotels in the area for spectators who fancy staying close to the ground, handy if the match is one of the regular night-time kick-offs.

Below: Stade de France has staged the biggest games in rugby union and football.

MATTER OF FACT

Stadium: Stade de France
Located: Paris, France
Address: Rue Henri Delaunay, 93200 Saint-Denis, Paris
Tel: +33 892 700 900 (info line)
or +33 1 55 93 00 00
Email: Via website
Website: www.stadefrance.com
Capacity: 81,338
To get there: Saint-Denis – Porte de Paris Station (métro), Stade de France-Saint-Denis or La Plaine-Stade de France Stations (RER)
Stands: Sud, Nord, Ouest, Est

Stadium tours
Open: Hourly from 10.00–18.00, tours in English 10.30 and 14.30, daily apart from event days; €12 adults, €8 concessions and under 12s, free under sixes, €32 family ticket, groups of 10 get one ticket free
Tel: +33 892 700 900

First match: France 24 England 17, 1998
First Test: France 24 England 17, 1998
Tests hosted: 53
France record: P 48, W 32, L 15, D 1

Bars in ground: Not named
Bars nearby: Au Pavillon (54 Rue Gabriel Péri, 93200 Saint-Denis, +33 1 48 09 49 25); **Paddy Wacks** (4 boulevard Anatole France, +33 1 42 43 10 74; **Le Maryland** (34 Rue Gabriel Péri, 93200 Saint-Denis, +33 1 48 20 22 55); **Au Soleil D'Or** (10 Rue de la Boulangerie, 93200 Saint-Denis, +33 1 48 20 17 97)

Finally . . . Stade de France is not the only attraction in Saint-Denis. All but three of the Kings of France are buried at the Basilica of Saint-Denis about a kilometre to the north of the ground. It is open from 10.00–18.15 in the summer (17.00 winter).

STADE FRANÇAIS

Pretty in pink

Love them or hate them, you can't ignore them. With the most colourful owner in France, and certainly the most colourful shirts, lurid pink garments never seen on a rugby pitch before, and a talent for self-promotion Stade Français attract both admiration and derision. The latter mostly from their rivals based in the south of France. They have a particularly intense rivalry with Biarritz and games between the two often turn into undignified fist fights.

The club were languishing in the lower divisions of French rugby when media mogul Max Guazzini took over in 1992 and immediately stamped his personality on the club. Within five years they were back in the top division and reeled off five titles between 1998 and 2007 as well as reaching two Heineken Cup finals with the brilliant Argentine place kicker, Diego Dominguez – who played internationally for Italy – contributing the majority of the points with his boot until he retired in 2004.

Stade Jean-Bouin is a 12,000-capacity stadium set in the shadows of Parc des Princes and close to Roland Garros, home of the French Open tennis and in 2010 underwent renovation with the club playing matches at Stade Charléty. Guazzini knows how to put on a show and regularly hires Stade de France for some home games, turning them into 80,000 strong extravaganzas more akin to something out of Moulin Rouge. Stade have also played at Parc des Princes and even entertained Ulster at King Baudouin Stadium in Brussels in December 2009. Guazzini's promotional skills extended to production of a calendar featuring semi-naked Stade players protecting their modesty with rugby balls that had them struggling to contain their laughter down south.

Below: Stade Français fans party in pink. Madonna and Naomi Campbell, both club godmothers, would approve.

MATTER OF FACT
Club: Stade Français Paris
Formed: 1883
Located: Paris, France
Administrative address: 2 Rue du Commandant Guilbaud, 75016 Paris
Tel: +33 892 46 75 75
Email: webmaster@stade.fr or via website
Website: www.stade.fr
Honours: French champions 13 times, French Cup 1999
Euro honours: None

Heineken Cup records
Best finish: Runners-up 2001, 2005
Record: P 79, W 52, L 26, D 1
Most appearances: 64 Sylvain Marconnet (1997–)
Most points: 581 Diego Dominguez (1997–2004)
Biggest win: 92-7 v L'Aquila, 2000
Biggest defeat: 42-16 v Toulouse, 2010

Ground: Stade Jean-Bouin
Address: 26 avenue du Général Sarrail, 75016 Paris
Capacity: 12,000
To get there: Métro Porte d'Auteil (Ligne 10) or Métro Porte de Saint-Cloud (Ligne 9)
Stands: Tribune Presidentielle, Virage Paris, Virage Pelouse, Tribune Parc des Princes

Bars in ground: Not named
Bars nearby: Bignon (71 Boulevard Exelmans, 75016 Paris, +33 9 71 50 19 60); **Les Deux Stades** (41 avenue du Général Sarrail, 75016 Paris, +33 1 47 43 12 35); **Le Padock** (53 Rue du Général Delestraint, 75016 Paris, +33 1 40 50 71 30); **Le Cardinal** (5 place de la Porte de Saint-Cloud, 75016 Paris, +33 1 45 27 38 63, www.lecardinalparis.com)

Legends
Christophe Dominici: Toulouse-born winger who played for Stade from 1997 to 2008. Won 65 French caps, starring in their defeat of New Zealand in the 1999 World Cup. Joined Stade coaching staff.
Sylvain Marconnet: Joined Stade in 1997 from Grenoble and became France's most capped prop when he made his 69th international appearance in the 2007 Six Nations. Bizarre skiing accident kept him out of 2007 World Cup. You don't get that in Gloucester.

Need to know: Stade adopted Gloria Gaynor's 'I Will Survive' before the national football team used it at the 1998 World Cup. Max Guazzini's contacts book has also seen Madonna and Naomi Campbell attend games. Both were appointed official 'godmothers' of the club.

MARSEILLE

City on the edge

Known as the 'city without name' during the French Revolution because of its support of Girondin Federalism, Marseille is the second most populated city in France and one of the most exciting. Marseille has a reputation for crime and violence so use your common sense but this is a great place for a rugby weekend.

While Paris is all chic and elegance, Marseille is its scruffy cousin, slightly down at heel with an edge other French cities don't possess. The Mediterranean climate helps as well and as a port, the varied mix of cultures, accents and ethnicities in the area make for a heady mix.

Home to Gene Hackman's detective, Popeye Doyle from the French Connection films, Marseille is also the birthplace of two of France's most talented and controversial footballers – Zinedine Zidane and Eric Cantona.

At night most of the action centres around the bars, restaurants and nightclubs of the Old Port (or Le Vieux Port). Fishing boats fill the harbour, not the super yachts you see elsewhere in France, and clubs are open all night and rocking. During the day you can wander around the port, see the old Town Hall (Hotel de Ville), Roman Docks Museum and the Garden of Ruins.

Above and below: It may be dubbed 'the city with no name', but Marseille is certainly not lacking in beauty.

Weather	Low (°C)	High (°C)	Rain (mm)	Sunset
January	3	11	53	17.14
February	4	13	44	17.50
March	6	15	40	18.28
April	9	18	58	20.05
May	13	22	41	20.40
June	16	26	25	21.12
July	19	30	12	21.23
August	19	29	31	21.01
September	16	25	61	20.14
October	12	20	85	19.20
November	7	15	50	17.31
December	4	12	52	17.04

3 THINGS YOU MUST DO...

1 BOUILLABAISSE

Bouillabaisse is a traditional soup of the region with local bony fish, shellfish, vegetables, spices such as saffron, fennel and orange peel. Served with *rouille* (spicy garlic sauce). Restaurants have different recipes for bouillabaisse and bicker among themselves about who has the most authentic dish.

2 LE CHATEAU D'IF

A short boat ride from the Vieux Port, this fortress was later a prison and was one of the scenes in Alexander Dumas' novel, *The Count of Monte Cristo*. The dangerous currents made it virtually impossible to escape from. When: daily Jan–Mar, Oct–Dec 09.30–17.30, Apr–Sept 09.30–18.30. Price: €4.

3 LE QUARTIER DU PANIER

In the heart of the old city follow the red marks on the floor and you will find the Maison Diamantee, la Place des Moulins, la Vielle Charite centre, which includes the Museum of Mediterranean Archaeology and the Museum of African, Oceanic and Amerindian Arts and the two major cathedrals.

STADE VÉLODROME

Le Vélodrome

Opened in 1937, the home of Olympique de Marseille FC, Stade Vélodrome is one of the most atmospheric grounds in the world when the French rugby team are in town. It was something of a fortress for Les Bleus, who beat New Zealand, England, South Africa and Australia on the ground before surprisingly losing to Argentina here in 2004.

Owned by Marseille City Council, the stadium was used in the 1938 and 1998 football World Cups and staged games at the 2007 Rugby World Cup, including England's quarter-final win over Australia. RC Toulonnais have also staged matches at the stadium and were beaten in the Challenge Cup final here by Cardiff in 2010.

As its name suggests, the arena has been used for cycling and its bowl-like structure gives a bear-pit atmosphere, especially at night matches with the bars opposite the ground always packed before matches. After games most of the action is found in the bars and restaurants of Le Vieux Port, a short hop away on the métro.

A redevelopment of the stadium, costing €150 million, was part of the French bid to host football's 2016 European Championship with the capacity planned to rise to 80,000.

Leave plenty of time to find your seats at the stadium as the directions and seat numbering are certainly not the clearest if you are not a French speaker. However, once inside and seated the atmosphere is one of the best you will find in world rugby. Marseille generally gets to see the French team once a year, in the autumn internationals, and the locals make the most of it when Les Bleus turn up.

MATTER OF FACT
Stadium: Stade Vélodrome
Located: Marseille, France
Address: 3 Boulevard Michelet, 13008 Marseille
Tel: +33 4 91 13 89 03 (Tourist Board)
Email: info@marseille-tourisme.com (Tourist Board)
Website: www.om.net (stadium info on football club's site) or marseille-tourisme.com (Tourist Board)
Capacity: 60,031
To get there: Rond-Point du Prado (métro, line 2), 200 metres from stadium
Stands: Virage Nord De Peretti, Virage Sud Chevalier Rose, Tribune Jean Bouin, Tribune Ganay

Stadium tours
(Operated by Marseille tourist board)
Open: Any day apart from match day and the day after.
Price: €106 for a group of 20 or less. €6 per person for more than 20
Tel: +33 4 91 13 89 03;
email: info@marseille-tourisme.com

First match: France XV 27 Italy 0, 1949
First Test: France 44 New Zealand 33, 2000
Tests hosted: 15
France record: P 10, W 8, L 2, D 0

Bars in ground: Not named
Bars nearby: Bar des Sports (164 Avenue de Mazargues, 13008 Marseille, +33 4 91 23 33 13); **Bar de l'Arret** (185 Avenue de Mazargues, 13008 Marseille, +33 4 91 77 83 00); **Shamrock of Marseille** (17 Quai de Rive Neuve, 13007 Marseille, + 33 4 91 33 11 01, www.shamrockofmarseille.fr); **Pub O'Malley** (9 Quai de Rive Neuve, 13001 Marseille, +33 4 91 33 65 50)

Finally . . . Gustave Ganay, who has a stand named after him at Stade Vélodrome and is also commemorated by a statue at the ground, was a Marseille-born cyclist who died in a race in Paris in 1926, aged 34. An electrician by trade he was reckoned to be one of the top cyclists of the 1920s and is buried in Marseille's Cemetery of St Peter.

Below: Stade Vélodrome's bowl-like design creates a fierce atmosphere come match day.

BRIVE

Seeing it black and white

The black and whites of Brive carried all before them in Europe in 1997 when they put on one of the best performances ever seen in the competition by destroying Leicester – with Martin Johnson and co in the side – 28-9 in the Heineken Cup final, in Cardiff. That win, with a side containing players such as Alain Penaud, Sebastien Carrat and Sebastien Viars has never been equalled although they did reach the final in 1998, only to go down by a single point to Bath in Bordeaux.

Brive's success in Europe was not mirrored domestically. Second Division champions in 1957, they reached four French cup finals up to 1996 without winning one and were relegated in 2000. They returned to the Top 14 in 2003 but did not seriously threaten for the French title for the rest of the decade.

CA Brive play at the Stade Amédée Domenech, a 15,000 capacity multi-purpose stadium that hosted one match in the 1991 Rugby World Cup and is due for renovation in 2011.

The club are pro-active in encouraging the many English-speaking residents of the Limousin area to attend matches and have recruited several high-profile England players. World Cup-winning hooker Steve Thompson, Ben Cohen, Jamie Noon, Riki Flutey, Andy Goode and Shaun Perry have all played for the club. This recruitment was bankrolled by a free-spending owner, Daniel Derichebourg, but the club was bought by a consortium known as Brive Rugby SAS, headed by pharmaceutical businessman Jean-Jacques Bertrand, in 2009. This, and the continued presence of foreign stars had little effect on the pitch as Brive lost all six of their Heineken Cup pool matches the following season.

Below: *Brive powered their way to Heineken Cup success in 1997.*

MATTER OF FACT
Club: CA Brive
Formed: 1913
Located: Brive, France
Administrative address: 116, Avenue du 11 Novembre, BP 181-19100 Brive-la-Gaillarde
Tel: +33 5 55 74 20 14
Email: contact@cabrive-rugby.com
Website: www.cabrive-rugby.com
Honours: French Cup 1996
Euro honours: Heineken Cup winners 1997

Heineken Cup records
Best finish: Winners 1997
Record: P 23, W 13, L 8, D 2
Most appearances: 12 Sebastien Carrat (1996–2001)
Most points: 196 Christophe Lamaison (1996–2000)
Biggest win: 56-18 v The Borders, 1997
Biggest defeat: 36-3 v London Irish, 2009

Ground: Stade Amédée Domenech (Stade Parc Municipal des Sports)
Address: 116, Avenue du 11 Novembre, BP 181, 19100, Brive-la-Gaillarde
Capacity: 15,000
To get there: Gare de Brive-la-Gaillarde (SNCF) 2.5 km (1.5 miles) from ground
Stands: Grande Iribune

Bars in ground: Not named
Bars nearby: Le Shamrock (13 Place Winston Churchill, 19100 Brive-la-Gaillarde, +33 5 55 87 61 08); **Bar Brasserie L'Ovalie** (86 Avenue John Kennedy, 19100 Brive-la-Gaillarde, +33 5 55 23 41 70), **Le Lord** (1 Avenue d'Alsace-Lorraine, 19100 Brive-la-Gaillarde, +33 5 55 74 16 74); **L'Envers du Decor** (Avenue Moliere, 19100 Brive-la-Gaillarde, +33 5 55 24 00 68)

Legends
Alain Penaud: 32 caps for France and fly-half at Brive for 15 years in two stints. He was lynchpin and captain of the 1997 Heineken Cup-winning side. In his second spell at the club he helped them to promotion in 2003.
Christophe Lamaison: Best known for his influence on France's epic World Cup semi-final win over the All Blacks in 1999 when playing fly-half. During his time at Brive (1996–2000) he mostly played at centre.

Need to know: Brive's stadium bears the name of their legendary prop Amédée Domenech, winner of 52 French caps, who played at the club in the 1950s and 1960s and was known as 'Le Duc'. The stadium was named after him on his death, aged 70, in 2003.

PERPIGNAN

Blood and Gold

Perpignan, the Catalan capital is yet another rugby hotbed and the local team, USA Perpignan, is the pride of both sides of the Pyrenees. The modern club is the by-product of six separate mergers, the last one in 1933. They promote their Catalan identity feverishly, have a partnership with soccer giants Barcelona and adopted a Catalan motto, *Sempre Endavant*, which translates as 'Always Going Forward'. The club's home kit bears the *Le Sang et Or* ('Blood and Gold') of the Catalan flag.

Sadly for their rabid supporters the motto has held up off the field, but not always on the pitch, so when they ended a 54-year title drought by beating Clermont 22-13 in the 2009 final it sparked huge celebrations.

Dan Carter was supposed to be part of these celebrations. The New Zealand fly-half joined the club for a six-month stint in December 2008, with the brief of delivering the title but an Achilles injury cut short his stay. As it turned out they didn't need him anyway, but Carter's arrival, on a huge salary, showed the ambition of the club. Other foreigners to be tempted by the big money on offer and the Catalan lifestyle include England's Perry Freshwater, Carter's compatriot Scott Robertson, South African World Cup-winner Percy Montgomery and Scotland's Nathan Hines.

Stade Aimé Giral, also the home of the Catalans Dragons rugby league team, is a brisk stroll out of the town centre and one of the most atmospheric grounds in France. There is a restaurant in the clubhouse, plus plenty of bodegas selling baguettes and beers. But these outlets do not take euros, so change your money into tokens, or tincsets, in the machines dotted around the stadium before getting fed and watered.

Below: Stade Aimé Giral, pride of the Pyrenees. Perpignan adopted a Catalan motto 'Always Going Forward'.

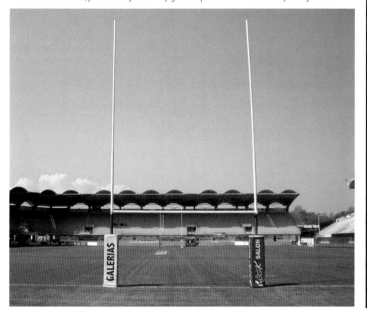

MATTER OF FACT
Club: Union Sporting Arlequins Perpignan
Formed: 1902
Located: Perpignan, France
Administrative address: Stade Aimé Giral, Allée Aimé Giral, 66000 Perpignan
Tel: +33 8 92 68 66 15
Email: infos@usap.fr
Website: www.usap.fr
Honours: French champions 1914, 1921, 1925, 1938, 1944, 1955, 2009
Euro honours: None

Heineken Cup records
Best finish: Runners-up 2003
Record: P 67, W 46, L 21, D 0
Most appearances: 55 Nicolas Mas (1999–)
Most points: 202 Manny Edmonds (2002–2007)
Biggest win: 67-8 v Petraca Padova, 1998
Biggest defeat: 54-15 v Leicester, 2001

Ground: Stade Aimé Giral
Address: Allée Aimé Giral, 66000 Perpignan
Capacity: 14,377
To get there: Gare de Perpignan (SNCF) 4 km (2.5 miles) from the ground. No 2 bus from station (free with match ticket)
Stands: Tribune Chevalier, Tribune Vaquer, Tribune Desclaux et Tribune Goutta

Bars in ground: La Buvette du Canigou, la Buvette Méditerranée, la Buvette Goutta et la Bodega
Bars nearby: O'Shannon (3 Rue de l'Incendie, 66000 Perpignan, +33 4 68 35 12 48); **Majid's Bar Eurl** (3 Place Résistance, 66000 Perpignan, +33 4 68 64 04 41, www.bar-66.com); **Chez Imbernon** (41, bis Quai Vauban, 66000 Perpignan, +33 4 68 51 27 78).

Legends
Aimé Giral: Giral was 18 when he kicked the late conversion that gave USAP an 8-7 win over Tarbes, and USAP their first French championship in 1914. A few months later he was dead, killed on the Western Front. The ground is named in his honour.
Marius Tincu: Romanian-born hooker who holds dual nationality. Hard nut who caused a storm when he turned out for his club in a championship match in 2008, despite serving an 18-week ban for eye-gouging against the Ospreys two months earlier.

Need to know: USAP have a group of fans known as the 'Ultras' who live, eat and breathe the club and will be decked out in the blood and gold colours on match day.

TOULOUSE

The pink city

Toulouse is known as the Ville Rose (Pink City) for its brick architecture. When the city was built the bricks were cheaper than white ones and it has retained its distinctive colourful décor to this day.

The town is a mixture of the ancient and the modern, with historical sights such as the 11th Century Basilica of St Sernin, a Romanesque church, which contains the tomb of St Thomas Aquinas and the art gallery, Hotel d'Assezat which houses the Bemberg Foundations, one of the major collections in Europe. By contrast most of the industry in Toulouse is related to the air travel and space industries, housing as it does the Airbus headquarters.

Toulouse has a vibrant nightlife, being home to over 100,000 students and is packed with clubs and bars. With most bars shutting at around 2am the clubs offer the chance to carry on the evening. The next morning you can wash away your hangover by heading to Place Saint-George's for a *croque monsieur* and give thanks that you can soothe your headache with a cheese and ham sandwich, unlike the 170-odd people who were beheaded in the square in the 18th century when it was a site for public executions.

Above: *Lights across the Garonne river.* ***Below:*** *The busy streets of Toulouse.*

Weather	Low (°C)	High (°C)	Rain (mm)	Sunset
January	2	9	58	17.28
February	3	11	51	18.05
March	5	14	54	18.43
April	7	16	67	20.21
May	10	20	77	20.56
June	13	24	64	21.29
July	16	28	45	21.40
August	16	28	51	21.17
September	13	24	52	20.30
October	10	19	52	19.36
November	5	13	51	17.46
December	3	10	52	17.19

3 THINGS YOU MUST DO...

1 CASSOULET

Have a cassoulet, a stew made of Toulouse sausages, white beans and duck legs at the superb restaurant Le Bon Vivre (15 Bis Place Wilson, tel: +33 5 61 230717), which opened in 1990. The square is a perfect spot for people watching. To get there: Métro to Jean Jaurès et Victor Hugo or Capitole.

2 SPACE CITY

Europe's top space museum is the Cité de l'Espace (Avenue Jean Gonord, tel: +33 8 20 377223) that houses the Russian Sputnik satellite launched in 1957, moon rock, old spacecraft, plus a huge model of the Ariane 5 rocket. You can sit in a gyroscope to get a feel of being in space. Price: €14–19.50.

3 AIRBUS FACTORY

Take a 90-minute tour of Europe's largest aeronautical plant (Village Aéroconstellation, Rue Franz Joseph Strauss, tel: +33 5 61 180601) where the huge airbuses are constructed. Book in advance and take your passport. Price: €9.50 adults, €8.00 children six-18, free for children under six.

TOULOUSE

Kings of Europe

Stade Toulousaln, winners of four Heineken Cups and 17 French championships, are one of the giants of French and European rugby.

Formed in 1907, they found much of their modern-day success under coach Guy Novès, one of the most eccentric men in rugby and a former Toulouse and France wing. After the 2005 Heineken Cup final at Murrayfield Novès was attempting to climb a fence to celebrate Toulouse's win over Stade Français to join his family when stewards intervened. His arrest and eviction from the ground only added to his legendary status among his side's fans.

Over the years the Toulouse side have been studded with the best players of French rugby from Pierre Villepreux and Jean-Claude Skrela to Yannick Jauzion and Thierry Dusautoir, who captained the side in their 2010 Heineken Cup final win over his old club Biarritz.

Toulouse's main ground is Stade Ernest Wallon, where in 2007 Irish lock Trevor Brennan, playing for Toulouse, jumped into the crowd and punched a fan during a Heineken Cup match against Ulster. Brennan was banned for five years and now runs a popular bar, De Danu, in the heart of Toulouse.

The ground is found on the Sept Deniers complex which includes three secondary pitches, a restaurant, clubhouse, tennis courts and a swimming pool.

Toulouse play some big matches at Stadium Municipal de Toulouse, which holds around 35,000, and is the home of Toulouse FC as well as hosting French international rugby Tests. It also staged six games in the 1998 soccer World Cup including Romania's victory over England.

Below: Toulouse fans have enjoyed one success after another, at home and in Europe.

MATTER OF FACT
Club: Stade Toulousain
Formed: 1907
Located: Toulouse, France
Administrative address: Stade Toulousain, 114 Rue de Troènes, 31200 Toulouse
Tel: +33 5 3442 2422
Email: accueil@stadetoulousain.fr
Website: www.stadetoulousain.fr
Honours: French champions 1912, 1922, 1923, 1924, 1926, 1927, 1947, 1985, 1986, 1989, 1994, 1995, 1996, 1997, 1999, 2001, 2008, French Cup 1946, 1947, 1984
Euro honours: Heineken Cup winners 1996, 2003, 2005, 2010

Heineken Cup records
Best finish: Winners 1996, 2003, 2005
Record: P 110, W 78, L 28, D 4
Most appearances: 76 Fabien Pelous (1997–2009)
Most points: 441 Jean-Baptiste Elissalde (2002–)
Biggest win: 108-16 v Ebbw Vale, 1998
Biggest defeat: 77-17 v Wasps, 1996

Ground: Stade Ernest Wallon
Address: 114 Rue des Troènes, 31200 Toulouse
Capacity: 18,754
To get there: Match day shuttle bus from métro station Barrière de Paris (line B). Every five minutes two hours before game and for an hour afterwards.
Stands: Nord, Sud, Est, Ouest

Bars in ground: Le Brasserie du Stade
Bars nearby: De Danu Irish Bar (9 Rue du Pont Guilhemery, 31000 Toulouse, +33 5 61 625879); **Bodega Bodega** (1 Rue Gabriel-Peri, 31000 Toulouse, +33 5 61630363); **Le Pere Louis** (45 Rue des Tourners, 31000 Toulouse, +33 5 61213345); **Le Rembrandt** (3 Rue Baour-Lormian, 31000 Toulouse, +33 5 61212252)

Legends
Jean-Pierre Rives: Blond bombshell flanker and French captain who is also a professional sculptor. Won 59 caps and his flowing locks were frequently streaked with blood due to his bravery.
Fabien Pelous: Second row who won 118 caps for France and two Heineken Cups. Captained France 42 times (including a Grand Slam in 2004). Retired in 2009 to make wine in a venture with footballer Djibril Cissé.

Need to know: Australian Tom Richards was Toulouse's first foreign player in 1912. The flanker won a Military Cross at Gallipoli and played for both Australia and the Lions. They now play for a trophy named after him.

TOULON

Hello sailor

With its dry, pleasant winters, cracking summers and beautiful beaches, it is no wonder so many top rugby players have settled in Toulon. Found around 65 km (40 miles) from Marseille, from which there is an hourly rail link, Toulon is France's main naval base and home of the French Navy's Mediterranean fleet with many of the residents being involved in the navy or the ship-building industry.

The old town is where you will find most of the points of historical interest. Souvenir hunters should head for the harbour and promenade, then take a look at the Place Puget, the nearby Saint Marie de la Seds Cathedral and the markets on Cours Lafayette which sell local produce every day except Mondays.

The new town, higher up, is north of the historical centre. Around Christmas time Place de la Liberté, the main square of the town which is close to the railway station, features an ice rink for children and a very busy market. The Opera House is also close by.

For a birds'-eye view of the town get up to the top of the Mont-Faron hill (you can take a cable car or drive) and once there view Toulon from 584 metres (1,916 feet) up and see the memorial commemorating the 1944 Allied landings and the liberation of the area.

Above and below: Toulon's setting and beautiful weather have helped attract many top rugby players.

Weather	Low (°C)	High (°C)	Rain (mm)	Sunset
January	6	13	91	17.12
February	6	14	73	17.49
March	7	16	51	18.25
April	9	18	62	20.03
May	13	22	43	20.38
June	16	26	29	21.08
July	18	29	7	21.20
August	19	29	30	20.58
September	16	26	47	20.12
October	13	21	103	19.19
November	9	16	72	17.29
December	7	13	71	17.03

3 THINGS YOU MUST DO...

1 NAVAL MUSEUM

Musée de la Marine (Place Monsenergue, Quai de Norfolk) has a collection of old model ships, etchings, drawings and an exhibition about military developments. When: 10.00-18.00 (closed Tues except Jul–Aug). Closed Jan, 1 May, 25 Dec. Price: €5.50 adults, €4 students, free for under 18s.

2 TAKE THE TRAIN

Les Petits Trains routes (185 bis, avenue de l'Infanterie de Marine, tel: +33 4 94 36 01 32) will show you all the scenes of Toulon. You will see Stade Mayol, Port Marchand, Port de Plaisance, Port Militaire, Arsenal du Mourillon and Pointe de la Mitre. Price: €5.

3 MAYOL CENTRE

Found near the rugby stadium, the Mayol Centre (Rue du Murier, tel: +33 4 98 00 91 91) is full of shops where you can fritter away your euros ahead of the match. All the major designer labels are represented and there are plenty of restaurants in the complex. When: Mon–Sat 09.30–19.30.

TOULON

Comic book heroes

What do you get if you mix together a comic strip businessman, a seaside location in the south of France and some of the world's best rugby players? President Mourad Boudjellal, who made his fortune in publishing, and is known as the 'Roman Abramovich' of rugby, decided to find out in the mid-2000s. Boudjellal, who dresses only in black and who once described a narrow Toulon defeat as 'the most shameful defensive point in the whole of rugby', spent vast sums luring some of the game's biggest names to the town. Megastars such as Jonny Wilkinson, George Smith, Tana Umaga and George Gregan have all felt the benefit of his largesse.

In the doldrums, and the French Second Division, for much of the decade after they were relegated because of money problems in 2000, Boudjellal's investment helped them qualify for the Heineken Cup for the first time for the 2010–11 season.

It is all a far cry from June 1908 when the club was founded in the Coq Hardi pub on the Boulevard de Strasbourg.

Stade Mayol, located just a Wilkinson punt from the sea, is surrounded by bars where generous Toulon fans will share a pastis with opposing fans and give them a rendition of their version of the 'Haka'. Known as the 'Pilou Pilou', it was created in the 1940s and depicts the Toulon players as ferocious warriors coming down towards the sea from the mountain. It is also heard at the start of the game and during periods of Toulon dominance in the scrum. Typically, the extrovert Boudjellal led the Pilou Pilou at the ground after his side gained promotion to the Top 14 in 2008.

Below: Many of the world's top players have graced Stade Mayol since the arrival of owner Mourad Boudjellal.

MATTER OF FACT
Club: Rugby Club Toulonnais
Formed: 1908
Located: Toulon, France
Administrative address: 53 Rue Melpomène, 83000 Toulon
Tel: +33 8 92 68 06 80
Email: contact@rctoulon.com
Website: www.rctoulon.com
Honours: French champions 1931, 1987, 1992
Euro honours: None

Heineken Cup: (First appearance 2010–11)

Challenge Cup records
Record: P 39, W 19, L 19, D 1
Most appearances: 16 Phillip Fitzgerald (1997–2010)
Most points: 106 Patrice Teisseire (1991–1998)
Biggest win: 73-3 v Rovigo, 2009
Biggest defeat: 76-3 v Gloucester, 2005

Ground: Stade Mayol
Address: Avenue de la Republique, 83000 Toulon
Capacity: 13,500
To get there: 15-minute walk from Gare de Toulon (SNCF) or bus network, 'le réseau Mistral' Numbers 3, 7, 23, 40 and 191 to Mayol stop
Stands: Tribune Bonnus, Tribune Finale, Tribune Lanfontan, Tribune Delangre

Bars in ground: Club House du RCT
Bars nearby: Brasserie du Stade (552 Avenue de la Republique, 83000 Toulon, +33 4 94 46 60 20);
Bar Hubac (1 Place de L'Hubac, 83000 Toulon, +33 4 94 62 85 09); **Le Gedari** (22 Rue des Bonnetières, 83100 Toulon, +33 4 94 62 07 64, www.gedari.com); **Bar Du Palais** (4 Place Louis Pasteur, 83000 Toulon, +33 4 94 36 13 590);

Legends
Jonny Wilkinson: English fly-half, who joined Toulon in the summer of 2009 and inspired them to the Challenge Cup final, where they lost to Cardiff.
Jérôme Gallion: Toulon-born scrum-half never played for any other club and won 27 caps for France. Key part of 1987 championship-winning side, was club president from 2000–2003 and practised dentistry in Toulon.

Need to know: Félix Mayol was a Toulon-born concert singer who made it big in Paris and helped nurture Maurice Chevalier's career. He bought land for RC Toulon to build a ground, giving up the rights to some of his songs to help fund the venture.

BIARRITZ

High rollers by the sea

You won't get the chance to mingle with the glitterati on too many rugby trips but a game in Biarritz offers an opportunity to see how the other half live. Away from the beaches you can risk your beer money standing shoulder-to-shoulder with the high rollers at the Casino Barrière de Biarritz before rounding off the night in one of the city's many nightclubs. Scuba diving, swimming, golf and horse riding enthusiasts are also well catered for in the area.

Set in the Basque region, at the bottom of southwest France, Biarritz was the favoured holiday destination of Queen Victoria while Edward VIII and his wife, Wallis Simpson, were regular visitors, as were the Russian Royal Family. Frank Sinatra and Ernest Hemingway also frequently stayed at the resort. Today the contrast between the well-heeled and the surfing types filling the beach bars is still marked.

For the rugby fan on a budget there are plenty of good, cheap brasseries and bars and other attractions such as the Maritime Museum (Musée de la Mer) that houses aquariums full of local fish and where you can see the seals being fed twice a day. Favourite bars for rugby heads to watch games include the Newquay Pub on Places Georges Clemenceau (near some high-grade clothes shops for shopping fans), and Red Café on Avenue Marechal Foch.

Above: Biarritz, where the other half live. *Below:* A quiet spot, a rarity in this party town.

Weather	Low (°C)	High (°C)	Rain (mm)	Sunset
January	3	9	104	17.41
February	4	10	96	18.18
March	5	14	107	18.55
April	8	17	102	20.33
May	10	17	86	21.08
June	14	20	81	21.41
July	17	23	66	21.51
August	15	23	80	21.29
September	13	22	110	20.42
October	10	18	163	19.48
November	8	14	145	17.58
December	5	11	119	17.31

3 THINGS YOU MUST DO...

1 STATUE OF THE MADONNA
Take a stroll to the end of Pointe Atalaye to see the Rock of the Virgin (so named because of the statue of the Madonna) that has stood there since 1865. She is said to protect the fisherman and sailors in the Bay of Biscay and is an icon of the city.

2 CHOCOLATE MUSEUM
Indulge your sweet tooth at Planète Musée du Chocolat (14 Avenue Beaurivage, tel: +33 5 5923 2772. When: Mon–Sat 10.00–12.30, 14.30–18.30 (school holidays, Mon–Sun 10.00–18.30). Price: €6 adult, €5 student, €4 children five–12 years old, €3 per person for groups of 15.

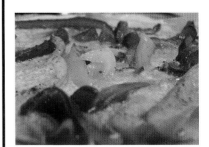

3 PIPERRADA
A Basque version of scrambled eggs made with onions, ham, garlic, tomatoes and red pepper. The Espelette pepper, brought back from Mexico by one of Columbus' men, is a mainstay of Basque cuisine. It is pureed, ground and pickled every autumn to keep locals going through the year.

Basque to the future

BIARRITZ

As a destination for a rugby weekend Biarritz, dubbed the 'Monte Carlo of the Atlantic coast', really does take some beating. You are spoilt for choice for bars and restaurants – some of which are owned by former Biarritz players such as Serge Betsen and Phillippe Bernat-Salles – while the rugby-mad fans turn the town into a sea of red on match days. Then there is the beach, the fantastic beach. In short, if your club draw Biarritz in any competition, just go.

Parc des Sports Aguiléra, a short trot from town, is a modern stadium with stands named after two of the most significant figures in the history of Biarritz: Serge Blanco and Serge Kampf. Kampf is one of the richest men in France who, with Blanco, revamped the club in the 2000s. In the brasserie at the stadium you can tuck into a solid three-courser to soak up the beer, a cheaper, and more filling, alternative to some of the snazzier establishments on the beach front. The ground, however, holds only 13,400, so Biarritz have played some big games over the Spanish border at Estadio Anoeta in San Sebastian, the home of the Real Sociedad FC.

Kampf's euros helped recruit players such as Imanol Harinordoquy, Dimitri Yachvili and Iain Balshaw and saw them reach Heineken Cup finals in 2006 and 2010, although they were beaten in both by Munster and Toulouse respectively.

The club's main rivals are Bayonne, based just a short distance away, who revel in their working-class reputation and see Biarritz as flashy upstarts. When Bayonne triumphed in one local derby they drove the team coach repeatedly around Parc des Sports Aguiléra taunting their vanquished opponents.

Below: The small capacity of Parc des Sport Aguiléra mean Biarritz play some big matches at Real Sociedad's home.

MATTER OF FACT
Club: Biarritz Olympique Pays Basque
Formed: 1913
Located: Biarritz, France
Administrative address: Parc des Sports Aguiléra, Rue Cino Del Duca, 64200 Biarrtiz
Tel: +33 5 59 01 64 60
Email: bopb@bopb.eu
Website: www.bo-pb.com
Honours: French champions 1935, 1939, 2002, 2005, 2006
Euro honours: None

Heineken Cup
Best finish: Runners-up 2006, 2010
Record: P 73, W 48, L 24, D1
Most appearances: 58 Julien Peyrelongue (2000–)
Most points: 517 Dimitri Yachvili (2002–)
Biggest win: 75-25 v Cardiff, 2003
Biggest defeat: 45-16 v Saracens, 2008

Ground: Parc des Sports Aguiléra
Address: Rue Cino Del Duca, 64200 Biarritz
Capacity: 13,400
To get there: Five-minute taxi from centre of town or 20-minute walk straight up Avenue de Verdun. Biarritz SNCF Station 2.5 km (1.5 miles) away.
Stands: Tribune Serge Blanco, Tribune Serge Kampf

Bars in ground: Bo Café Clubhouse
Bars nearby: Red Café (9 Avenue du Maréchal Foch, 64200 Biarritz, +33 5 59 24 21 02 www.redcafe.fr); **Bar Tabac Pot Ana** (93 Avenue de Biarritz, 64600 Biarritz, +33 5 59 23 93 34); **Hôtel Le Caritz** (14 Esplanade du Port Vieux, 64200 Biarritz, +33 5 59 24 41 84, www.lecaritz.com); **Bar L'Excuse** (7 Avenue d'Etienne, 64200 Biarritz, +33 5 59 03 25 36)

Legends
Serge Blanco: Venezuelan-born full-back played 93 times for France while reputedly smoking 60 cigarettes a day. Superb attacking force who played for Biarritz for 18 years to 1992 and later became club president.
Imanol Harinordoquy: Brilliant back rower who epitomizes the spirit of Biarritz. In 2010 he played a Heineken Cup semi-final, which Biarritz won against Munster, with a broken nose and broken ribs, with a Phantom of the Opera style mask protecting his face.

Need to know: Have a beer at Hotel Le Caritz and you may see owner Pascal Ondarts, the ferocious Basque prop, who made his French debut in the 'Battle of Nantes' against New Zealand in 1986. Don't expect a smile.

CASTRES

Olympique games

I n 1898 Castres Olympique rugby club were formed, appropriately in a city bar, by old boys of the local college and took their current name eight years later. At first rugby was just one sport of many on offer but members, disgruntled about the dominance of cycling, broke away and formed a club dedicated to rugby in 1906.

Fifteen years later they were in the top flight of French rugby and have been there virtually ever since but apart from two French championships, in 1949 and 1950, the club were generally underachievers.

Then Pierre Fabre, who founded the local pharmaceutical company, which is the third biggest firm of its type in France, took over the club in 1988. Results improved and in 1993 Castres won the title, beating Grenoble 14-11 in the final at Parc des Princes. That side included Laurent Labit, the All Black second row Gary Whetton and was captained by fly-half Francis Rui, who was killed in a road accident in 2001 and has a stand named after him at Stade Pierre-Antoine. Later players such as Raphael Ibanez, Thomas Castaignède and New Zealander Kees Meeuws would turn out for Castres.

Found in the Midi-Pyrénées, Castres, is an industrial town, about 65 km (40 miles) east of Toulouse, with the ground about a 20-minute walk out of the city centre. The stadium is pretty basic with bars underneath the two main stands. It is a daunting place for visiting teams but in 2007, however, Wasps triumphed 16-13 at Stade Pierre-Antoine, with one of the best defensive displays ever seen in the Heineken Cup. Castres had their revenge two years later.

Fans should fly to Toulouse or Carcassone airports. Castres does have its own airport but it only has connections to Paris Orly and Lyon.

Below: Castres was one of five clubs French hooker Rafael Ibanez (seen here playing for Wasps) represented.

MATTER OF FACT
Club: Castres Olympique
Formed: 1898
Located: Castres, France
Administrative address: 205 Avenue Charles de Gaulle, 81100 Castres
Tel: +33 5 63 51 45 00
Email: maurice.bille@castres-olympique.fr (or via web)
Website: www.castres-olympique.fr
Honours: French champions 1949, 1950, 1993
Euro honours: European Shield winners 2003

Heineken Cup records
Best finish: Semi-finals 2002
Record: P 40, W 17, L 22, D 1
Most appearances: 22 Alexandre Albouy (1998–)
Most points: 161 Romain Teulet (2001–)
Biggest win: 58-13 v Harlequins, 2005
Biggest defeat: 46-9 v Munster, 2006

Ground: Stade Pierre-Antoine
Address: Rue des Frères Nicouleau, 81100 Castres
Capacity: 10,000
To get there: Taxi from Castres station about 3.5 km (2 miles) or 40-minute walk through town and out again
Stands: Tribune Sud, Tribune Nord, Tribune Rui, Tribune Gabarrou

Bars in ground: Not named
Bars nearby: **The Quay** (23 Rue Frédéric Thomas, 81100 Castres, +33 5 63 71 91 80, www.sortir. tarnpratique.com/spip.php?article214); **Le Baron** (15 Rue de l'Orphelinat, 81100, +33 5 63 51 32 84); **Via Notte** (18 Rue d'Empare, 81100 Castres, +33 5 63 35 98 27); **Super Bar** (2 Boulevard Magenta, 81100 Castres, +33 5 63 59 04 82)

Legends
Gerard Cholley: 'Le Guv'nor'. Described by Stephen Jones of *The Sunday Times* (UK) as 'the baddest man ever'. 1970s' prop who was a paratrooper and French Army boxing champion prepared to use his fists on the pitch.
Alexandre Albouy: Two stints at Castres, the first from 1998 to 2006 before returning to the club in 2009 after a spell at Stade Français. The scrum-half played once for France, against Italy in 2002, but is a hero at Castres where he won the European Shield in 2003.

Need to know: Follow the crowd. Most fans going to games in Castres stay in Toulouse about an hour away by train. Make your way by rail on match day, go into town for a few beers then head out in the other direction following local fans to the ground on the outskirts.

CLERMONT

Michelin men

O riginally formed as a work team for his staff by the tyre magnate Marcel Michelin in 1911, ASM Clermont Auvergne qualified for 10 French Championship finals, the first in 1936, before finally winning one, in 2010.

There were several near misses on the way, including a last-minute defeat to Stade Français in 2007, being humbled by Toulouse, who they had beaten twice in the regular season in 2008 and blowing a half-time lead against Perpignan in 2009.

They finally came good by taking revenge on Perpignan, 19-6, a year later. On the way there were a couple of European Challenge Cup titles – triumphs over Bourgoin in the 1999 final and Bath in 2007 – but it was the domestic pot they yearned for. It is a poor return for a club who have had players such as Australian centre Pat Howard, France's Benoît Baby, New Zealander-turned Frenchman Tony Marsh and Philippe Saint-André, the scorer of 'The Try from the End of the World' against New Zealand in 1994.

The Stade Marcel Michelin, with the Puy de Dôme (lava dome) dominating the skyline, is a thoroughly modern stadium after renovations in 2006 and again for the start of the 2011–12 season that means it is up there with Europe's best club grounds.

In a town which is twinned with a similar industrial area, Salford in England, rugby fans migrate towards Le Café Pascal, near the cathedral, which was opened by a former Clermont second row. Before and after games the banter with the ardent Clermont supporters, known as 'The Vulcans', but without the big ears and green blood of Star Trek's Dr Spock, keeps the visitors occupied.

Clermont does have an airport but it is not served very well from Britain. Most fans fly to Lyon instead and drive for about two hours to get to the city. If you fancy seeing bit more of the French countryside then take the train from Paris Gare du Lyon with the journey taking around three and a half hours.

Below: The fans at Stade Marcel Michelin never tire of a good game.

MATTER OF FACT

Club: ASM Clermont Auvergne
Formed: 1911
Located: Clermont-Ferrand, France
Administrative address: 35 Rue du Clos Four, 63028 Clermont-Ferrand, Cedex 2
Tel: +33 4 73 14 63 66
Email: mireille.charrier@asm-rugby.com
Website: www.asm-rugby.com
Honours: French champions 2010, French Cup 2001
Euro honours: Challenge Cup winners 1999, 2007

Heineken Cup records
Best finish: Quarter-finals 2000, 2002, 2010
Record: P 45, W 22, L 22, D 1
Most appearances: 36 Alexandre Audebert (1999–)
Most points: 208 Brock James (2006–)
Biggest win: 41-0 v Scarlets, 2008
Biggest defeat: 57-23 v Leicester, 2005

Ground: Stade Marcel Michelin
Address: Rue du Clos Four, 63028 Clermont-Ferrand, Cedex 2
Capacity: 15,857
To get there: 1.5 km (1 mile) from Gare de Clermont-Ferrand, seven minutes by tram
Stands: Tribune Volvic, Tribune Philiponeau, L'espace Edouard

Bars in ground: Not named
Bars nearby: The Oval (107 Avenue de la République, 63000 Clermont-Ferrand, +33 4 73 25 15 15, www.theoval.fr); **Le Matchiko** (56 Avenue de la République, 63000 Clermont-Ferrand, +33 4 73 14 15 35); **Le Café Pascal** (4 Place de la Victoire, 63000 Clermont-Ferrand, +33 4 73 91 86 08)

Legends
Aurelien Rougerie: Winger who captained Clermont to the their first title in 2010 after years of heartache. A powerful runner with over 50 French caps, he sued Phil Greening of Wasps after a windpipe injury left him needing three operations in 2002.
Olivier Magne: Big back rower who won 89 caps and played in four French Grand Slam winning sides. After a spell at London Irish, he went into coaching and in 2009 was given the job of sparking Greek rugby into life. It was beyond him.

Need to know: The club was originally known as Association Sportive Michelin Clermont Auvergne until the French government banned sports teams from having business names in their title in 1922.

IRELAND
(INCLUDES NORTHERN IRELAND)

 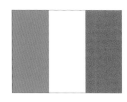
Below: Ireland regularly send a side out to contest the Churchill Cup in the USA and were winners in 2009.

The long wait ends

The Irish Grand Slam of 2009 ended a wait of 61 years, and bridged the gap between the hero of 1948, the legendary fly-half Jackie Kyle, and the dominant Irish player of his generation, the centre Brian O'Driscoll. In between, although the Irish had some stellar performers, in particular Mike Gibson and Keith Wood, and they contributed hugely to the Lions, they fell short in the Five (then Six) Nations consistently. Irish sides always 'gave it a lash' and weekends watching international rugby at Lansdowne Road, or Croke Park, prior to the rebuilding of the Aviva, were memorable, but the national side could not compete at the top table of international rugby.

However, a system of what amounts to player central contracts with the IRFU, changed all that and Ireland looked primed to have a decent crack at the World Cup in 2007. Their campaign was hampered by a tough group and reports of player disharmony, and they failed to improve on their previous best of a place in the quarter-finals when they were eliminated at the pool stage. The talk was that a golden era of Irish players such as O'Driscoll, Paul O'Connell and Ronan O'Gara had missed the boat but the team of 2009 put that theory to bed.

Willie John McBride, Ciaran Fitzgerald, O'Driscoll and O'Connell have all captained the Lions since 1974 but only McBride, with his 1974 squad, has managed a series victory. O'Driscoll's pre-eminence is such that he was voted player of the decade by *Rugby World* magazine in 2010.

Above: *The futuristic Aviva Stadium, on the site of Lansdowne Road, hosted its first Test match in 2010.*

TEST RECORD (capped internationals only)

Versus	First Test	Played	Won	Lost	Drawn
Argentina	Oct 1990	11	6	5	0
Australia	Nov 1927	29	8	20	1
England	Feb 1875	123	45	70	8
France	Mar 1909	86	29	52	5
Italy	Dec 1988	18	15	3	0
New Zealand	Nov 1905	23	0	22	1
Scotland	Feb 1877	124	55	64	5
South Africa	Nov 1906	19	4	14	1
Wales	Jan 1882	115	47	62	6

Most international caps: Brian O'Driscoll (1999–) 103 Tests
Most international points: Ronan O'Gara (2000–) 963 points, 99 Tests
(14t, 154c, 181p, 14d)
Most international tries: Brian O'Driscoll (1999–) 40 tries, 103 Tests

WORLD CUP RECORD

Year	Venue	Finished
1987	Australia & NZ	Quarter-finals
1991	England	Quarter-finals
1995	South Africa	Quarter-finals
1999	Wales	Pool
2003	Australia	Quarter-finals
2007	France	Pool

Most World Cup appearances: Brian O'Driscoll 13 matches (1999, 2003, 2007)
Most World Cup points: David Humphreys 70 points, 7 matches (1999, 2003)
Most World Cup tries: Brian O'Driscoll 6 tries, 13 matches (1999, 2003, 2007)
Record World Cup win: 64-7 v Namibia, Sydney, 2003
World Cup coaches: 1987 Mick Doyle; 1991 Ciaran Fitzgerald; 1995 Gerry Murphy; 1999 Warren Gatland; 2003 Eddie O'Sullivan; 2007 Eddie O'Sullivan

DUBLIN

Above: *The appropriately harp-shaped Samuel Beckett Bridge spans the River Liffey in Dublin. It is supported by 31 cable stays.*

A sleepy capital city, that for many years was resigned to watching its residents head off in search of prosperity in Britain, the USA, Canada and beyond, Dublin burst into action in the mid-1990s as the country boomed economically.

Rapid growth rates (sometimes reaching double digits annually) earned Ireland the tag 'the Celtic Tiger', a reference to the countries such as Singapore, Taiwan and South Korea, who were dubbed 'the East Asian Tigers', because they also enjoyed rapid growth rates. It was only natural the country's capital would see the economic benefits, as for the first time the country had to become a net importer of people to keep up momentum.

However, the growth screeched to an alarming halt in the late 2000s and some locals moan the rapid growth they enjoyed has killed the city's soul (people getting greedy, too many foreigners, high prices and so on).

Dublin is served by many of the budget airlines, significantly Ryanair,

and has an efficient transport network on the ground, particularly the Dublin Area Rapid Transit trains and the Luas light railway.

Although home to more than a million people, the city has retained a friendly charm and remains small enough to navigate easily enough. Which is just as well, because this being Dublin, you'll be looking for a Guinness as soon as your feet touch the ground no doubt?

The visitor hot-spot for drinks, food and general revelry is the Temple Bar area. Its narrow streets make it an ideal place to simply wander around until you find a pub that takes your fancy so you can try a pint of Ireland's famous stout.

Shoppers should head to the busy Henry Street, O'Connell Street and Grafton Street (where you will also see the famous Trinity College and central landmark St Stephen's Green).

3 THINGS YOU MUST DO...

1 GAELIC GAMES

Visit Experience Gaelic Games (32 Claude Road, Drumcondra, tel: +353 1 830 0730) to try your hand at something new. Sessions last three and a half hours. Price: €25-€35.
To get there: public sessions are held at Na Fianna GAA Club (St Mobhi Rd, Glasnevin), 10 minutes north of the city centre.

2 GUINNESS STOREHOUSE

Take the Guinness tour (St James Gate, tel: +353 1 408 4800), learn how to pour a pint (and get a certificate), then relax once you hit the Gravity Bar to enjoy 360-degree views of Dublin. When: daily 09.30–17.00 (09.30–19.00 Jul, Aug). Price: €15 adult. To get there: bus 51B, 78A, 123 or Luas to James's St.

3 LITERARY PUB CRAWL

Combine the great literary history of Dublin with a pub crawl and a show performed as you go from pub to pub. Meet at the Duke Pub (Duke St, bookings tel: +353 1 670 5602). When: Apr–Oct daily 19.30, Nov–Mar Thur–Sun 19.30. Price: €12 adult, €10 students. To get there: bus to Grafton St, Nassau St or Dawson St.

Above: Is there a better reason to visit Ireland's capital city?

Weather	Low (°C)	High (°C)	Rain (mm)	Sunset
January	2	7	61	16.17
February	3	7	50	17.08
March	3	9	54	18.03
April	5	11	42	20.00
May	7	13	54	20.55
June	10	16	56	21.43
July	12	18	64	21.57
August	11	18	71	21.21
September	10	16	60	20.15
October	7	12	70	19.02
November	5	10	63	16.53
December	3	8	61	16.11

AVIVA STADIUM

Lansdowne Road reborn

Aviva Stadium, built on the site of the old Lansdowne Road, opened on 14 May 2010, and on 31 July that year staged its first rugby match when a combined Leinster/Ulster XV beat Connacht/Munster 68-0. Its first Test match followed on 6 November that year when Ireland lost 21-23 to South Africa.

Home of the Irish rugby team and Irish football team, the ground was up and running three years after the demolition of the rickety old Lansdowne Road stadium had begun and, in a lesson to those involved at Wembley, came in under its budget of €410 million.

In the three years the site was not operational Ireland played their home matches at Croke Park, the 82,000-seater home of the Gaelic Athletic Association, and the move back to their old patch, with a capacity of just over 50,000 meant fewer rugby fans could watch their team as Croke Park regularly sold out for Six Nations games.

Despite the reduced capacity the ground is an impressive structure with three of the four stands having four tiers for spectators, although the north stand has only one level because of a nearby residential area.

It is a huge improvement on the old stadium, the brainchild of Henry William Dunlop, an athlete who organized the first All-Ireland Athletics Championships. The stadium first opened for athletics in 1872.

Below: The Aviva Stadium, the new home of Irish rugby, built on the site of Lansdowne Road.

MATTER OF FACT
Stadium: Aviva Stadium
Located: Dublin, Ireland
Address: 62 Lansdowne Road, Dublin 4
Tel: +353 1 238 2300
Email: info@avivastadium.ie
Website: www.avivastadium.ie
Capacity: 51,700
To get there: Two-minute walk from Lansdowne Road Station (DART),
Stands: West, North, East, South

Stadium tours
Open: Mon–Sun 10.00–16.00 on the hour (varies); €10 adults, €5 children (12 and under), free infants (under 3), family (2 adults, 2 children) €25, groups over 20 get 10 per cent discount, max 25. Must pre-book.
Tel: +353 1 238 2300
Email: tours@avivastadium.ie or roisin.walsh@avivastadium.ie

First match (Lansdowne Road): Leinster v Ulster, 1876
First match (Aviva): Leinster/Ulster 68 Connaught/Munster 0, 2010
First Test (Lansdowne Road): Ireland 0 goals England 2 goals and 1 try, 1878
First Test (Aviva): Ireland 21 South Africa 23, 2010
Tests hosted: 247
Ireland record: P 244, W 118, L 109, D 17

Bars in ground: Not named
Bars nearby: The Baggot Inn (143 Lower Baggot Street, Dublin 2, +353 1 661 8758, www.thebaggotinn.ie); **Slattery's Public Bar** (62 Upper Grand Canal Street, Dublin 4, +353 1 668 5481); **O'Sheas Merchant Hotel** (12 Bridge Street Lower, Dublin 8, +353 1 679-3797, www.osheashotel.com); **The Lansdowne Hotel** (27-29 Pembroke Road, Dublin 4, +353 1 668 2522, www.lansdownehotel.ie)

Finally. . . Even the thirstiest fans have no problem getting the beers at Aviva Stadium. The ground's 18 bars can pour 2,000 pints a minute and 16 food outlets sell everything from oysters to burgers to soak up the black stuff.

LEINSTER

Dublin glory boys

Leinster lived in the shadows of Munster on the European stage until everything clicked for them in 2009. Not only did they beat their red-shirted rivals in the semi-finals of the Heineken Cup – a 25-6 tonking in front of more than 82,000 people at Croke Park – but they overcame Leicester 19-16 in the final at Murrayfield to be crowned champions for the first time.

That side, containing the inspirational Australian flanker Rocky Elsom, the peerless Brian O'Driscoll and hard heads such as Shane Jennings and Jamie Heaslip, went on to provide five members of the Lions touring party to South Africa that summer. The Heineken Cup win supplemented success in the Magners League in 2002 and 2008 and proved the players were worthy successors to the likes of Karl Mullen, Fergus Slattery and Ronnie Dawson.

Leinster play home matches at RDS Arena, in the suburb of Ballsbridge, having moved their Heineken Cup games there from Donnybrook in 2005. The new ground had nearly three times the capacity of the dilapidated Donnybrook, although nowadays the province will play their biggest European games at Aviva Stadium, the ultra-modern reincarnation of Lansdowne Road. Renovated in 2007, RDS became Leinster's official home for the 2007–08 season and they took an immediate liking to the place, winning 11 out of 12 home games on their way to the Magners League title.

RDS Arena, which hosts the Dublin Horse Show every year, is 4.5 km (3 miles) from O'Connell Street but there are plenty of bars within a grubber kick of the ground for pre- and post-match entertainment.

Below: The legendary centre Brian O'Driscoll helped Leinster to Heineken Cup success in 2009.

MATTER OF FACT
Club: Leinster Rugby
Formed: 1875
Located: Dublin, Ireland
Administrative address: Leinster Rugby, 55 Main Street, Donnybrook, Dublin 4
Tel: +353 1 269 3224
Email: information@leinsterrugby.ie
Website: www.leinsterrugby.ie
Honours: Celtic/Magners League winners 2002, 2008, Irish Interprovincial Champions 22 times
Euro honours: Heineken Cup winners 2009

Heineken Cup records
Best finish: Winners 2009
Record: P 97, W 61, L 34, D 2
Most appearances: 78 Shane Horgan (1998–)
Most points: 348 Felipe Contepomi (2003–2009)
Biggest win: 92-17 v Bourgoin, 2004
Biggest defeat: 43-7 v Toulouse, 2002

Ground: RDS Arena (Royal Dublin Society)
Address: Ballsbridge, Dublin 4, Ireland
Capacity: 18,500
To get there: Lansdowne Road Station (DART), Sandymount Aircoach from Dublin Airport or bus 5, 7, 45
Stands: Bank of Ireland North, Bank of Ireland South, Anglesea, Grandstand

Bars in ground: Ring Bar, Centurion Bar, Laighin-Out Bar
Bars nearby: The Horseshoe House (34 Merrion Rd, Ballsbridge, Dublin 4, +353 1 6689424); **Bellamy's** (13 Ballsbridge Terrace, Dublin 4, +353 1 6680397)
Paddy Cullen's (14 Merrion Rd, Ballsbridge, Dublin 4, +353 1 6684492, www.paddycullens.com);
O'Donoghue's Bar (15 Merrion Row, Dublin 2, +353 1 660 7194, www.odonoghues.ie)

Legends
Karl Mullen: Doctor who played hooker and captained Ireland to the Grand Slam in 1948. Also led the 1950 Lions to Australia and New Zealand and was president of Leinster. He died in 2009 aged 82.
Brian O'Driscoll: Centre who could just be Ireland's best-ever player. Helped the province to the 2009 Heineken Cup, won over 100 caps for his country and captained the Lions in 2005.

Need to know: Donnybrook the traditional home of Leinster is now used for Ireland A, women's, school games and friendlies. Renovated in 2008 (capacity 11,200) it is a short walk from the Aviva Stadium.

BELFAST

City reborn

Belfast is probably better known around the world for the wrong reasons, a legacy of the Troubles that scarred the city from the late 1960s onwards and which reached their height in the 1970s.

Belfast people love their sport – hundreds of thousands turned out for the funerals of local heroes George Best and Alex Higgins – and rugby union has a big part in that enthusiasm.

Away from the 80 minutes of action at Ravenhill, Belfast offers plenty of distractions for the travelling fan. It has an industrial heritage and you can see the shipyards where the Titanic was built, take a Black Cab Tour of the city, visit Belfast Castle or if you have youngsters with you, or you are just a big kid yourself, take in W5, at the Odyssey, a science and discovery exhibition that has something for everyone.

At night Belfast is a far different place than it was three decades ago when many areas were off-limits to visitors. West and South Belfast have busy pub and club scenes and The Culturlann, near the Falls Road, central to a revival of the Irish language culture, with art galleries, a theatre and a club, is a magnet of for tourists.

Above: Belfast City Hall. *Below:* Looking down on the City Hall grounds from the big wheel.

Weather	Low (°C)	High (°C)	Rain (mm)	Sunset
January	4	7	80	16.09
February	5	7	52	17.01
March	6	8	50	18.00
April	6	10	48	20.01
May	9	13	52	20.58
June	11	15	68	21.49
July	13	17	94	22.03
August	12	17	77	21.25
September	11	15	80	20.16
October	8	11	83	19.00
November	5	8	72	16.48
December	5	7	90	16.03

3 THINGS YOU MUST DO...

1 TITANIC DOCK AND PUMPHOUSE

Check out the world's most infamous ship at the Northern Ireland Science Park (Queen's Road, Queen's Island, tel: +44 28 9073 7813). When: visitor centre 10.30-16.30 daily. Tours Sat, Sun, Mon, Weds 14.00. Price: tours £6 adult, £4 child. To get there: metro to Queen's Rd.

2 BELFAST MURALS

Belfast is famous for its murals that depict the history and politics of the city. Guides will take you around these and the peace walls in a 90-minute tour that gives a sense of the city's troubled past. (Tel: +44 28 90 294345, +44 7964 734862.) Price: £10 per person, £30 minimum tour charge.

3 BUSHMILLS DISTILLERY

Ireland's oldest whiskey distillery (2 Distillery Road, Bushmills, Co Antrim, tel: +44 28 2073 3218/3272. When: Nov–Feb, Mon–Fri 09.30–15.30 (Sat–Sun 12.30–15.30), Mar Mon–Sat 09.15–17.00 (Sun 12.00–16.00) Apr–Oct, Mon–Sat 09.15–17.00, Sun 12.00–17.00. Price: £6 adults, £5 over 60s, £3 children (8–17).

ULSTER

Red Hand Gang

Ulster, perhaps the least celebrated of the three major Irish provinces were, nonetheless, the first team from Ireland to become European champions. They landed the trophy in 1999 and although some carp that English teams were not involved that year, try telling them that down at Ravenhill. In that campaign, when they were captained by David Humphreys, the record-breaking fly-half, they beat Toulouse twice, Stade Français and Colomiers, in the final 21-6, so they didn't exactly have an easy ride.

A Magners League title found its way to Ravenhill in 2006, with notorious Australian second row Justin Harrison lending his weight to the cause although the final, a 19-17 win over the Ospreys, wasn't decided until a late Humphreys drop goal went over after hitting both posts.

Ravenhill has an intimidating atmosphere but was a slightly ramshackle ground until redevelopment got underway. The New Stand that opened in September 2009 and cost £4.5 million (€5.3 million), on the Mount Merrion side of the venue, has a covered terrace and 20 corporate boxes. More improvements were planned as Ulster tried to maximize revenue to compete with the best in Europe rather than just rely on their famous 'Friday-Night Feeling'.

The atmosphere of Ravenhill did not appeal to the almost all-conquering Australians of 1984. Then, a touring side including names like Lynagh, Campese and Hawker were beaten 15-13 by an Ulster team (captained by David Irwin) who probably dine out on the memories of the match to this day.

There are lively pubs within walking distance from the ground and visitors are guaranteed a warm welcome at Malone Rugby Club, nearby, on Gibson Park Avenue.

Below: Ulster looked down on Europe in 1999 when becoming the first Irish side to win the Heineken Cup.

MATTER OF FACT
Club: Ulster Rugby
Formed: 1879
Located: Belfast, Northern Ireland
Administrative address: Ravenhill Grounds, 85 Ravenhill Park, Belfast BT6 0DG
Tel: +44 28 949 3222
Email: marketing@ulsterrugby.com
Website: www.ulsterrugby.com
Honours: Magners League winners 2006, Celtic Cup winners 2004, Irish Interprovincial Champions 26 times
Euro honours: Heineken Cup winners 1999

Heineken Cup records
Best finish: Winners 1999
Heineken Cup record: P 87, W 36, L 48, D 3
Most appearances: 57 David Humphreys (1994–2008)
Most points: 564 David Humphreys (1994–2008)
Biggest win: 59-3 v Benetton Treviso, 2002
Biggest defeat: 56-3 v Wasps, 1997

Ground: Ravenhill Stadium
Address: 85 Ravenhill Park, Belfast BT6 0DG
Capacity: 12,300
To get there: 3 km (1.8 miles) from Belfast Central Station or 78 bus
Stands: Main, New

Bars in ground: Scoop Bar (members), Marquee Bar
Bars nearby: The Rosetta (71-75 Rosetta Road, Belfast BT6 0LR, +44 28 9064 9297, www.rosettabar.com); **Errigle Inn** (312-320 Ormeau Road, Belfast BT7 2GE, +44 28 9064 1410, www.errigle.com); **Pavilion Bar** (296 Ormeau Road, Belfast BT7 2GD, +44 28 9028 3283, www.laverysbelfast.com); **The Eastender** (426 Woodstock Road, Belfast BT6 9DR, +44 28 9073 2443)

Legends
Jack Kyle: Fly-half who inspired Ireland to the Grand Slam in 1948. Lion in 1950, he was also a doctor who practised in Zambia for many years. In 2010 became first player to be inducted into the Ulster Hall of Fame.
Willie John McBride: Second row who went on five Lions tours, including skippering 'The Invincibles' of 1974. Invented the infamous '99' call that led to mayhem and many fist fights in South Africa.

Need to know: The Red Hand of Ulster depicted on the team's badge reputedly dates back to the arrival of the three sons of King Milesius of Spain in Ireland. One apparently chopped off his hand and threw it ashore from the boat to have first claim on the land.

LIMERICK

The lively city

Limerick is a perfect city for a rugby weekend. Enjoy the raucous atmosphere at Thomond Park, follow up with an evening on the black stuff in a selection of good pubs around the ground and then head to one of the many decent restaurants offering solid Irish food to soak it all up. What more do you need?

Around 25 km (15 miles) from Shannon Airport, Limerick is also full of historical places of interest if you don't want to spend all day drinking. The Flying Boat Museum, King John's Castle (an 800-year-old Anglo-Norman fort on the River Shannon) and the Jim Kemmy Municipal Museum, in Castle Lane, which has information about local history, are all worth a visit.

Rugby and pubs are intertwined in Limerick. The family of Munster hooker Jerry Flannery own a popular bar in Catherine Street and former prop Peter Clohessy owns another drinking establishment. Dolan's Pub on Dock Road is the place to go if live music is your thing. Limerick has a famous musical heritage – the Cranberries hail from the city and in 2010 played a homecoming concert at Thomond Park.

JP McManus, the billionaire currency dealer and owner of 2010 Grand National winner Don't Push It is a Limerick man while actor and Munster fan Richard Harris, was another local.

Above: *Limerick Castle.* ***Below:*** *Merry Munster men mutter manly type things ahead of the match. Mmmm.*

Weather	Low (°C)	High (°C)	Rain (mm)	Sunset
January	3	8	97	16.30
February	3	8	72	17.20
March	4	10	72	18.13
April	5	13	56	20.09
May	7	15	60	21.02
June	11	19	62	21.48
July	13	18	57	22.01
August	11	17	82	21.28
September	11	17	82	20.23
October	7	13	92	19.12
November	4	10	95	17.05
December	0	6	100	16.24

3 THINGS YOU MUST DO...

1 THE TREATY STONE

Limerick's most famous monument (Clancy's Strand, tourist office tel +353 61 317552), on which the Treaty of Limerick, which ended the war between the Jacobites and William of Orange, was signed in 1691. To get there: it's opposite King John's Castle.

2 LIMERICK RACECOURSE

One of the best racecourses (Greenmount Park, Patrickswell, tel: +353 61 320000) in a country that knows a thing or two about racing. Price: €10-€20 adult, €10-€15 concessions, free: children under 16. To get there: 12 km (7 miles) south on the N20. Shuttle buses from Colbert Station (train) on race days.

3 HUNT MUSEUM

The Hunt Museum (Rutland Street, tel: + 353 61 312833) is home to one of Ireland's greatest collections of art with work by Picasso, Renoir and Yeats. When: Mon–Sat 10.00–17.00, Sun 14.00–17.00. Price: €8 adults, €6.25 concessions, €4.25 children, €18 family ticket. To get there: to the north of Colbert Station.

MUNSTER

Stand up and fight

Men of a certain age get misty eyed recounting the day when Munster beat Graham Mourie's All Blacks at Thomond Park in 1978. Visit Limerick and you would think there were about 200,000 in the ground that day for all the 'I was there' blarney you hear. The match has spawned a West End play and a successful book, *Stand Up and Fight*. The attendance on the day was given as 13,000 but everyone in Limerick and for miles around seems to think they were present.

Australia had also been beaten 11-8 by a Munster side led by Tom Kiernan in 1967 (the Wallabies, then world champions, were defeated again in 1992). But it was when the Heineken Cup started in 1995 that the real Munster crusade began...

Out with the washing initially, Munster were beaten quarter-finalists in 1999, lost the final by a point to Northampton in 2000, were victims of a dodgy touch-judge decision in a semi-final defeat in Lille in 2001 and some skulduggery by Neil Back in the 2002 final. Semi-final heartache – by a solitary point to Toulouse in 2003 – and a 37-32 defeat to Wasps, again in the last four, in one of the best club matches ever, plus quarter-final agony a year later followed. It seemed it would never end for the travelling army but then, in 2006, they annexed the big one when the men of Munster, led by Anthony Foley, beat Biarritz in the final. The city of Limerick went mad.

Paul O'Connell's team of 2008 followed the success up by which time the redevelopment of Thomond Park was well under way. It was a very basic venue and although it has now become one of the best club grounds in Europe for visiting fans it remains one of the most hostile for visiting teams.

Below: Ronan O'Gara, Munster's all-time leading points scorer.

MATTER OF FACT
Club: Munster
Formed: 1879
Located: Limerick, Ireland
Administrative address: Musgrave Park, Ballyphenane, Pearse Road, Cork
Tel: +353 2 1432 3563
Email: info@munsterrugby.ie
Website: www.munsterrugby.ie
Honours: Magners League 2003, 2009, Celtic Cup 2005, Irish Interprovincial Champions 22 times
Euro honours: Heineken Cup winners 2006, 2008

Heineken Cup records
Best finish: Winners 2006, 2008
Record: P 109, W 77, L 31, D 1
Most appearances: 93 John Hayes (1998–)
Most points: 1,138 Ronan O'Gara (1997–)
Biggest win: 64-0 v Viadana, 2002
Biggest defeat: 60-19 v Toulouse, 1996

Ground: Thomond Park (website: www.thomondpark.ie)
Address: Thomond Park, Limerick
Capacity: 26,000
To get there: 3 km (1.8 miles) from Colbert Station (train)
Stands: East, West, North Terrace, South Terrace

Bars in ground: The Dug Out
Bars nearby: Ardhú Bar (Ennis Road, Limerick, +353 61 329 869, www.ardhubar.com); **Quilty's** (79 Sexton Street North, Thomondgate, Limerick, +353 61 326 543); **Dolan's Pub** (Dock Road, Limerick, +353 61 314 483, www.dolanspub.com); **Curragower Pub** (Clancy's Strand, Limerick, +353 61 321 788, www.curragower.com)

Legends
Mick Galwey: Second row who captained Munster and won 41 Ireland caps. Led Munster to two Heineken Cup finals without success and was in retirement when the glory days arrived.
Moss Keane: He definitely was there when Munster beat the All Blacks – he was playing. The accomplished Gaelic footballer, who died in 2010, turned to rugby and played for Kerry as a full-back before switching to lock, winning 51 Irish caps and a place on the 1977 Lions tour.

Need to know: Owned by former Munster prop, Peter 'The Claw' Clohessy, the aptly named Sin Bin, part of Clohessy's pub, on Howley's Quay, less than a kilometre from Thomond Park, is chock-a-block as the post-match evening wears on.

ITALY

THE

3

MINUTE GUIDE

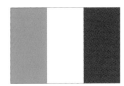

Capital: *Rome.* **Language:** *Italian.* **Beer:** *Peroni, Nastro Azzurro.* **Food:** *Pizza, pasta, antipasto.* **National anthem:** *Il Canto degli Italiani (The Song of the Italians).* **Population:** *58 million.* **Time zone:** *GMT + 1.* **Emergency number:** *112.* **Did you know?** *You can see the actual middle finger of Galileo Galilei in the museum Museo di Storia del Scienza in Florence.* **Rugby body:** *Federazione Italiana Rugby, Foro italico, Stadio Olympico, Curva Nord, Roma 00194. Tel: +39 6685 7309. Web: www.federugby.it.*

Below: Finding some quiet along the waterways of Venice.

The latecomers

Italy should have been admitted to the Five Nations at least four years before the organizers finally made it six countries in 2000 and they shamed those who had dragged their feet by winning their first match against Scotland, then the reigning champions, 34-20, in Rome.

Federazione Italiana Rugby joined the International Rugby Board in 1987, played in the inaugural World Cup the same year and had their first major scalp in 1995 when they beat Ireland (they also defeated them twice in 1997).

The 1980s and 1990s saw expansion for Italian rugby, always the poor relation to its round-ball cousin in this country, when tax breaks encouraged investment in rugby clubs. Superstars such as Michael Lynagh, John Kirwan and David Campese were lured to play club rugby by the Italian lifestyle and gradually local players, who could hold their own on the world stage, such as Massimo Giovanelli and Mauro Bergamasco, started to emerge. But to the frustration of every Italian coach, the leading names were constantly tempted by moves abroad and consequently the national side had no control over their biggest assets.

Benetton Treviso and new 'super club' Aironi were admitted into the Magners League for the 2010–11 campaign in the hope that the prospect of playing in a competition stronger than the existing domestic Super 10 would encourage better home-grown players to stay.

In 11 Six Nations' tournaments from 2000–2010 Italy managed seven wins, five of those against Scotland.

Above: *An intricately sculpted door at Milan Cathedral.*

TEST RECORD (capped internationals only)

Versus	First Test	Played	Won	Lost	Drawn
Argentina	Oct 1978	16	5	10	1
Australia	Nov 1973	14	0	14	0
England	Oct 1991	16	0	16	0
France	Oct 1937	31	1	30	0
Ireland	Dec 1988	18	3	15	0
New Zealand	May 1987	11	0	11	0
Scotland	Dec 1996	16	6	10	0
South Africa	Nov 1995	12	0	12	0
Wales	Oct 1994	17	2	14	1

Most international caps: Alessandro Troncon (1994–2007) 101 Tests
Most international points: Diego Dominguez (1991–2003) 983 points
(9t, 127c, 209p, 19d)
Most international tries: Marcello Cuttitta (1987–1999) 25 tries, 54 Tests

WORLD CUP RECORD

Year	Venue	Finished
1987	Australia & NZ	Pool
1991	England	Pool
1995	South Africa	Pool
1999	Wales	Pool
2003	Australia	Pool
2007	France	Pool

Most World Cup appearances: Alessandro Troncon, 14 matches (1995, 1999, 2003, 2007)
Most World Cup points: Diego Dominguez, 98 points, 9 matches (1991, 1995, 1999)
Most World Cup tries: Marcello Cuttitta 5 tries, 7 matches (1987, 1991, 1995)
Record World Cup win: 31-5 v Portugal, Paris, 2007
World Cup coaches: 1987 Marco Bottesan; 1991 Bertrand Fourcade; 1995 Georges Coste; 1999 Massimo Mascioletti; 2003 John Kirwan; 2007 Pierre Berbizier

ROME

Above: *Famous classical statue anyone?*

The seven hills of history

This legendary city, which was at the centre of the Roman Empire, is steeped in history. Famously built on seven hills, it is home to world-famous landmarks such as the sweeping Spanish Steps, linking Piazza Trinità dei Monti and Piazza di Spagna; the Trevi Fountain, where you can toss coins for luck and romance; the Colosseum, the former gladiatorial arena; and temple of the gods, the Pantheon.

Rome also encompasses the tiny city-state of Vatican City (the smallest country in the world), centre of the Catholic Church and home to its head, the Pope. It is here where you will find the skyline's iconic St Peter's Basilica, St Peter's Square, the Apostolic Palace and the Sistine Chapel.

It is easy enough to join the throngs in paying homage to the city's amazing history as these attractions are clustered closely together either side of the river.

At the end of all the history, you'll be in need of food, and there is no better way to do it than to grab a huge slice of Italy's finest pizza from a vendor or café, find somewhere to sit and eat away while watching the rest of Rome go about its business and pleasure. Wash it down with gelato (Italian ice cream) a refreshing Peroni beer or a glass of the country's excellent Chianti.

The capital of Italy is centrally located in the country towards the western coast and sits on the River Tiber. Its history stretches back over two and a half thousand years although there is evidence of human activity in the area stretching back thousands of years prior to that. Today just over 2.7 million people call this historic city home and it remains one of the most visited places in the world as people around the world continue to flock to its attractions

3 THINGS YOU MUST DO...

1 THE SPANISH STEPS
Get some exercise up the famous steps built between 1723–26 with the church Trinità dei Monti at the top. A lot of the designer shops are based around here, too. To get there: metro to Spagna.

2 THE COLOSSEUM
See gladiators fight to the death and the Christians fed to the lions at the Colosseum (Piazza del Colosseo, tel: +39 6 3996 7700). In your imagination, anyway. When: daily 09.00–16.00 (later some months). Price: €15.50, concessions €10.50 and €4.50. To get there: metro to Colosseo.

3 VATICAN CITY
Visit the world's smallest state, home to the Roman Catholic Church and its head, the Pope. It has a population of less than a thousand people and covers just 44 hectares. To get there: metro to Ottaviano or Cipro-Musei Vaticani, bus 40 and 64.

Above: A staircase in the Vatican, centre of the Catholic faith.

Weather	Low (°C)	High (°C)	Rain (mm)	Sunset
January	3	12	80	16.50
February	4	13	74	17.25
March	6	15	65	18.00
April	8	17	54	19.35
May	12	21	31	20.09
June	16	25	16	21.39
July	18	28	15	20.49
August	19	28	33	20.29
September	16	26	68	19.47
October	13	21	93	18.52
November	7	16	110	17.05
December	5	13	89	16.40

STADIO FLAMINIO

The place of gladiators

Located 4 km (2.5 miles) northwest of Rome's city centre and just 300 metres (328 yards) from the Parco di Villa Glori, the current Stadio Flaminio was opened in 1959 for the Olympics held in Rome a year later. You can see the five rings of the Olympics above the players' tunnel.

At just over 32,000 it has the smallest capacity of any of the Six Nations main grounds but redevelopment, scheduled to finish in time for the 2012 tournament was to take that figure up to 42,000. With the trees lining the hills at the back of the stands it proves that small can indeed be beautiful.

Rome is hardly a hotbed of Italian rugby. The football teams Roma and Lazio, who used to play at Stadio Flaminio, attract most attention and the ground has had to fight off challenges from Bologna, Padua and Genoa to host major Italian matches.

The stadium is home to one of Rome's less glamorous soccer clubs, Cisco Roma, and the rugby outfit Capitolina. The ground staged Italy's first Six Nations win, over Scotland, in their first Six Nations game in 2000, plus further wins over the Scots in 2004 and 2008 and victories over Wales in 2003 and 2007.

There are bars around the stadium with many fans drinking in the Piazzale Flaminio and then taking the short walk to the ground for kick-off.

Below: The picturesque Stadio Flaminio is flanked by trees and hills.

MATTER OF FACT
Stadium: Stadio Flaminio
Located: Rome, Italy
Address: Viale dello Stadio Flaminio, 00196
Rome, Italy
Tel: +39 63 6851
Email: turismo@comune.roma.it.
Website: www.federugby.it
or www.romaturismo.it
Capacity: 32,000 (42,000 by 2012)
To get there: Take metro 'A' for Flaminio, or Tram 225 to Flaminio then Tram 2 to ground
Stands: Tribuna Coperta, Tribuna Scoperta, Curva Sud, Curva Nord

First Test: Italy 6 France 44, 1935
Tests hosted: 40
Italy record: P 40, W 10, L 30, D 0

Bars in ground: Not named
Bars nearby: Mad Jack's (Via Arenula 20, 00186 Rome, +39 6 6830 1060, www.madjacks.it);
Stella – Bar Stadio (Via Flaminia, 231, 00196 Rome, +39 6 322 7492); **Kilmoon Pub Di Andrea Filippi** (Via Giovanni Battista Tiepolo, 2, 00196 Roma, +39 6 321 5457); **Pink Panter** (Via Luigi Poletti 10, 00196 Rome, +39 6323 6473, www.pinkpanter.it)

Finally... Lawrence Dallaglio's Italian heritage meant he could have been playing at Stadio Flaminio instead of Twickenham. In 2010 the English World Cup winner set off from the ground on an 2,900 km (1,800 mile) bicycle ride taking in all the Six Nations grounds. With numerous celebrities for company the 'Cycle Slam' raised £1 million (€1.1 million) for charity.

BENETTON TREVISO

United colours

Benetton Treviso, who have been sponsored by the clothing and accessory company since 1979 and owned by them since 1999, were the dominant Italian club for two decades and they were invited to join the Magners League for the 2010–11 season. Although powerful domestically, and consistently supplying more players to the national side than any other Italian outfit, they have struggled in the Heineken Cup with their best result being the 9-8 shock win against Perpignan in their opening match of the 2009–10 campaign.

That victory took place at Stadio Comunale di Monigo, Treviso's ground, sited 4 km (2.5 miles) from the city centre, which was redeveloped in 1973 and up until 2001, when Italy hosted Fiji, regularly staged Test matches. In 1998, prior to Italy's admission to the Six Nations, Scotland were beaten 25-21 at the ground, a sign of things to come from the Italians...

Before heading to the ground, which has four bars, most fans start off at one of the rugby bars in town. One of these, Osteria Trevisi, in the middle of Treviso, is covered in rugby memorabilia and the staff are able to argue with you about anything from the make-up of the England front row to whether the Wallabies should employ a blitz defence.

Traditionally Treviso have been a haven for foreign stars with players such as Australia's Michael Lynagh, New Zealander John Kirwan and Englishmen Fraser Waters enjoying stints in a town tagged 'Benettonville' because of the impact of the fashion business on the area.

Below: *Treviso legend Alessandro Troncon (right) addresses his troops on national duty.*

MATTER OF FACT
Club: Benetton Treviso
Formed: 1932
Located: Treviso, Italy
Administrative address: Strada del Nascimben, 1/B 31100 Treviso
Tel: +39 4 2232 4238
Email: info@benettonrugby.it
Website: www.benettonrugby.it
Honours: Super 10 champions 1956, 1978, 1983, 1989, 1992, 1997, 1998, 1999, 2001, 2003, 2004, 2006, 2007, 2009, 2010, Coppa Italia winners 1970, 1998, 2005, 2010
Euro honours: None

Heineken Cup records
Best finish: Pool (13 times)
Record: P 72, W 16, L 56, D 0
Most appearances: 40 Massimiliano Perziano (1991–2007)
Most points: 227 Marius Goosen (2004–)
Biggest win: 86-8 v Farul Constanta, 1995
Biggest defeat: 71-5 v Wasps, 2006

Ground: Stadio Comunale di Monigo
Address: Viale Olimpia, 1, 31100 Treviso
Capacity: 9,000
To get there: Treviso Centrale Station (train) 3.2 km (2 miles)
Stands: Central, Side

Bars in ground: Not named
Bars nearby: Osteria Trevisi (Via Avogari Vicolo Trevisi, 6, 31100 Treviso, +39 4 22 545308); **Bar Botolo** (Via Castagnole, 13, 31100 Treviso, +39 4 22 230500); **Snak Passaparola** (Via Castagnole, 53, 31100 Treviso, +39 4 22 210884); **Charlie Pub** (Via Tre Venezie, 19, 31100 Treviso, +39 4 22 23698, www.charliepub.net)

Legends
Alessandro Troncon: Treviso-born scrum-half who was the first Italian to win 100 caps. Had two spells at his local club, spanning a decade, before retiring in 2007 and joining the Italian coaching staff.
John Kirwan: Big All Black wing who spent four years at Treviso from 1986 and scored 35 Test tries. In retirement he coached the Italian national team from 2002 to 2005 before taking over the Japanese squad.

Need to know: For a bit of culture take a trip to Venice, about 45 km (30 miles) from Treviso. See the intricate paintings of the Doge's Palace, the Bridge of Sighs, St Mark's Square and take a trip in a gondola.

AIRONI

New kids in the ruck

Aironi Rugby are a franchise club, formed to compete in the Magners League and the Heineken Cup from the start of the 2010–11 season. Eight rugby clubs came together to create Aironi. Rugby Viadana are the biggest stakeholder with 54 per cent while Gran Parma Rugby, Rugby Parma and Colorno are the other major players. The new franchise attracted many players already playing in Italy and financial support from the Italian Federation meant they were also able to lure big names such as former national captains Marco Bortolami and Fabio Ongaro to the club and foreigners of the calibre of ex-Gloucester and France fly-half Ludovic Mercier plus Munster's Nick Williams.

Based at Viadana MN's Stadio Luigi Zaffanella, they play big Heineken Cup games at the near-30,000 capacity Stadio Giglio, in Reggio Emila, the home of AC Reggiana 1919 soccer club which is a 50-minute drive from their normal base.

Viadana MN, not to be confused with the Viadana near Brescia, is a small, quiet, industrial town with a population of 17,000 and a surprising choice for the base of a new club as it is basically in the middle of nowhere. It has very little accommodation for travelling fans, no railway service, a limited bus service and no taxi company. Apart from that lot it's a delight to visit . . .

Most fans base themselves in Parma, about a 40-minute drive away, but make sure your return journey is booked otherwise you will find yourself stranded in Viadana for the evening.

Below: Aironi (Italian for heron) became European rugby's new boys when they joined the party in 2010.

MATTER OF FACT
Club: Aironi Rugby
Formed: 2010
Located: Viadana MN, Italy
Administrative address: Via Learco Guerra, 12, 46019 Viadana
Tel: +39 375 771 225
Email: info@aironirugby.eu
Website: www.aironirugby.eu

Heineken Cup records (First season 2010–11)

Ground: Stadio Luigi Zaffanella
Address: Via Learco Guerra 12, 46019 Viadana MN
Capacity: 6,000
To get there: Parma Station (train) 25 km (20 miles) away. By car take SP 62 R
Stands: West, East, Montepaschi

Bars in ground: Club House Acqua & Vent
Bars nearby: Bar Centrale (13, Piazza Manzoni Alessandro, 46019 Viadana MN, +39 375 781 215); **Bar Jolly** (Largo Alcide De Gasperi, 36, 46019 Viadana MN, +39 375 781 132); **Bini Giuseppe Bar** (Via Giuseppe Garibaldi, 25, 46019 Viadana MN, +39 375 781 426); **Bar Sport** (67, Via Milano, Viadana MN 46019, +39 375 88 220)

Legends:
Luigi Zaffanella: Captain of Viadana when they won their first promotion to Division B of Italian rugby in 1981. A back rower, he did not have time to savour his team's historic feat as he was killed in a car accident on 29 April that year, aged 29. The ground is named in his memory.
Kaine Robertson: Nine years at Viadana before the formation of Aironi. New Zealand-born back who helped Viadana to the 2002 Italian Championship, scoring 12 tries and gained eligibility for the Italian national team in 2004.

Need to know: Aironi means heron in Italian and the bird features on the badge of the franchise. Games against the Ospreys should be known as the 'Battle of the Birds'.

ROVIGO

Culture Club

Founded by a medical student, Dino Lanzoni, in 1935, Rovigo have traditionally been one of the strongest sides in Italian rugby with 11 national titles between 1951 and 1990. However, they failed to add to that number in the following two decades and decisions in European rugby mean it will be even harder for them to climb to the top table again.

The elevation of Benetton Treviso and the amalgamation of teams to form Aironi Rugby, both entered in the Magners League, means they have no prospect of Heineken Cup rugby and are condemned to life in the second-tier Challenge Cup, at least for the time being.

In the past the lifestyle in Rovigo attracted players such as Naas Botha, the South African fly-half, who joined in 1987 and guided the side to two championships, Gert Smal, the Springbok flanker and Nick Mallett who would go on to coach South Africa and the Italian national side. Nairn McEwan, the Scottish flanker and national coach, also did a stint in charge of the side from 1982 to 1984.

Match days are enlivened by the presence of Bersagliotto, a bear who acts as the club mascot and whose theme tune is a slightly irritating jingle, while the supporters glory under the name of Rugby Club Posse Rossoblu.

Away from the rugby, Rovigo is a 45-minute train journey from Venice and is the home of Accademia dei Concordi, which houses over 220 works of art and Chiesa La Rotonda, an octagonal-plan church built in 1594 that houses the famous Virgin with Child fresco.

There are plenty of restaurants and bars in the town but some fans stay in nearby Padova, or in Venice, although getting back from night matches is not easy in the latter's case and Venice is hardly the choice for the budget rugby fan.

MATTER OF FACT
Club: Femi-CZ Rugby Rovigo
Formed: 1935
Located: Rovigo, Italy
Administrative address: Viale Vittorio Alfieri, 46, 45100 Rovigo (RO)
Tel: +39 425 168 7060
Email: info@rugbyrovigo.com
Website: www.rugbyrovigo.com
Honours: Super 10 champions 1951, 1952, 1953, 1954, 1962, 1963, 1964, 1976, 1979, 1988, 1990
Euro honours: None

Heineken Cup records (Never appeared)

Challenge Cup records
Record: P 36, W 3, L 33, D 0
Most appearances: 34 Marco Barion (1998–)
Most points: 141 Andrea Scanavacca (1998–2004)
Biggest win: 34-14 v Caerphilly, 1998
Biggest defeat: 78-3 v London Irish, 2008

Ground: Stadio Mario Battaglini
Address: Via Vittorio Alfieri, 46 45100 Rovigo (RO)
Capacity: 5,000
To get there: 2 km (1.2 miles) from Rovigo Station (train)
Stands: Lanzoni Tribune, Quaglio Tribune

Bars in ground: Not named
Bars nearby: Bar Celio (Via Lodovico Ricchieri detto Celio, 5, 45100 Rovigo RO, +39 425 22211);
Bar Sport Di Cappello Mario (Via Adige, 60, 45100 Rovigo RO, +39 425 1922125); **Bar Stazione FS** (Piazza Riconoscenza, 3, 45100 Rovigo RO, +39 425 33326); **Bar La Fenice Snc** (Via del Sacro Cuore, 15, 45100 Rovigo RO, +39 425 27125)

Legends
Elio De Anna: Wing who won two titles with Rovigo and 27 caps for Italy between 1972 and 1980. A doctor, he turned to politics and was elected president of the province of Pordenone, for Forza Italia, a right-of-centre coalition.
Carlo Checchinato: Locally-born number eight and lock who won 83 caps for Italy, scoring 21 tries while playing for Rovigo and Benetton Treviso between 1990 and 2004. Went on to become Italian team manager.

Need to know: The town of Rovigo is twinned with, among others, Bedford in England. The link started when Bedford Blues played Rovigo in a European tie in 1999–2000. The two clubs have organized exchange visits for young players.

Below: Rovigo look like being frozen out of the Heineken Cup for the foreseeable future.

SCOTLAND

THE 3 MINUTE GUIDE		**Capital:** *Edinburgh.* **Language:** *English.* **Beer:** *Tennents Lager, Deuchars IPA (Indian Pale Ale).* **Food:** *Shortbread, porridge, haggis, deep-fried Mars bar.* **National anthem:** *Flower of Scotland.* **Population:** *5.1 million.* **Time zone:** *GMT.* **Emergency number:** *999.* **Did you know?** *In 1832 Scottish physician Neil Arnott invented the water bed.* **Rugby body:** *Scottish Rugby Union, Murrayfield Stadium, Roseburn Street, Edinburgh EH12 5PJ. Tel: +44 131 346 5000. Web: www.scottishrugby.org*

Below: Whisky must be aged for a minimum of three years to earn the right to be called Scotch.

Scotland the Brave

S cotland initiated the first rugby union international, played in 1871, when they challenged England to a match – via the pages of *Bell's Life*, a sporting weekly. The match played at Raeburn Place, the home of Edinburgh Academicals, ended in a win for the Scots and started a rivalry with the English that is just as passionate today as it ever was.

The Calcutta Cup, made from the melted-down rupees left in the kitty of the disbanded Calcutta Rugby Club, has been contested by the two nations since 1879 and Scotland wins, particularly those that thwarted English Grand Slams in 1990 and 2000 are still talked about with reverence north of the border.

Scotland have provided their fair share of notable Lions, including Gordon Brown, Gavin Hastings, Finlay Calder and Andy Irvine, plus Ian McGeechan, who played on two tours and coached on five. However, they have had just three Grand Slams to their name up to 2010, although they have the distinction of being the last winners of the Five Nations, under Jim Telfer in 1999.

In World Cups Scotland have been perennial quarter-finalists, apart from 1991, when they were beaten in the semi-finals by, of all teams, England, with Hastings who had been heroic throughout the tournament missing a penalty in front of the posts with the scores level.

Scotland is also the birthplace of Sevens, the brainchild of a Melrose butcher, Ned Haig, who was looking for ways to raise extra funds for his club in 1883.

Above: *Callanish stone circle on the isle of Lewis in the Outer Hebrides, one of many ancient sites in Scotland. The circle is believed to be about 5,000 years old.*

TEST RECORD (capped internationals only)

Versus	First Test	Played	Won	Lost	Drawn
Argentina	Nov 1990	12	4	8	0
Australia	Dec 1927	26	8	18	0
England	Mar 1871	127	42	67	18
France	Jan 1910	84	34	46	3
Ireland	Feb 1877	124	64	55	5
Italy	Dec 1996	16	10	6	0
New Zealand	Nov 1905	27	0	25	2
South Africa	Nov 1906	20	4	16	0
Wales	Jan 1883	115	48	64	3

Most international caps: Chris Paterson (1999–) 100 Tests
Most international points: Chris Paterson (1999–) 752 points, 100 Tests
(22t, 87c, 153p, 3g)
Most international tries: Ian Smith (1924–1933) 24 tries, 32 Tests
and Tony Stanger (1989–1998) 24 tries, 52 Tests

WORLD CUP RECORD

Year	Venue	Finished
1987	Australia & NZ	Quarter-finals
1991	England	Semi-finals
1995	South Africa	Quarter-finals
1999	Wales	Quarter-finals
2003	Australia	Quarter-finals
2007	France	Quarter-finals

Most World Cup appearances: Doddie Weir 14 matches (1991, 1995, 1999)
Most World Cup points: Gavin Hastings 227 points, 13 matches (1987, 1991, 1995)
Most World Cup tries: Gavin Hastings, 9 tries, 13 matches (1987, 1991, 1995)
Record World Cup win: 89-0 v Ivory Coast, Rustenburg, 1995
World Cup coaches: 1987 Derrick Grant; 1991 Ian McGeechan; 1995 Jim Telfer; 1999 Jim Telfer; 2003 Ian McGeechan; 2007 Frank Hadden

EDINBURGH

Above: *Looking out across the capital of Scotland from Edinburgh Castle.*

The relaxed capital

It's not hard to like Edinburgh. Smart and sophisticated, the Scottish capital boasts an easy air that comes from a city that seems at ease with its place in history and modern life in Scotland

While the much-bigger city of Glasgow to the west has a rough and tough image, providing the drive behind the country's industry, Edinburgh relaxes in its status as the centre of government, culture and tourism.

Since devolution in 1999, the Scottish Parliament has been based here and sits in what is known as Holyrood, the area to the east of the centre in which the parliament building is situated.

The building, which was completed in 2004, is at one end of the famous Royal Mile, the main throughfare which runs (not surprisingly for a mile) from here to Edinburgh Castle. The Royal Mile (made up of Abbey Strand, Canongate, High Street, Lawnmarket, Castle Hill and Castlegate), with its granite paved streets and lined with its imposing old buildings is just one of the reason why more than a million people flock to the city each year.

And while they are here many of them will no doubt sample Scotland's greatest export: whisky (the Scotch Whisky Experience can be found towards the Castle). Although other regions are more famed for whisky-making (Glenkinchie is one malt distillery close by, as is the huge North British distillery, which produces huge quantities of the less glamorous grain for the blended market) you will certainly have no selection problems due to the ranges available in the bar and pubs.

Select a famed whisky bar, such as the Bow Bar in West Bow or the Albanch in the High Street, choose a few whiskies that take your fancy (the local Glenkinchie would not be a bad place to start) and slowly start working your way through them. Taxi!

3 THINGS YOU MUST DO...

1 THE SCOTCH WHISKY EXPERIENCE
Whisky courses, a shop, and the whole whisky-making process can be enjoyed in this replica distillery (354 Castlehill, tel: +44 131 220 0441). When: daily 10.00–18.00 (18.30 Jun–Aug) Last tour an hour before close. Price: from £11.50 adult, £8.95 concessions. To get there: along the Royal Mile near the Castle.

2 CAIRNAPPLE HILL
One of the most important prehistoric monuments in Scotland (Bathgate Hills, Bathgate, tel: Historic Scotland +44 131 668 8600), this ancient burial ground and ceremonial site was used from 3000–1400BC. When: Apr–Oct but hill can be accessed all year. Price: free. To get there: Bus 20 (27, 28 on Sun).

3 JAMIE'S SCOTTISH EVENING
Get the full taste of Scottish entertainment (bookings tel: +44 131 556 0111) with four-course banquet, pipers, dancers and the Ceremony of the Haggis. Price: £45 adult, £30 child under 14. When: April–Oct.

Above: The busy streets of Edinburgh's Royal Mile.

Weather	Low (°C)	High (°C)	Rain (mm)	Sunset
January	0	6	57	15.49
February	0	7	42	16.46
March	2	9	51	17.47
April	3	11	41	19.50
May	6	14	52	20.50
June	9	17	51	21.47
July	10	18	57	22.01
August	10	18	65	21.21
September	8	16	67	20.08
October	6	14	65	18.49
November	2	9	63	16.33
December	1	7	58	15.45

MURRAYFIELD

The tower of Scotland

Renovated in 1995 Murrayfield, just 1.5 km (1 mile) from Edinburgh's Haymarket Station, has been used for rugby union since 1925.

Although it is never full for club matches the ground is packed out for internationals with the roar of the anthem *Flower of Scotland* providing a spine-tingling moment that has often inspired great home victories for the men in blue.

In 1990 Will Carling's England travelled to Murrayfield as hot favourites for a Grand Slam but a Tony Stanger try helped Scotland to a 13-7 win and they took the Slam themselves. Ten years later, in a torrential downpour, they rained on England's parade again when Duncan Hodge scored all the points in a 19-13 victory to deny Clive Woodward's side a clean sweep.

The ground has hosted the 2005 and 2009 Heineken Cup finals, matches in three Rugby World Cups, the Rugby League Challenge Cup final from 2000 to 2004, as well as football matches and many top concerts.

There are bars all around the ground and a Famous Grouse Tent, which is a recent boost to rugby fans who enjoy a drink because from 1982 to 2007 the sale of alcohol was banned in the stadium under the 1980 Criminal Justice Act.

For pre- and post-match refreshment spectators will find plenty of bars in the Haymarket area, Grassmarket and Rose Street but the heaving Murrayfield Hotel and the Roseburn are the main focal points for a singsong.

Below: Clouds have gathered over Murrayfield for many visiting teams.

MATTER OF FACT
Stadium: Murrayfield Stadium
Located: Murrayfield, Edinburgh
Address: Roseburn Street, Edinburgh EH12 5PJ
Tel: +44 131 346 5000 or +44 131 346 5044 (store)
Email: feedback@sru.org.uk
Website: www.scottishrugby.org
Capacity: 67,500
To get there: 15-minute walk from Haymarket Station (train) or buses 12, 16, 22, 26, 30, 31, 38
Stands: North, West, East, South

Stadium tours
Open: Mon–Fri (weekends and public holidays by arrangement, minimum 10 people); £6 adults, £3.50 concessions, £14 family ticket, free under-5s; Groups (15 or more) £5.50 adults, £3 concessions
Tel: +44 131 346 5160 (book 48 hours in advance)
Email: stadiumtours@sru.org.uk

First match: Scotland 14 England 11, 1925
First Test: Scotland 14 England 11, 1925
Tests hosted: 237
Scotland record: P 236, W 120, L 106, D 10

Bars in ground: Famous Grouse Tent, Triangle Bar, Clock Tower Bar
Bars nearby: Murrayfield Hotel & Lodge (18 Corstorphine Road, Murrayfield, Edinburgh EH12 6HN, +44 131 337 1884, www.festival-inns.co.uk); **Roseburn Bar** (1 Roseburn Terrace, Edinburgh EH12 5NG, +44 131 337 1067); **The Haymarket Bar in Edinburgh** (11–14a West Maitland Street, Edinburgh EH12 5DS, +44 131 228 2537, www.greatvaluepubs.co.uk); **The Caledonian Ale House** (1–3 Haymarket Terrace, Edinburgh EH12 5ES, +44 131 337 1006)

Finally . . . Bill McLaren, the rugby commentator who died aged 86 in January 2010, was synonymous with Scottish rugby. Journalists watch the action from the Bill McLaren Press Gallery, which was opened in 2002.

EDINBURGH

Edinburgh not rocking

The original Edinburgh district side played as far back as 1872, but the team was revived in 1996 when the Scottish Rugby Union decided their clubs were too weak to compete against the English and French in the Heineken Cup. They did not exactly cover themselves in European glory in the subsequent years, however, making the Heineken Cup quarter-finals just once in the first 14 years of the competition.

Life is never simple in Scottish sport, and in 2006 Edinburgh were transferred to private ownership headed by local businessmen, but the new owners soon fell into a row with the SRU over, you guessed it, money. Some Edinburgh players – including Chris Paterson – were withdrawn from a national training squad ahead of the 2007 World Cup and the club opted out of membership of the SRU. It all came to a head with the SRU regaining control in 2007 and the cancellation of the franchise agreement.

Former Scotland and Lions captain Gavin Hastings was made chairman in 2007 and Andy Robinson, an Englishman, was appointed coach. The improvement under Robinson was almost immediate with Edinburgh finishing fourth and second in the Magners League and scoring Heineken Cup wins over Leinster and Leicester before Robinson took on the Scotland job in 2009.

Considering that Murrayfield is such a cauldron of passion on Six Nations days it can be disappointing to sit there when there are a few thousand fans rattling around the ground for a Heineken Cup match. Attendances of only 5,000 are not uncommon in an arena built for over 67,000 and it can be like watching a County Championship cricket match fizzle out at Lord's or the Oval. A bit of a damp squib.

Below: *Edinburgh's Chris Paterson piles in against Cardiff Blues in the Heineken Cup in 2010.*

MATTER OF FACT

Club: Edinburgh Rugby
Formed: 1996
Located: Edinburgh, Scotland
Administrative address: Murrayfield, Edinburgh, EH12 5PJ
Tel: +44 131 346 5252
Email: info@edinburghrugby.org
Website: www.edinburghrugby.org
Honours: Scottish League 2003
Euro honours: None

Heineken Cup records
Best finish: Quarter-finals 2004
Record: P 77, W 27, L 47, D 3
Most appearances: 57 Allan Jacobsen (1997–)
Most points: 236 Chris Paterson (1999–)
Biggest Heineken Cup win: 43-16 v Ebbw Vale, 1998
Biggest Heineken Cup defeat: 69-12 v Dax, 1996

Ground: Murrayfield Stadium
Address: Roseburn Street, Edinburgh EH12 5PJ
Capacity: 67,500
To get there: 15-minute walk from Haymarket Station (train) or buses 12, 16, 22, 26, 30, 31, 38
Stands: North, West, East, South

Bars in ground: Famous Grouse Tent, Triangle Bar, Clock Tower Bar
Bars nearby: Auld Hundred (100 Rose Street, Edinburgh EH2 2NN, +44 131 225 1809, www.auldhundred.co.uk); **The Black Rose Tavern** (49 Rose Street, Edinburgh EH2 2NH, +44 131 220 0414, www.blackrosetavern.com); **The Oxford Bar** (8 Young Street, Edinburgh EH2 4JB, +44 131 539 7119, www.oxfordbar.com); **Athletic Arms** (1–3 Angle Park, Edinburgh EH11 2JX, +44 131 337 3822)

Legends:
Allan Jacobsen: Front row anchorman who made his 200th Edinburgh appearance in 2008 and kept on racking up the caps. Nicknamed 'Chunk', for obvious reasons, Jacobsen, made his Edinburgh debut in 1997.
Duncan Hodge: Former Edinburgh fly-half still revered in Scotland for scoring all the points in his country's 19-13 win over England that denied them the Grand Slam in 2000. Went on to work as Scotland's kicking coach.

Need to know: Edinburgh are nicknamed, and were officially known for a short time, as the Gunners, because of the howitzer gun that is fired on the ramparts of Edinburgh Castle every day, barring Sundays, Good Friday and Christmas Day.

GLASGOW

Europe's tough City of Culture

Universally known as a rough, tough city, Glasgow is built on the River Clyde in central Scotland. The city is an important industrial and cultural centre (it was the European City of Culture in 1990) and is the country's largest city, with a population of around 650,000, although the greater urban area is well over a million.

Sauchiehall Street is the main, and most well-known strip in Glasgow for business, shopping and nightlife. The 2.5 km (1.5 mile) street runs from the Buchanan Galleries, the city's large shopping complex at its eastern end, passing near the Charing Cross (Glasgow) rail station before crossing the M8 motorway, and ending eventually at the Kelvingrove Park, which adjoins the University of Glasgow. It is along this street that locals and visitors head to for a drink or three and there are certainly no shortage of bars.

The Buchanan Galleries is situated near the heart of the city and is one of the UK's largest retail centres, housing most of the top outlets when the need for a shopping fix bites.

*Above: Cloisters at Glasgow University. **Below:** The River Clyde runs from east to west across the city.*

Weather	Low (°C)	High (°C)	Rain (mm)	Sunset
January	0	6	141	15.54
February	1	6	99	16.50
March	2	8	109	17.51
April	3	10	60	19.55
May	6	15	62	20.56
June	8	17	63	21.51
July	11	18	68	22.05
August	10	18	84	21.24
September	8	15	116	20.12
October	6	12	131	18.53
November	2	8	130	16.35
December	1	6	137	15.50

3 THINGS YOU MUST DO...

1 AUCHENTOSHAN DISTILLERY

Tour the Auchentoshan Distillery (tel: +44 1389 878 561) to learn more about the country's national drink, and taste a few whiskies. When: Mon–Sat 10.00–17.00, Sun 12.00–17.00. Price: £4.50 adult. To get there: by car on the Great Western Road (A82) or by train to Kilpatrick.

2 HAMPDEN PARK

This 52,000-seater stadium (tel: +44 141 616 6139) is home to the Scottish national football side. When: tours daily 11.00, 12.30, 14.00 and 15.00 (15.30 Apr–Oct). Price: stadium and museum tour, £9 adult, £4.50 under 16s. To get there: buses 31, 37 and 75, or train to Kings Park or Mount Florida.

3 CLYDE AUDITORIUM

There is some impressive architecture in Glasgow but the stand-out is the Armadillo, as the Clyde Auditorium (Finnieston Street, tel: +44 8700 404000 for box office) is known locally. Designed by Sir Norman Foster, it has drawn comparisons with the Sydney Opera House.

GLASGOW WARRIORS

Glasgow kiss

It is tough trying to make a big noise when your neighbours are Celtic and Rangers and in truth Glasgow did little initially to promote rugby's cause in the city. Attendances for Heineken Cup matches, which sometimes amount to little more than 3,000, at Firhill Stadium, are not uncommon and Glasgow's and Edinburgh's, automatic places in Europe's top competition rankle with English clubs who sweat blood all year just to qualify.

Glasgow Warriors, as they have been known since 2005, share Firhill with Partick Thistle FC, a club with a similar history of underachievement. It became their permanent home in 2007, taking over from Hughenden. Glasgow's best effort in the first 15 years of the Heineken Cup was a place in the quarter-final play-off in 1997–98 although when they got there they were walloped by Leicester.

But in the 2009–10 season Glasgow showed some improvement, finishing third in the Magners League regular season table with coach Sean Lineen, the original 'Kilted Kiwi' and a member of Scotland's Grand Slam team of 1990, relying more on Scottish players rather than foreign imports. He did, however pull off a coup when luring the Argentinian back Federico Aramburu, a star at the 2007 World Cup, to Firhill.

Most home fans at the ground are found in the Jackie Husband Stand, named after a former Partick Thistle footballer who spent almost his entire adult life at the club as player, coach, kit man and any other task that came at him.

In 1996 rugby league, even more of a minority sport in Glasgow than union, came to Firhill when Scotland beat Ireland, while 2000 World Cup games were also played at the ground.

Below: Alastair Kellock has captained both Glasgow Warriors and Scotland.

MATTER OF FACT
Club: Glasgow Warriors
Formed: 1996
Located: Glasgow, Scotland
Administrative address: Firhill Arena, 80 Firhill Road, Glasgow G20 7AL
Tel: +44 141 954 5100
Email: info@glasgowwarriors.org
Website: www.glasgowwarriors.org
Honours: None
Euro honours: None

Heineken Cup
Best finish: Quarter-final play-offs 1998
Record: P 67, W 20, L 46, D 1
Most appearances: 41 Gordon Bulloch (1996–2005)
Most points: 388 Tommy Hayes (1997–2003)
Biggest win: 33-11 v Gloucester, 2009
Biggest defeat: 90-19 v Leicester, 1997

Ground: Firhill Stadium
Address: 80 Firhill Road, Glasgow G20 7AL
Capacity: 10,988
To get there: Kelvinbridge or St George's Cross Stations (metro, both 600 metres), Glasgow Queen Street or Glasgow Central Stations both 1.5 km (1 mile) from ground
Stands: North, Main, Jackie Husband

Bars in ground: Alan Rough Lounge, Aitken Suite
Bars nearby: Star & Garter (687 Garscube Road, Glasgow G20 7JX, +44 141 332 4358; **Crosslands** (182 Queen Margaret Drive, Glasgow G20 8NX, +44 141 576 0127); **Strathmore Bar** (775 Maryhill Road, Glasgow G20 7TL, +44 141 945 6402); **Royalty Ale House** (144 Maryhill Road, Glasgow G20 7QS, +44 141 332 1321)

Legends:
Max and Thom Evans: 20th pair of brothers to play for Scotland. Max was briefly a professional golfer, Thom a member of boy band Twen2y4Se7en. The latter retired with a serious neck injury incurred on Scotland duty in 2010.
Gordon Bulloch: Scotland and Lions hooker who won 75 caps for Scotland, a record for a hooker, before retiring from international rugby in 2005. Left Glasgow that year for an unhappy spell at Leeds that ended in relegation.

Need to know: The North Stand at Firhill was built in 2002 to bring the ground up to Scottish Premier League standards. At first it only ran for two thirds of the length of the pitch and Partick Thistle fans christened it 'The Viagra Stand'. It was only half-erect.

WALES

THE 3 MINUTE GUIDE

Capital: *Cardiff.* **Language:** *English, Welsh.* **Beers:** *Brains SA, Brains Bitter.* **Food:** *Faggots and peas, lamb with laver (seaweed) sauce, cawl (stew), leeks.* **National Anthem:** *Hen Wlad Fy Nhadu (Land of My Fathers).* **Population:** *3 million.* **Time zone:** *GMT.* **Emergency number:** *999.* **Did you know?** *Cardiff was once the largest coal-exporting port in the world. Today, just a handful of mines remain in Wales.* **Rugby body:** *Welsh Rugby Union, The Millennium Stadium, Westgate Street, Cardiff, CF10 1ES. Tel: +44 29 2082 2000. Web: www.wru.co.uk*

Below: The Welsh players know their fans expect nothing but 100 per cent passion.

Dragon's breath

Wales is the only country in the Home Nations where rugby union can genuinely be called the national sport and results in Six Nations and World Cups affect the mood of the population. Welsh papers are full of rugby and international players are under constant scrutiny. Although this passion has never been translated into world dominance, Wales have certainly had their high moments.

From 1900 to 1914 Wales were dominant in Britain, winning three Triple Crowns up to 1905 and three Grand Slams to 1911, after France were admitted to the championship. The economic downturn after the World War I, however, saw players such as Jim Sullivan, defect to rugby league.

In the 1970s legendary names such as Barry John, Gareth Edwards and JPR Williams brought the glory days back and Wales won four straight Triple Crowns from 1976. John, a lynchpin of the 1971 Lions retired at just 27 a year later but Phil Bennett was a ready-made replacement while scrum-half Edwards was voted the Greatest Player of All Time in one poll in 2003.

In the late 1980s and 1990s rugby league claimed the likes of Jonathan Davies, Scott Gibbs and Alan Bateman although some returned when union turned professional. In 2005 Mike Ruddock coached the side to their first Grand Slam since 1978, and was rewarded with a player revolt and the loss of his job. New Zealander Warren Gatland repeated the trick in 2008 but in-between there was an embarrassing World Cup exit in 2007, culminating in a 38-34 defeat to Fiji.

Above: *The spectacular ruins of Tintern Abbey, Monmouthshire, were founded in the 12th century and has inspired poets such as Alfred Lord Tennyson and William Wordsworth.*

TEST RECORD (capped internationals only)

Versus	First Test	Played	Won	Lost	Drawn
Argentina	Oct 1991	12	8	4	0
Australia	Dec 1908	29	10	18	1
England	Feb 1881	119	53	54	12
France	Mar 1908	87	43	41	3
Ireland	Jan 1882	115	62	47	6
Italy	Oct 1994	17	14	2	1
New Zealand	Dec 1905	27	3	24	0
Scotland	Jan 1883	115	64	48	3
South Africa	Dec 1906	24	1	22	1

Most international caps: Gareth Thomas (1995–2007) 100 Tests
Most international points: Neil Jenkins (1991–2002) 1049 points, 87 Tests (11t, 130c, 235p, 10d)
Most international tries: Shane Williams (2000–) 51 tries, 73 Tests

WORLD CUP RECORD

Year	Venue	Finished
1987	Australia & NZ	Third
1991	England	Pool
1995	South Africa	Pool
1999	Wales	Quarter-finals
2003	Australia	Quarter-finals
2007	France	Pool

Most World Cup appearances: Gareth Thomas 14 matches (1995, 1999, 2003, 2007)
Most World Cup points: Neil Jenkins 98 points, 7 matches (1995, 1999)
Most World Cup tries: Shane Williams 7 tries, 6 matches (2003, 2007); Ieuan Evans 7 tries, 11 matches (1987, 1991, 1995); Gareth Thomas 7 tries, 14 matches (1995, 1999, 2003, 2007)
Record World Cup win: 72-18 v Japan, Cardiff, 2007
World Cup coaches: 1987 Tony Gray; 1991 Alan Davies; 1995 Alex Evans; 1999 Graham Henry; 2003 Steve Hansen; 2007 Gareth Jenkins

CARDIFF

Above: The Millennium Centre, in the regenerated Bay area of Cardiff, is home to the Welsh National Opera and has hosted many art performances including dance, music, ballet.

When horizons sing

Situated on the south coast of the country, Cardiff is the capital of Wales, with a city population of about 350,000. Known as a tough port and industrial city, Cardiff grew rapidly on the back of its coal exporting and was made the country's capital only in 1955. It has also been the seat of the Welsh Assembly Government since devolution in 1999. Parliament meets at the hi-tech, glass-dominated Senedd building that is situated at Cardiff Bay.

The Bay area is the regenerated former dockland area to the south and includes many other impressive buildings including the tube-like Visitor Centre, the Wales Millennium Centre with its giant inscription spelling out the words 'In These Stones Horizons Sing' in both English and Welsh, as well as the older Pierhead Building and Norwegian Church (which author Roald Dahl used to attend as a child).

In such a rugby-mad country it's no surprise to discover that the Millennium Stadium would easily be classed as one of the 'landmarks' of the city by its locals. But away from sport, Cardiff Castle stands tall in both stature and history. Although rebuilt and added to over the years in various styles, it is believed to be the site of a Roman fort dating back about 2,000 years and today the grounds and building continue to be a major attraction for visitors to this city.

Castell Coch, another castle on the the outskirts of the city, the domed City Hall with its impressive marble hall and the large, centrally located Bute Park are other popular attractions. For more modern culture, Techniquest in the Bay area has numerous science and technology attractions for nerds at heart.

Attractions of a liquid kind can be found in St Mary Street and Greyfriars Road, both popular haunts to try a cold Brains SA, the beer that is brewed in the city.

3 THINGS YOU MUST DO...

1 CARDIFF BAY
Home of the Welsh rugby team and scene of the 1999 Rugby World Cup final. Stadium tours (Westgate St, tel: +44 29 2082 2228) last one hour. When: Mon–Sat 10.00–17.00, Sun 10.00–16.00. Price: £6.50 adult, £4 child. To get there: train to Cardiff Central Rail Station, bus to Cardiff Central Bus Station.

2 ST MARY STREET
One of the busiest streets for nightlife with a host of bars, restaurants and clubs. Try the stylish 411 (3–6 St Mary St, tel: +44 29 2066 7996). When: Thur 09.00–03.00, Fri–Sat 10.00–04.00. Price: free until midnight, £10 after.

3 CARDIFF CASTLE
The castle (Castle St, tel: +44 29 2087 810) has over 2,000 years of history and beautiful grounds. Try to allow three hours. When: Mar–Oct 09.00–18.00, Nov–Feb 09.00–17.00. Price: £8.95 adult, £6.35 child 5–16. To get there: near Cardiff Central Rail Station and Cardiff Central Bus Station.

Above: Cardiff is famed for its many beautiful shopping arcades.

Weather	Low (°C)	High (°C)	Rain (mm)	Sunset
January	2	7	108	16.16
February	2	7	72	17.02
March	3	10	63	17.54
April	6	13	65	19.46
May	8	16	76	20.36
June	12	19	63	21.20
July	13	20	92	21.33
August	13	21	99	21.02
September	11	19	99	19.59
October	8	15	109	18.51
November	5	10	118	16.46
December	3	8	108	16.07

MILLENNIUM STADIUM

Lifting the lid

Sitting bang in the middle of town, almost next to the train station and surrounded by the bars and restaurants of Cardiff, the Millennium Stadium is probably the most fan-friendly ground in the British Isles. The only drawback is when the rail authorities decide not to run trains out of Cardiff on days when late kick-offs take place, leaving some fans stranded in the city. There are, however, worse places to spend a night out than in the hostelries of Westgate Street.

Built for the 1999 Rugby World Cup, the stadium has also been used for, among other things, rugby league, FA Cup finals, Welsh international football, indoor cricket and concerts. It was also rostered to host soccer matches during the 2012 London Olympics.

Inside, the steep stands and the roof, when it is closed, create an amphitheatre that reverberates with the lyrics of *Bread of Heaven* when the Welsh team are playing.

As well as the 1999 Rugby World Cup final, the Millennium Stadium hosted games in the 2007 World Cup, most memorably the quarter-final that saw France defeat New Zealand 20-18, and staged its first Heineken Cup final in 2002. Then, 'the Hand of Back' enraged Munster fans as Leicester's Neil Back knocked the ball out of Peter Stringer's grasp at a scrum and the Tigers held on to win their second European title.

Below: Venue of the 1999 Rugby World Cup, the Millennium Stadium hosted England's FA Cup final six times.

MATTER OF FACT
Stadium: Millennium Stadium
Located: Cardiff, Wales
Address: Westgate Street, Cardiff CF10 1NS
Tel: +44 2929 822000 (main)
or 08442 777888 (tickets)
Email: info@millenniumstadium.com
Website: www.millenniumstadium.com
Capacity: 74,500
To get there: Five-minute walk from Cardiff Central Station (train)
Stands: BT East, South, North, West

Stadium tours
Open: Mon–Sat 10am–5pm, Sun 10am–4pm; £6.50 adults, £4.50 concessions, £4 children (5–15), free under-5s, family ticket (2 adults, 3 children £18)
Tel: 02920 822228
Email: tours@millenniumstadium.com
or book at website

First match: Wales 29 South Africa 19, 1999
First Test: Wales 29 South Africa 19, 1999
Tests hosted: 79
Wales record: P 73, W 39, L 32, D 2

Bars in ground: Pontypool Front Row Bar, The Baa Bar, The Phil Bennett Bar, The Three Feathers Bar, The Gareth Edwards Bar, The Barry John Bar
Bars nearby: The Queens Vaults (29 Westgate Street, Cardiff CF10 1EH, +44 29 2022 7966); **The Goat Major** (33 High Street, Cardiff, CF10 1PU, +44 29 2033 7161, www.sabrain.com/goatmajor); **The Gatekeeper** (9–10 Westgate Street, Cardiff CF10 1DD, +44 2920 646020, www.jdwetherspoon.co.uk/home/pubs/the-gatekeeper); **The City Arms** (10–12 Quay Street, Cardiff CF10 1EA, +44 29 2022 5258)

Finally . . . The ground has had well-documented problems with the pitch and employs hawks to scare pigeons and seagulls away. The best known bird of prey, 'Dad', is a full-time resident at the stadium although he gets match days off when the crowd noise is considered too much.

CARDIFF BLUES

Blue is the colour

Cardiff Blues, formed in 2003 when regionalization was the flavour of the month in Welsh rugby, have never quite lived up to the feats of some of their predecessors in a city used to watching the likes of Gareth Edwards, Gerald Davies and Wilfred Wooller.

In 1996 Cardiff reached the first Heineken Cup final only to be beaten by the Toulouse of Emile Ntamack, Thomas Castaignède and Philippe Carbonneau. That season's competition, a dip-a-toe-in-the-water affair, is historically diminished as it contained no teams from England or Scotland and pools were two-match contests.

It was a bit different in 2009 when the Heineken Cup had established itself as the premier club competition in the world. Cardiff, led by the combustible New Zealander Paul Tito and with Xavier Rush, Jamie Roberts and Ben Blair in the side, they won all six group games – including a double over Biarritz. A quarter-final win over Toulouse was followed by heartbreak in the last four when Cardiff lost rugby's first penalty shoot-out to Leicester. Martyn Williams, a back row man to his boots, was the unfortunate Welshman doing the Gareth Southgate impression.

Although the Blues were eliminated from the Heineken Cup at the pool stage in 2010 they were one of the best losers and joined the Challenge Cup, which they won, beating Jonny Wilkinson's Toulon in the final 28-21.

Cardiff share the Cardiff City FC Stadium with the city's football club. The ground is the second biggest sports arena in Wales, opened in the summer of 2009, and in 2010 pressure and finance from supporters led to plans to erect a statue of Fred Keenor at the ground. Keenor captained Cardiff City to their FA Cup win in 1927, the only time the trophy has left England.

Below: Scrum-half Richie Rees (passing ball), supported by legendary Cardiff prop Gethin Jenkins.

MATTER OF FACT
Club: Cardiff Blues
Formed: 2003
Located: Cardiff, Wales
Administrative address: Cardiff City Stadium, Leckwith Road, Cardiff, CF11 8AZ
Tel: +44 2920 643600
or 0845 345 1400 (from UK only for tickets)
Email: enquiries@cardiffblues.com
Website: www.cardiffblues.com
Honours: Anglo-Welsh Cup 2009
Euro honours: Amlin Challenge Cup 2010

Heineken Cup records
Best finish: Runners-up 1996
Record: P89, W 45, L 40, D 4
Most appearances: 58 Martyn Williams (1999–)
Most points: 279 Ben Blair (2006–)
Biggest win: 62-20 v Rugby Calvisano, 2009
Biggest defeat: 75-25 v Biarritz, 2003

Ground: Cardiff City Stadium
Address: Leckwith Road, Cardiff CF11 8AZ
Capacity: 26,828
To get there: Ninian Park station 1 km (0.6 miles) from ground. Match day shuttle bus from city centre
Stands: Grandstand, Canton, Ninian, Grange

Bars in ground: Not named
Bars nearby: Landsdowne Hotel (71 Beda Road, Cardiff CF5 1LX, +44 2920 398306, www.lansdownepubcardiff.co.uk); **Cornwall Hotel** (92 Cornwall Street, Cardiff CF11 6SR, +44 2920 303947); **King's Castle Hotel** (74 Cowbridge Road East, Cardiff CF11 9DU, +44 2920 372697); **Butchers Arms** (29 Llandaff Road, Cardiff CF11 9NG, +44 2920 227927)

Legends
Martyn Williams: Ball-playing flanker lured out of international retirement by Warren Gatland to help Wales to 2008 Grand Slam. Captained Cardiff from 2002 to 2005 and in 2009 he beat Gareth Edwards' Welsh record of 45 Six Nations' appearances.
Gethin Jenkins: Prop joined Cardiff after Celtic Warriors were disbanded in 2004. Adept on both sides of the scrum and the hands of a centre despite being about 120 kg (264 lb), skills that should get him banned from the front-row union.

Need to know: Cardiff RFC, almost consigned to history since the advent of the Blues, count Barry John and Bleddyn Williams as former players. They still play at Cardiff Arms Park in the Welsh Premiership.

SWANSEA

With beauty on its doorstep

A visit to Swansea offers the best of both worlds: city and country. The city itself, home to about a quarter of a million people, has all the vibrancy you'd hope for in a place of its size and nightlife that challenges many much bigger. And yet on its doorstep are attractions of a different kind – the resort of Mumbles, a former fishing village, and the spectacular Gower Peninsula, the first place in Britain to be designated as an Area of Outstanding Natural Beauty.

For scenes of the liveliest kind, especially on the weekends, everyone heads to the Kingsway, where bars and clubs compete for the attention of the throngs of partygoers. For more bars, and a good variety of restaurants, head to Wind Street, while if you exhaust these options then Brynymor Road is another popular area for a night out, especially among the city's lively student population.

When its time to wind down there is always Mumbles, the seaside village just minutes from the city centre. And beauty can never be far from Swansea as its located on the stunning Gower Peninsula with its many kilometres of lush countryside, dramatic cliffs and long sandy beaches. It's the perfect place to blow away the cobwebs after a night out in urban Swansea.

Above: *Swansea nestles on the sandy southwest coast of Wales.* **Below:** *The Liberty Stadium*

Weather	Low (°C)	High (°C)	Rain (mm)	Sunset
January	4	6	71	16.16
February	4	6	52	17.02
March	7	9	45	17.54
April	8	11	49	19.47
May	12	15	36	20.40
June	14	17	42	21.24
July	16	19	51	21.37
August	16	18	50	21.02
September	13	16	55	19.59
October	11	13	80	18.51
November	8	9	71	16.48
December	6	8	71	16.07

3 THINGS YOU MUST DO...

1 FAGGOTS AND PEAS
Faggots, a speciality of Wales, are made of pig livers and offal. Just think of them as giant, tasty meatballs. Add, thick gravy, peas and often mashed potato.

2 GOWER PENINSULA
Kilometre upon kilometre of unspoilt countryside surround the city of Swansea, with its long sandy beaches to walk on and its castles and small villages to explore. It's also a popular area for surfers.

3 THE KINGSWAY
If you can't find the type of bar or club you are looking for along the Kingsway then you're not looking hard enough. The street parties and parties hard into the night. Join the action.

OSPREYS

Flying in 'Ospreylia'

The Ospreys, the Neath-Swansea Ospreys until 2005, were formed in 2003 when the top level of Welsh rugby was reduced to five regions, from nine clubs, in a attempt to mimic the success of the Irish provinces. Ospreys extended east when Bridgend were added in 2004 and they won their first Celtic League title in 2005.

Described by one newspaper as 'the Real Madrid of rugby,' the Ospreys attracted big foreign names such as Justin Marshall and Marty Holah, and a string of Welsh talent spearheaded by James Hook, Shane Williams, Gavin Henson, Ryan Jones and Mike Phillips.

This nurturing of Welsh talent was seen in February 2008 when they provided 13 of the starting line-up for the Six Nations game against England and the same year the region reached the quarter-finals of the Heineken Cup for the first time.

For a side with such a galaxy of talent, although Henson's contribution was sporadic, three successive European quarter-final defeats at the hands of Saracens, Munster and Biarritz, the latter by a single point, represented something of a letdown. A third Celtic title was collected in 2010 when they beat Leinster 17-12 in the final in Dublin and provided some consolation, although that year they were fined €25,000 for having 16 men on the pitch in a European game against Leicester. They also landed a £100,000 (€110,000) fine and were docked points for failing to fulfil a Magners League fixture against Ulster.

Initially the Ospreys played home games at St Helen's, the base of Swansea RFC, and The Gnoll, the famous Neath ground. In 2005 they moved to the 20,000-seater Liberty Stadium, which is shared with Swansea FC. The ground is modern and slightly out of town although easily reachable by bus from Swansea station.

Below: Shane Williams (right), the Rugby Union Writers' Club player of the season in 2007–8.

MATTER OF FACT
Club: The Ospreys
Formed: 2003
Located: Swansea, Wales
Administrative address: Liberty Stadium, Landore, Swansea SA1 2FA
Tel: +44 1792 616 5000
Email: b.harper@ospreysrugby.com
Website: www.ospreysrugby.com
Honours: Celtic/Magners League 2005, 2007, 2010, EDF Energy Cup 2008
Euro honours: None

Heineken Cup records
Best finish: Quarter-finals 2008, 2009, 2010
Record: P 45, W 23, L 20, D 2
Most appearances: 41 Adam Jones (2003–)
Most points: 198 James Hook (2004–)
Biggest win: 68-8 v Benetton Treviso, 2008
Biggest defeat: 43-9 v Munster, 2009

Ground: The Liberty Stadium
Address: Landore, Swansea SA1 2FA
Capacity: 20,520
To get there: 2.2 km (1.4 miles) from Swansea Station (train). Buses 4, 4a, 120, 122, 125, 132
Stands: North, South, Tesco, West

Bars in ground: Riverside Bar (members)
Bars nearby: Morfa Parc (Unit 19, Morfa Shopping Parc, Brunel Way, Swansea SA1 2FB, +44 1792 475 605, www.harvester.co.uk); **The Alma Inn** (10 Bennet Street, Landore, Swansea SA1 2QH, +44 1792 411 311); **The Wern Inn** (48 Siloh Road, Landore, Swansea SA1 2PE, +44 1792 465 365); **The Manselton** (Penfilia Road, Swansea SA5 9HX, +44 1792 472 224)

Legends
Shane Williams: Jinking wing who flies the flag for rugby's little men. IRB International Player of the Year in 2008, he stands 1.70m (5ft 7in) and scored his 51st international try, a Welsh record, against Italy in 2010.
Marty Holah: Kiwi flanker who landed at the Ospreys when he realized he would not oust Richie McCaw from the All Blacks side. 2009–10 Ospreys Player of the Year, he would have walked into any other Test side.

Need to know: The region around Swansea is now officially known as 'Ospreylia'. Seriously. In 2010 Ordnance Survey produced a map covering Swansea, Neath-Port Talbot, Bridgend and southern Powys. They measured 'Ospreylia' as an area 59 km by 38 km (37 miles by 24 miles), with 243 km (151 miles) of boundaries.

SCARLETS

Scarlet fever

Formed in 2003, mostly out of the powerful Llanelli side of the previous years, the Scarlets kicked off by winning the Celtic League in their first year, captained by Leigh Davies, but in Europe their results have not lived up to the proud tradition of rugby in West Wales.

As Llanelli they were knocked out in the semi-finals of the Heineken Cup in 2000 and 2002, both times by the eventual winners of the tournament (Northampton and Leicester) and in 2007 by Leicester again. In 2003, in Nottingham, a 58-metre penalty from Tigers full-back Tim Stimpson hit the bar and a post before denying Llanelli victory.

In November 2008 the Scarlets moved from their historic ground, Stradey Park, to a new base, Parc y Scarlets, in Pemberton. The ground has a pub, and the lounges and boxes are named after famous figures from the rich history of Llanelli such as Phil Bennett, former coach Carwyn James, who masterminded the Lions win in New Zealand in 1971, the Quinnell family, Ray Williams and Ieuan Evans.

The Ken Jones Museum contains the final ball kicked at Stradey Park while the clock and scoreboard from the old ground have been moved to the new stadium where a 10-tonne statue of the late Scarlet great, Ray Gravell, stands.

On match days the indoor centre at Parc y Scarlets is turned into a 'Supporters' Village' with hog roasts, bar, beer garden plus music and entertainment. Despite this, and the gleaming facilities at the venue, some supporters still pine for the old days of Stradey Park, which was sold to developers in 2008, to much public outcry.

MATTER OF FACT
Club: The Scarlets
Formed: 2003
Located: Llanelli, Wales
Administrative address: Parc y Scarlets, Parc Pemberton, Llanelli, Carmarthenshire SA14 9UZ
Tel: +44 1554 783900
Email: comments@scarlets.co.uk
Website: www.scarlets.co.uk
Honours: Celtic League 2004
Euro honours: None

Heineken Cup records
Best finish: Semi-finals 2000, 2002, 2007
Record: P 93, W 50, L 42, D 1
Most appearances: 70 Stephen Jones (1996–2003 and 2006–)
Most points: 762 Stephen Jones (1996–2003 and 2006–)
Biggest win: 93-14 v Rugby Calvisano, 2001
Biggest defeat: 49-3 v Stade Francais, 1998

Ground: Parc y Scarlets
Address: Llanelli, Carmathenshire, SA14 9UZ
Capacity: 15,180
To get there: 2.4 km (1.5miles) from Llanelli Station (train), 2.1 km (1.3 miles) from Bynea Station (train)
Stands: Castell Howell South, Gravells North, Link Telecom East, KL Plant West

Bars in ground: The Delme Thomas
Bars nearby: The Bush Inn (5 Maescannar Road, Llanelli SA14 8LR, +44 1554 749095); **Joiners Arms** (56–58 Llwynhendy Road, Llanelli SA14 9HR, +44 1554 754594); **Halfway Hotel** (33 Glyncoed Terrace, Llanelli SA15 1EZ, +44 1554 773571); **Nevills Arms** (21 Maescannar Road, Llanelli SA14 8LR, +44 1554 774 618)

Legends
Ray Gravell: Llanelli centre for 15 years from 1970, playing 485 games, he was a Lion in 1980. President of Llanelli he later turned to broadcasting and acting, starring with Peter O'Toole in *Rebecca's Daughters*.
Phil Bennett: Fly–half who instigated the 'greatest try ever' playing for the Barbarians against New Zealand in 1973. Lions captain in 1977 and star of 1974, Bennett is a member of International Rugby Hall of Fame.

Need to know: The pub at Parc y Scarlets is named after Delme Thomas, the second row who captained Llanelli to a 9-3 win over the All Blacks in 1972. The day was commemorated in a poem by Welsh comedian Max Boyce called *The Day the Pubs Ran Dry.*

Below: *The modern-day Scarlets have struggled to live up to the feats of their famous predecessors.*

NEWPORT GWENT DRAGONS

Dragons breathe

The formation of the four Welsh regions in 2003 left many fans feeling the soul of their local club had been ripped out and in Newport, the birth of the Newport Gwent Dragons was far from painless. As Stephen Jones, of *The Sunday Times* and a Newport man, once wrote:'I used to be a member of a real rugby club – Newport. In the villages and suburbs of Newport and district, we held ownership... We are no more. The Welsh Rugby Union forgot what made Wales great. They took our club away.' In 2002–03 Newport were the best supported club in Wales, two years later the Dragons were averaging a little of 5,000 at home games. Many thought the inclusion of Newport in the name alienated other fans from the region while Newport fans were resentful of their club being diluted.

Newport were a proud club, the scourge of touring national sides and in 1891–92 won 29 of 32 games, drawing the other three. Later, players such as David Watkins, Ken Jones and William 'Bunner' Travers all represented the 'Black and Ambers'.

The Dragons were formed in 2003 when Welsh rugby embraced regionalization and came third in the Celtic League in their first season when coached by Mike Ruddock. Ruddock went on to take charge of Wales, and masterminded a Grand Slam in 2005, while Paul Turner took over the reins at Rodney Parade. Turner's first few seasons were not a great success but in 2009–10 the Dragons' form improved significantly. They were unbeaten at home until the final match and narrowly missed out on qualification for the knock-out stages of the Heineken Cup.

Home for the Dragons is Rodney Parade, on the east bank of the River Usk. It was due to be redeveloped and plans were put together for a £40 million project to have been finished at the start of the 2010 season but by then work had not even started.

Below: Backrower Dan Lydiate came through the Newport system and made his Welsh debut in 2009.

MATTER OF FACT
Club: Newport Gwent Dragons
Formed: 2003
Located: Newport, Wales
Administrative address: Rodney Parade, Rodney Road, Newport, Gwent NP19 0UU
Tel: +44 1633 670690
Email: sharon.dennison@rodneyparadeltd.com
Website: www.newportgwentdragons.com
Honours: None
Euro honours: None

Heineken Cup records
Best finish: Pool
Record: P 36, W 7, L 29, D 0
Most appearances: 29 Adam Black (2003–2009)
Most points: 97 Ceri Sweeney (2004–2008)
Biggest win: 48-5 v Edinburgh, 2005
Biggest defeat: 37-0 v Stade Francais, 2004

Ground: Rodney Parade
Address: Rodney Road, Newport, Gwent NP19 0UU
Capacity: 10,059
To get there: Newport Station (train) 1.5 km (1 mile)
Stands: Hazell Stand, Hazel Terrace, Family, Argus Terrace,

Bars in ground: Rodney Hall, Snelling Lounge, Watkins
Bars nearby: Riverside Tavern (63 Clarence Place, Newport NP19 7AB, +44 1633 666 699); **The Dodger** (6–8 Chepstow Road, Newport NP19 8EA +44 1633 212 910); **The Ivy Bush Inn** (65 Clarence Place, Newport NP19 7AB, +44 1633 267 571); **Ye Olde Murenger House** (52–53 High Street, Newport NP20 1GA, +44 1633 263 977)

Legends
David Watkins: Fly-half who helped Newport to 1963 win over the All Blacks and captained the Lions twice in Australia in 1966. Switched to rugby league with Salford, captained Great Britain and scored more than 2,000 points in league.
Keith Jarrett: Newport's boy wonder who ran 75 metres to score on his Test debut against England in 1967, aged 18. A 1968 Lion in South Africa, he turned to rugby league, with Barrow, in 1969, but a stroke forced his retirement aged 25.

Need to know: The original Newport side beat all three of the southern hemisphere Test sides. They defeated South Africa in 1912 and 1969, Australia in 1957 and New Zealand in 1963. They provided 15 Lions from 1945 to 2003.

ARGENTINA

THE

3

MINUTE
GUIDE

Capital: *Buenos Aires.* **Language:** *Spanish.* **Beers:** *Cerveza Quilmes.* **Food:** *Beef, beef and beef, empanada (filled pastry).* **National Anthem:** *Himno Nacional Argentino (Argentine National Anthem).* **Population:** *40.5 million.* **Time zone:** *GMT -3.* **Emergency number:** *101 (police), 107 (medical), 100 (fire).* **Did you know?** *The revolutionary leader Che Guevara was born in Rosario, Argentina and then studied medicine at the University of Buenos Aires.*
Rugby body: *Unión Argentina de Rugby, Reconquista 150, 3° Piso C1003 ABD, Capital Federal Buenos Aires. Tel: +54 11 4515 3500. Web: www.uar.com.ar*

Below: *Back rower Juan Martín Fernández Lobbe, who made his Test debut in 2004.*

Los Pumas

When the International Rugby Board finally cleared the way for Argentina to enter a Four Nations tournament with Australia, New Zealand and South Africa in time for the 2012 season, the rugby world said 'about time too!' *Los Pumas* have to compete for attention in a soccer-mad country but have beaten all the teams in the Six Nations and the Wallabies more than once.

Rugby union was introduced to Argentina by the British and has been played in the country since the 1870s. Nowadays the main centre of interest is around Buenos Aires, an area that can boast over 80 clubs although most top Argentine players ply their trade in Europe. The Tucumán area is also fanatical about rugby and has supplied a host of top-notch forwards to the national side.

Traditionally their sides were built on supremacy at the scrummage but in later years gifted backs such as Juan Martin Hernandez, dubbed the 'Maradona of Rugby', Agustin Pichot and Felipe Contepomi have starred at World Cups.

South African coach Izak van Heerden helped revolutionize the sport in the late 1960s and then fly half Hugo Porta, a Puma from 1971 to 1990, came along. He was the inspiration behind the 1985 side that drew 21-21 with the All Blacks and is still regarded as the best Puma player.

Argentina came third at the 2007 World Cup, beating the hosts France twice and sparking a clamour for their inclusion in more tournaments. That bore fruit with admission to the expanded SANZAR competition.

Above: *The famous colourful homes in La Boca neighbourhood of Buenos Aires.*

TEST RECORD (capped internationals only)

Versus	First Test	Played	Won	Lost	Drawn
Australia	Oct 1979	14	4	12	1
England	May 1981	15	4	10	1
France	Aug 1949	43	11	31	1
Ireland	Oct 1990	11	5	6	0
Italy	Oct 1978	16	10	5	1
New Zealand	Oct 1985	13	0	12	1
Scotland	Nov 1990	12	8	4	0
South Africa	Nov 1993	13	0	13	0
Wales	Oct 1991	12	4	8	0
British & Irish Lions	May 2005	1	0	0	1

Most international caps: Lisandro Arbizu (1990–2005) 87 Tests
Most international points: Hugo Porta (1971–1999) 592 points,
60 Tests (11t, 85c, 101p, 26d)
Most international tries: José Nunez Piossek (2001–2008) 29 tries, 29 Tests

WORLD CUP RECORD

Year	Venue	Finished
1987	Australia & NZ	Pool
1991	England	Pool
1995	South Africa	Pool
1999	Wales	Quarter-finals
2003	Australia	Pool
2007	France	Third

Most World Cup appearances: Agustin Pichot 14 matches (1999, 2003, 2007)
Most World Cup points: Gonzalo Quesada 135 points, 8 matches (1999, 2003)
Most World Cup tries: Pablo Bouza 4 tries, 2 matches (2003), Ignacio Corleto 4 tries,
12 matches (1999, 2003, 2007), Martin Gaitan 4 tries, 2 matches (2003)
Record World Cup win: 63-3 v Namibia, Marseille, 2007
World Cup coaches: 1987 Hector Silva and Angel Guastella; 1991 Luis Gradín and
Guillermo Lamarca; 1995 Alejandro Petra and Ricardo Paganini; 1999 Alex Wyllie;
2003 Marcelo Loffreda; 2007 Marcelo Loffreda

BUENOS AIRES

Above: *Built in May 1936, the obelisk of Buenos Aires celebrates the 400th anniversary of the founding of the city. Pedestrians must be patient when crossing Avenida 9 de Julio.*

The city that knows how to dance

Second only to Brazil's Sãu Paulo when it comes to largest populations in South America, the greater metropolitan area of Buenos Aires is a huge 13 million and counting.

The city itself, though, is a much more agreeable three million or so. Large it may be, but Argentina's capital is far from a sprawling Sãu Paulo. In fact first-time visitors to the city, used to the clichéd impressions of South American cities are struck by just how stylish Buenos Aires is.

And is it any wonder really from a city smack in the middle of the region that gave us the sensual tango dance? Although there have been adaptations and variations of the tango, Argentina (and Uruguay) remains the home of the dance. Visitors to the city can enjoy displays of the dance in venues all over the city or go one step further and learn from the masters. Courses of varying lengths are on offer twinkle toes . . .

In fact you are going to need nimble footwork while staying here,

if only to cross the massive Avenida 9 de Julio. There are so many lanes that pedestrians have to cross in stages via various safe crossing islands. Now you know what those frogs in the early PC games felt like.

When not dancing the tango, or crossing Avenida 9 de Julio, you'll be needing a beer, which is handy because Argentina produces the very agreeable Cerveza Quilmes. For popular and busy nightlife areas head to San Telmo and Puerto Madero.

The city has a stylish café scene that will remind you of France or Italy and these cafés are a great place to start off the afternoon or evening because this city parties late. Try a mate (an infused drink enjoyed through an elaborate 'straw') or if you fancy something stronger simply ask for a *aguardiente* (firewater). Hey, now you're dancing . . .

3 THINGS YOU MUST DO...

1 PARQUE LEZAMA

See monuments where Mendoza founded Buenos Aires, and join chess-playing, flag-waving, book-reading locals, with a second-hand clothes stalls at the weekend (cnr Defensa and Av Brasil San Telmo). To get there: buses 10, 22, 29, 45, 74.

2 FLORALIS GENÉRICA

This needs to be seen – the petals of this giant metallic flower open every morning and close at dusk It was designed by architect Eduardo Catalano in 2002 (Plaza de las Naciones Unidas, Av Pres Figueroa Alcorta). When: petals open at 8.00, close at sunset.

3 PERU BEACH

A short trip out of the city (Peru y el rio, Acassuso, tel: +54 11 4793 5986) you will find football fields, a roller rink, a climbing wall, water sports such as kite-surfing, a grassy lawn and refreshments. To get there: 20 km (12 miles) north of the city centre.

Above: *Tango till the early hours in the home of the dance.*

Weather	Low (°C)	High (°C)	Rain (mm)	Sunset
January	20	30	121	20.10
February	20	29	122	20.01
March	17	26	153	19.33
April	14	23	106	18.50
May	10	19	92	18.13
June	7	16	50	17.51
July	7	15	53	17.53
August	9	17	63	18.11
September	10	19	78	18.35
October	13	23	139	18.56
November	16	25	131	19.22
December	18	28	103	19.52

ESTADIO JOSÉ AMALFITANI

Lair of the Puma

Effectively the national rugby stadium of Argentina, although Los Pumas do play elsewhere, Estadio José Amalfitani, commonly known as Velez Sarsfield, was built in 1947, remodelled for the 1978 soccer World Cup and is home of the football team Velez Sarsfield, the third team of Buenos Aires. Nicknamed 'El Fortin' (The Fort) by locals, the stadium is about 14 km (9 miles) to the west of the centre of the town, where the best nightlife is found after games.

The steep-sided ground is not all-seater and some fans can stand at each end. It was first used by the Argentine rugby team in 1986 after they had played at other grounds in the city.

In 1990 it saw the first visit to the country by an English sporting team since the Falklands conflict. Prop Jason Leonard made his Test debut in a 25-12 England win that was marked by the hostility of the crowd to the tourists with smoke and firecrackers everywhere.

In 2002 Phil Vickery, then propping at Gloucester, captained England to victory at the ground and described the atmosphere as 'putting Kingsholm in the kindergarten'. Since then the ground has seen wins over Australia, England, Ireland, Wales and a 41-13 thumping of France in 2010. The atmosphere has not changed since the days of Leonard and Vickery.

MATTER OF FACT
Stadium: Estadio José Amalfitani
Located: Buenos Aires, Argentina
Address: Avenue Juan B Justo 9200, CP 1408, Liniers, Buenos Aires
Tel: +54 11 4641 5663/5763
Email: rrpp@velezsarsfield.com.ar
Website: www.velezsarsfield.com.ar
Capacity: 49,540
To get there: Liniers Station (train) 750 metres (0.5 miles)
Stands: North, South, East Grandstand, West Grandstand

First Test: Argentina 15 France 13, 1986
Tests hosted: 29
Argentina record: P 29, W 13, L 15, D 1

Bars in ground: Not named
Bar nearby: Cafe de Garcia (Sanabria 3302, Villa Devoto, Buenos Aires, +54 11 4501 5912, www.cafedegarcia.com.ar). Other city bars: **The Shamrock** (Rodriguez Pena 1220, Buenos Aires, +54 11 4812 3584); **The Kilkenny** (Marcelo T de Alvear 399, Buenos Aires, +54 11 4312 7291, www.thekilkenny.com.ar); **Unico** (Honduras 5604, Palermo Hollywood, Buenos Aires, + 54 11 4775 6693)

Finally... Football is still the number one sport in Buenos Aires, despite the valiant efforts of Los Pumas, and there are 24 professional teams of various standards in the city headed by Boca Juniors and River Plate. Rugby does well to get a look-in.

Below: Although Tests are played at other stadiums, Estadio José Amalfitani is effectively home to Argentine rugby.

ESTADIO MONUMENTAL

Puma stronghold

Estadio Monumental Presidente José Fierro is the home of Club Atletico Tucumán football side but has hosted the Argentine rugby side for several Tests and until the summer of 2010 the Pumas were unbeaten at the venue.

Tucumán is a rugby-mad area and the fans know a thing or two about the game. When Andy Robinson's Scotland beat Argentina 24-16 at the ground the home fans stayed and cheered the tourists as they paraded around the pitch after the match. You don't get that at Old Trafford...

The ground holds over 32,000 spectators with three steep banks of terracing and, probably because it is mainly a football ground, the crowd are penned in and have exceeded 40,000 for football matches. Health-and-safety fiends would probably not stand for that elsewhere.

Built in 1922 the ground originally had room for just 5,000 spectators and opened with a football match between Racing Club de Avellaneda and Club Atletico Tucumán. It is found in the northern part of the city which has a train service from Buenos Aires and is close to the airport for supporters wanting to base themselves in the capital.

MATTER OF FACT
Stadium: Estadio Monumental Presidente José Fierro
Located: Tucumán, Argentina
Address: 25 de Mayo 1351 y República de Chile, Barrio Norte, San Miguel de Tucumán
Tel: +54 381 431 4925
Email: correa@clubatleticoTucumán.com or uarugby@uar.com.ar
Website: www.clubatleticoTucumán.com
Capacity: 32,700
To get there: Sante Fe Station (metro)
Stands:

First match: Argentina 78 Brazil 6, 1977
First Test: Argentina 78 Brazil 6, 1977
Tests hosted: 15
Argentina record: P 8, W 7, L 1, D 0

Bars in ground: Not named
Bars nearby: Hotel Italia (Corrientes 999, 4000 San Miguel de Tucumán, +54 381 421-5873); Merco Bar De Camandona Ernest (Blas Parera 999, 4001 San Miguel de Tucumán, +54 381 428 0704); Künstner (Crisóstomo Álvarez 456, 4000 San Miguel de Tucumán, +54 381 497 5597); Quincas Berro Bar (Corrientes 936, 4000 San Miguel de Tucumán, +54 381 15 402 5635)

Finally... When Scotland visited in 2010 they were surprised to find mushrooms growing on the pitch when they had their captain's run the day before the Test. Flanker John Barclay remarked that the stadium was 'not exactly a new-build'.

Below: Los Pumas have a formidable record at the Estadio Monumental.

AUSTRALIA

THE

3

MINUTE
GUIDE

Capital: *Canberra.* **Language:** *English.* **Beers:** *Tooheys (New South Wales), XXXX (Queensland), Swan (Western Australia), Victoria Bitter (Victoria).* **Food:** *Barbecues, Chiko roll, meat pie, Vegemite on toast.* **National Anthem:** *Advance Australia Fair.* **Population:** *22 million.* **Time zones:** *GMT +10 (Sydney, Melbourne, Brisbane, Hobart), GMT +9.30 (Adelaide), GMT +8 (Perth).* **Emergency number:** *000.* **Did you know?** *The Super Pit, Australia's biggest open cut gold mine is 3.5 km (2 miles) long, 1.5 km (1 mile) wide and 360- metres deep.* **Rugby body:** *Australia Rugby Union, Ground floor, 29–57 Christie Street, St Leonards, NSW 2065. Tel: +61 2 8005 5555. Web: www.rugby.com.au*

Below: Young Australian fans are waiting for more success to follow the 1991 and 1999 World Cup wins.

The bouncing Wallabies

Rugby union may be only the fourth-most popular sport in Australia but the Wallabies have punched well above their weight since their first international in 1903. The first side to win the World Cup twice, after victories in 1991 and 1999, Australia were first invited to join the International Rugby Board in 1948 and the Australian Rugby Football Union was formed a year later.

In 1963 the touring Wallabies, captained by John Thornett, beat South Africa in consecutive Tests, becoming the first side to do so in South Africa since the British team of 1896.

But it was the 1984 Wallabies who captivated the rugby public on their tour of Britain and Ireland by becoming the first Australian team to beat all four home nations with the brilliant Aboriginal fly-half Mark Ella scoring a try in every Test. Coached by Alan Jones they had future World Cup winners such as Michael Lynagh, Simon Poidevin, Nick Farr-Jones and David Campese in their line-up, although Ella, one of three rugby-playing brothers, retired at the age of 25.

John Eales, considered the finest lock of the modern era along with England's Martin Johnson, gained a winners' medal in 1991 and skippered the side in 1999. In 2001, Eales got one over Johnson by leading the Wallabies to victory over the Lions when the hosts came back from the shock of losing the first Test in Brisbane.

Australia co-hosted the 1987 World Cup, with New Zealand, but staged the tournament in its entirety in 2003.

Above: *One of the world's great city views. But how many of you have actually been to the opera there?*

TEST RECORD (capped internationals only)

Versus	First Test	Played	Won	Lost	Drawn
Argentina	Oct 1979	17	12	4	1
England	Jan 1909	39	23	15	1
France	Jan 1928	40	22	16	2
Ireland	Nov 1927	29	20	8	1
Italy	Oct 1983	12	12	0	0
New Zealand	Aug 1903	139	39	95	5
Scotland	Dec 1927	26	18	8	0
South Africa	Jun 1921	71	29	41	1
Wales	Dec 1908	29	18	10	1
British & Irish Lions	Jun 1899	20	5	15	0

Most international caps: George Gregan (1994–2007) 139 Tests
Most international points: Michael Lynagh (1984–1995) 911 points, 72 Tests
(17t, 140c, 177p, 9d)
Most international tries: David Campese (1982–1996) 64 tries, 101 Tests

WORLD CUP RECORD

Year	Venue	Finished
1987	Australia & NZ	Fourth
1991	England	Winners
1995	South Africa	Quarter-finals
1999	Wales	Winners
2003	Australia	Runners-up
2007	France	Quarter-finals

Most World Cup appearances: George Gregan 20 matches (1995, 1999, 2003, 2007)
Most World Cup points: Michael Lynagh, 195 points, 15 matches (1987, 1991, 1995)
Most World Cup tries: Chris Latham 11 tries, 7 matches (1999, 2003, 2007)
Record World Cup win: 142-0 v Namibia, Adelaide, 2003
World Cup coaches: 1987 Alan Jones; 1991 Bob Dwyer; 1995 Bob Dwyer;
1999 Rod Macqueen; 2003 Eddie Jones; 2007 John Connolly

CANBERRA

Grey suits you, Sir

Canberra might not get the worldwide attention of Sydney and Melbourne but it is the capital of Australia, and was selected as such as compromise between the country's two largest cities. Canberra itself was designed by, of all people, architects from Chicago at the start of the 20th Century. It thrived after the World War II and although it may have a slightly dour reputation for those who have not been there, if you know what you are doing then it is worth the trip.

First a down side: nowadays it is swarming with public servants being the seat of the Australian government and the High Court. But it is not all grey suits. The Australian Institute of Sport, or should that be conveyor belt, has its home in Canberra, as do the National Library, National Museum and numerous sites of historical interest including the Australian War Memorial, the Captain James Cook Memorial and the National Carillon (a gift from the British government), which contains 55 bells, some of which weigh up to six tonnes.

If all that seems a bit dull to the rugby tourist then head to areas such as Dickson and Kingston for the liveliest bars. At the Kingston Pub, on Giles Street, one of the oldest pubs in Canberra, you can barbecue your own steaks before having a couple of cold ones and hitting the nightclub.

Above: *Australian War Memorial.* ***Below:*** *Floriade, Canberra's annual flower show.*

Weather	Low (°C)	High (°C)	Rain (mm)	Sunset
January	13	28	61	20.22
February	13	27	54	20.12
March	11	24	52	19.42
April	7	20	49	17.58
May	3	15	48	17.21
June	1	12	39	16.59
July	0	11	42	17.02
August	1	13	47	17.20
September	3	16	53	17.47
October	6	19	65	18.06
November	9	22	64	19.34
December	11	26	52	20.03

3 THINGS YOU MUST DO...

1 AUSTRALIAN INSTITUTE OF SPORT

See what makes the Aussie sports stars tick with a tour round the complex that churns out the country's sporting heroes. (Leverrier Street, Bruce, tel: +61 2 6214 1010. When: daily at 10.00, 11.30, 13.00, 14.30. Price: $16 adult, $9 child, $11 concessions, $44 family ticket).

2 BLACK MOUNTAIN TOWER

See the spectacular 360-degree night-and-day views of Canberra's region from Black Mountain Tower (Black Mountain Drive, Acton, tel: +61 2 6219 6120) on open viewing platforms, then dine at Alto, the tower's revolving restaurant.

3 ZIERHOLZ PREMIUM BREWERY

Brewery tours available (Unit 7/19–25 Kembla St, Fyshwick, tel: +61 2 6162 0523), plus a pub serving food and beers such as Amber Ale, Porter and Weizen, all made in Canberra. When: tours by arrangement. Pub open Tues–Weds, Sun 11.00–17.00, Thurs–Sat 11.00–19.00).

BRUMBIES

Capital gains

Named after the wild horses found around Canberra, the Brumbies were the third Australian team in the-then Super 12 in 1996 and were widely assumed to be cannon fodder for the rest of the contestants. However, they were the first Australian side to win two titles, in 2001 and 2004, successes founded on outstanding players such as George Gregan, George Smith, Joe Roff and Stirling Mortlock. They had reached five finals up to 2010.

The 2001 vintage were coached by Eddie Jones, who oversaw a memorable match the same year with virtually a second team against the Lions. The tourists needed a last-ditch conversion from Matt Dawson to win the game. Jones moved on to international duty and it was down to David Nucifora to take them to the 2004 Super 12 title with a 47-38 win over their fierce rivals, the Crusaders, in the final. The Brumbies also have a bitter rivalry with the Waratahs as they were perceived as being made up of NSW cast-offs when they were formed.

At the time the franchise were known as the ACT Brumbies but the structure of the ACT Rugby Union was changed that off-season to embrace the Far South Coast and Southern Inland Unions. ACT Rugby Union became the ACT and Southern NSW Rugby Union in November 2004 and the team name became simply 'Brumbies Rugby'. For sponsorship reasons they subsequently became known as the CA Brumbies.

The Brumbies play at Canberra Stadium, formerly known as Bruce Stadium, which was redeveloped initially for the 1985 World Cup Athletics. In 1990 it was renovated once more when the Canberra Raiders, the local NRL team moved in.

The ground, which hosted four matches in the 2003 Rugby World Cup, is found in the bushland of North Canberra, next to the Australian Institute of Sport. The main stand is named after Raiders and Kangaroo rugby league legend Mal Meninga and a statue of Laurie Daley, another Canberra league superstar, is found at the main grandstand entrance.

Below: Fans at the Canberra Stadium, formerly the Bruce Stadium, enjoyed Super Rugby success in 2001 and 2004.

MATTER OF FACT
Club: CA Technologies Brumbies
Formed: 1996
Located: Canberra, Australia
Administrative address: Austin Street, Griffith, ACT 2603
Tel: +61 2 260 8588
Email: info@canberrastadium.com (ground)
Website: www.brumbies.com.au
or www.canberrastadium.com

Super Rugby records
Honours: Winners 2001, 2004
Best finish: Winners 2001, 2004
Record: P 186, W 112, L 72, D 2
Most appearances: 136 George Gregan (1996–2007)
Most points: 996 Stirling Mortlock (1998–2010)
Biggest win: 64-0 v Cats, 2000 and 73-9 v Bulls, 1999
Biggest defeat: 44-10 v Waratahs, 1996

Ground: Canberra Stadium (formerly Bruce Stadium)
Address: Battye Street, Bruce ACT 2617
Capacity: 25,011
To get there: ACTION shuttle bus (982, 983, 984)
Stands: Mal Meninga, Gregan-Larkham, Western, Eastern

Bars in ground: Not named
Bars nearby: All Bar Nun (O'Connor Shops, Macpherson St, O'Connor, ACT, 2601, +61 2 6257 9191, www.allbarnun.com.au); **O'Neills of Dickson** (8/30–36, Woolly St, Dickson, ACT, 2602, +61 2 6262 8253; **Trinity Bar** (28 Challice St, Dickson, ACT, 2602, +61 2 6262 5010, www.lovetrinitybar.com)

Legends
George Gregan: Zambian-born scrum-half with 139 Wallaby caps and a foundation player for the Brumbies. Played four World Cups, winning one in 1999.
Joe Roff: Aussie wing whose interception try turned the 2001 series against the Lions. Played for Oxford University after quitting Test rugby in 2004.

Need to know: Brumby Jack is the mascot of the rugby union franchise – a comic figure wearing a T-shirt and board shorts who was named after a vote among 10,000 fans. Pre-match antics include sky-diving, driving his hovercraft and throwing gifts to the crowd.

SYDNEY

Above: *The monorail nips around the city of Sydney.*

The city of plenty

Sydney is one of the great modern cities in the world with a reputation for energy and beauty. Situated on the southeast coast of the country, it is the largest city in Australia with a population of about 4.5 million, and a hub for tourism, commerce and entertainment. The waterside central business district, dominated by the iconic Sydney Opera House and Harbour Bridge is one of the great urban backdrops.

The city is also famed for its many beaches – Bondi and Manly are well-known names among many – plus its many parks, rivers and attractive points jutting out into the inlet from the Tasman Sea on which the city is built.

Add to this a climate of warm summers and cool winters, an energetic multi-cultural population, plus a vibrant cultural and nightlife scene, and it is easy to see why Sydney is consistently ranked as one of the most livable cities according to various economic indicators. Head to the vibrant Rocks area for old pubs, tucked-away boutique shops and the weekend night market.

Like all Australian cities, sport is integral to life and Sydney has hosted the 1938 Empire Games, the 2000 Olympic Games and the 2003 Rugby World Cup. As well as the Waratahs rugby union side the city is also home to top-level sides in various sports such as the Sydney Swans (Australian Rules), Sydney FC (football) while the NSW Blues compete in cricket's Sheffield Shield. The city hosted the 1992 Cricket World Cup and will also host the 2015 competition.

Stadium Australia, officially the ANZ Stadium, which was built for the Olympics in 2000, is 16 km (10 miles) to the west.

3 THINGS YOU MUST DO...

1 STADIUM AUSTRALIA

Built to host the 2000 Olympic Games (Edwin Flack Avenue, Sydney Olympic Park, tel: +61 2 8765 2000). When: weekdays 11.00, 12.30, 14.00, 15.30, weekends 11.00, 13.00, 15.00. Price: $28.50 adults, $18.50 concessions. To get there: trains to Sydney Olympic Park Station, buses 525, 401/404.

2 ROYAL RANDWICK

No-one enjoys a bet more than the Australians. Visit The Royal Randwick (Alison Road, Randwick, tel: +61 2 9663 8400) for horse racing action. When: race days usually Wed and Sat. Price: weekdays sometimes free, otherwise $15. To get there: bus from Central Station to Royal Randwick Racecourse.

3 MONORAIL

See the city as the monorail (tel: +61 2 8584 5288) winds through Chinatown, the Spanish Quarter and Darling Harbour. When: every three to five mins from Mon–Sat 07.00–22.00, Sun 08.00–22.00. Price: $4.90 per trip. To get there: Darling Park is a good place to start and finish your loop.

Above: A replica of Captain James Cook's HMS Endeavour, in which he sailed to Australia in 1770.

Weather	Low (°C)	High (°C)	Rain (mm)	Sunset
January	18	26	95	20.09
February	18	26	104	20.01
March	18	24	129	19.36
April	14	22	135	18.53
May	12	18	128	17.17
June	9	17	122	16.56
July	8	16	122	16.59
August	9	17	79	17.20
September	11	20	77	17.37
October	12	22	75	17.57
November	16	23	79	19.22
December	17	25	79	19.50

STADIUM AUSTRALIA

Where Cathy is a Freeman

Stadium Australia, officially ANZ Stadium due to sponsorship, and previously Telstra Stadium, was built for the 2000 Olympics and lies about 16 km (10 miles) west of Sydney's Central Business District. Easily accessible by train, the stadium crammed in 109,874 fans to watch the 2000 Bledisloe Cup match, when a late Jonah Lomu try gave New Zealand a 39-35 win over the Wallabies.

The Olympic closing ceremony saw 114,714 people in the ground, but in 2002 the arena was reconfigured to its current capacity, with roofs put on over the northern and southern ends a year later. Now the stadium can be changed from a rectangular lay-out to an oval lay-out (to host Australian Rules and cricket) in just 12 hours.

The ground was the centrepiece of the 2003 Rugby World Cup, hosting the final in which Jonny Wilkinson's last-ditch drop goal gave England the trophy. It has staged all four forms of what Australians call football, as well as cricket (first in 2003) and the 2000 Paralympics.

Wilkinson added to his legendary status here, and guaranteed infamy among the Australian fans, when he kicked the final penalty for England as they won their summer tour match 21-20 against the Wallabies in 2010. For fans of the 13-a-side code the ground also hosts State of Origin matches, when New South Wales and Queensland rugby league sides scrap it out, each year.

There are plenty of bars, many in the chain hotels around the ground, although some fans prefer to stay in central Sydney bars before making the journey to Homebush Bay. Most public transport out to the ground is free if you are holding a match ticket.

Below: Built for the 2000 Olympics, the Stadium Australia now holds over 83,000 fans.

MATTER OF FACT
Stadium: ANZ Stadium
Located: Olympic Park, Homebush Bay, Sydney
Address: Edwin Flack Avenue, Sydney Olympic Park, New South Wales 2127
Phone: +61 2 8765 2000
Email: admin@anzstadium.com.au
Website: www.anzstadium.com.au
Capacity: 83,647
To get there: Olympic Park Station (rail), Homebush Bay Ferry Wharf (ferry)
Stands: Western, Eastern, North, South

Stadium tours
Open: Weekdays 11.00, 12.30, 14.00, 15.30; weekends, public holidays 11.00, 13.00, 15.00; may vary on event days, closed 25 December; $28.50, $18.50 concessions and children, $70 family ticket
Tel: +61 2 8765 2300
Email: tours@anzstadium.com.au

First match: Australia 22 England 15, 1999
First Test: Australia 22 England 15, 1999
Tests hosted: 32
Australia record: P 28, W 21, L 7, D 0

Bars in ground: Tooheys New Bars
Bars nearby: The Brewery (Dawn Fraser Avenue, Homebush Bay NSW 2127, +61 2 8762 7693);
Hotel Concord (39 Victoria Avenue NSW 2138, +61 2 9736 1891, www.hotelconcord.com.au);
Horse & Jockey Hotel (70 Parramatta Road, NSW 2140, +61 2 9746 6110); **The Wentworth Hotel** (195 Parramatta Road NSW 2140, +61 2 9746 6000, www.thewentworth.com.au)

Finally... Cathy Freeman provided the highlight of the 2000 Sydney Olympics when winning the 400 metres gold. Freeman, wearing a striking green and white all-in-one suit in front of an expectant crowd, became only the second Australian Aboriginal Olympic champion.

WARATAHS

Tah very much

The Waratahs, named after the state flower of New South Wales, were formed in 1996 for Super Rugby purposes although the New South Wales Rugby Union, originally the Southern Rugby Union, has been in existence since 1874. As amateurs NSW beat the touring Springboks in 1937 and later boasted players such as Ken Catchpole, Ron Graham and Nick Shehadie.

In the professional era the Waratahs reached the Super 12 final in 2005 and the Super 14 final in 2008, losing to the Crusaders on both occasions.

The Waratahs play home games at the Sydney Football Stadium, found next to the Sydney Cricket Ground in Moore Park, which they share with the Sydney Roosters NRL outfit and Sydney FC. They also play some big games at ANZ Stadium, the venue for the 2003 Rugby World Cup final.

The Sydney Football Stadium was opened in 1988 to provide a venue for sports needing a rectangular field – games had previously been staged at the cricket ground. It was used for football matches in the 2000 Olympics and five matches in the 2003 Rugby World Cup. The passion for sport in the area was emphasized during this tournament when over 28,000 fans turned up for a pool match between Georgia and Uruguay.

In 1994 the Australian football side played out a 1-1 draw in a World Cup qualifier at the ground against an Argentina side including Diego Maradona. The same year George Gregan pulled off a last-ditch tackle on All Black wing Jeff Wilson, which is still talked about, to help Australia retain the Bledisloe Cup.

The ground is close to the bars of Paddington for pre- and post-match entertainment, with the Captain Cook Hotel, a short stroll from the ground across Moore Park, the pick.

Below: *The Sydney-based Waratahs have twice reached the Super Rugby final.*

MATTER OF FACT
Club: HSBC Waratahs
Formed: 1996 (as NSW 1882)
Located: Sydney, Australia
Administrative address: Gold Members' Car Park, Sydney Football Stadium, Driver Avenue, Moore Park NSW 2021
Phone: +61 2 9323 3300
Email: enquiries@nswrugby.com.au
Website: www.nswrugby.com.au

Super Rugby records
Honours: None
Best finish: Runners-up 2005, 2008
Record: P 182, W 98, L 80, D 4
Most appearances: 123 Phil Waugh (2000–2010)
Most points: 959 Matt Burke (1996–2004)
Biggest win: 73-12 v Lions, 2010
Biggest defeat: 96-19 v Crusaders, 2002

Ground: Sydney Football Stadium
Address: Driver Avenue, Paddington, Sydney NSW 2021
Capacity: 45,500
To get there: 20-minute walk from Central Station (train) or match day shuttle (Moore Park Link ticket covers train and bus), or bus 339, 374, 376, 391
Stands: Western Grandstand, Eastern Grandstand

Bars in ground: Not named
Bars nearby: Captain Cook Hotel (162 Flinders Street, Paddington NSW 2021, +61 2 9360 4327, www.thecaptaincookhotel.com.au); **Paddington Inn** (338 Oxford Street, Paddington NSW 2021, +61 2 9380 5913, www.paddingtoninn.com.au); **Olympic Hotel Bar & Bistro** (308 Moore Park Road, Paddington NSW 2021, +61 2 9361 6315, www.olympichotel.com.au); **The Saint Hotel** (384 Oxford Street, Paddington NSW 2021, +61 2 9360 9668)

Legends
Matt Burke: Full-back with 81 Wallaby caps and Waratahs stalwart until dropped in 2004. Came back as coach and Waratahs' Player of the Season now receives the Matt Burke Trophy.
Chris Whitaker: Sydney boy was Waratah scrum-half for nine years, and played 118 Super Rugby games, but restricted to 31 Wallaby caps by George Gregan.

Need to know: Trevor Allan played rugby union for Australia between 1946 and 1949, and league for North Sydney and Leigh in England and his statue, on the forecourt of stadium is one of several in the complex to celebrate local sporting heroes.

BRISBANE

Above: *Brisbane is capital of Queensland and its metropolitan area is home to around two million people.*

Sun, sand and sport

Situated on the east coast of Australia, the two-million strong population of Brisbane has a worldwide reputation for being lovers of the sun and the sea.

And yet the central part of the city, although close to the sea, is actually inland a few kilometres, the city development winding itself around the aptly named Brisbane River. In fact, the names best associated with sand and bronzed bodies in this area, the Gold Coast and Surfer's Paradise, are actually about 75 km (47 miles) to the south.

The Botanic Gardens, situated on the north bank and jutting out into the river, are centrally located, with the streets off it forming the CBD of Brisbane. Across the river is the South Bank, a more cosmopolitan area with a wide range of cafés and restaurants featuring food from different ethnic backgrounds.

On this side of the river you will also find South Bank Parklands,

which is on the site of the World Expo 88. Here you can enjoy grasslands, rainforest and plazas to stroll around, or if that sounds too energetic then simply join the locals in soaking up some sun at the man-made beach, commonly referred to as Streets Beach. Remember the sun block now, won't you? Close by is the West End, an area of eclectic shops and cafes beloved by the art crowd.

And this being Australia need we mention that this is also a sport-loving city? As well as the rugby stadium Lang Park, where you can watch union, rugby league and football, there is cricket's legendary stadium the Gabba, which is found south of the river in the wonderfully named area of Woolloongabba. The city also boasts top-level national hockey, netball, and baseball teams. You certainly won't be short of your sporting fix when you've had enough of the sun and the sand.

3 THINGS YOU MUST DO...

1 NORMANBY HOTEL
Great setting, great fun. When: Sunday afternoon is the best time for drinks at the popular Normanby Hotel (1 Musgrave Road, Red Hill, tel: +61 7 3831 3353) where you could rub shoulders with players from the Lions (AFL) and the Broncos (rugby league).

2 WEST END
This is an area thick on the ground with bars, restaurants and clubs. Try Über (100 Boundary Road, tel: +61 7 3846 6680). When: Tue–Sat, 19.00–late). To get there: South Brisbane Train Station is close or bus 190, 191.

3 THE WHEEL OF BRISBANE
Ride a gondola to a height of 60 metres (197 feet) and see a panoramic view of Brisbane. Situated in the South Bank (tel: South Bank Visitor Centre, +61 7 3867 2051). Price: $15 adult, $10 child aged 3–12. To get there: South Brisbane Train Station.

Above: Diving the Tangalooma wrecks in Moreton Bay off the coast of Brisbane.

Weather	Low (°C)	High (°C)	Rain (mm)	Sunset
January	22	30	166	18.47
February	20	29	160	18.43
March	19	28	148	18.20
April	17	27	94	17.48
May	13	23	72	17.17
June	12	21	66	17.01
July	9	20	58	17.06
August	10	22	48	17.19
September	14	25	48	17.34
October	16	27	68	17.49
November	18	28	94	18.05
December	19	29	127	18.29

LANG PARK

A stadium for all sports

Lang Park, now officially Suncorp Stadium, is one of four Test venues that have been used for rugby union in Brisbane along with the Gabba, the Brisbane Exhibition Ground and Ballymore. Home of the Brisbane Broncos rugby league team and Brisbane Roar soccer outfit, the ground is built on the site of a cemetery and served as a rubbish dump before being designated a sporting area. In a nod to its previous life the ground was originally named after the late Reverend John Dunmore Lang, who founded the cemetery.

A short walk from the Brisbane's central business district, and close to the Castlemaine Brewery (which offers tours), the stadium is now the city's foremost rugby union venue, as internationals have not been played at Ballymore since 2000.

The stadium hosted nine games in the 2003 Rugby World Cup, including two quarter-finals, and has also staged State of Origin rugby league games since 1980. It is also infamous as the venue for England's 76-0 drubbing by Australia on Clive Woodward's 'Tour of Hell' in 1998.

In that 2003 World Cup the ground was lit up by one of the greatest tries ever seen in a global tournament when France took on Fiji. The Fijian-wing Rupeni Caucaunibuca ran in from 70 metres, making the French defence look like novices, but then blotted his copybook by punching Olivier Magne and earning himself a two-match suspension. Fiji eventually went down 61-18 but Caucau's brilliance was the highlight of the night.

After the upgrade for the 2003 event the ground is one of the most modern in world rugby, has 32 bars dotted around and the many bars of Caxton Street are just a stroll away. A State of Origin Walk of Fame leading up to the stadium commemorates famous Queensland rugby league figures.

Below: It used to be the site of a rubbish dump, but today Lang Park is one of the best rugby venues in the world.

MATTER OF FACT
Stadium: Suncorp Stadium
Located: Brisbane, Queensland
Address: 40 Castlemaine Street, Milton, Queensland 4064
Phone: +61 7 3331 5000
Email: info@suncorpstadium.com.au
Website: www.suncorpstadium.com.au
Capacity: 52,500
To get there: Milton/Roma Street stations then shuttle bus or short walk
Stands: Eastern, Western, Northern, Southern

Stadium tours
Open: Wed 10.30 (take 90 mins approx). $12.50 adults, $7.50 concessions, $32.50 family ticket; groups (15 and over) $10 adult, $6 concessions
Tel: +61 7 3331 5000

First Test: Australia 12 South Africa 8, 1965
Tests hosted: 26
Australia record: P 19, W 15, L 4, D 0

Bars in ground: Not named
Bars nearby: The Paddington Tavern (186 Given Terrace, Paddington, Qld 4064, +61 7 3369 0044, www.mcguireshotels.com.au/paddo); **The Caxton Hotel** (38 Caxton Street, Qld 4000, +61 7 369 5544, www.caxton.com.au); **Kitty O'Shea's** (25 Caxton Street, Qld 4000, +61 7 3368 1932); **Mirasoul Bar** (55 Caxton Street, Qld 4064, +61 7 3367 1333, www.mirasoul.com.au)

Finally… Wally Lewis was a legendary Queensland rugby league player before retiring from State of Origin games in 1991. There is a statue of the 'King of Lang Park' outside the ground.

REDS

Brisbane's Red Army

Queensland Rugby Union was formally constituted in 1893 and the annual state trophy, the Hospital Cup, was first played for in 1899. In the early 1900s the QRU banned players who had played rugby league in Sydney which led to the birth of league in Queensland. It affected many clubs in the area and although the game in the state has recovered the Super Rugby franchise have not had the success of the Brumbies or the Waratahs.

Queensland won the Super 10 in 1994 and 1995 but have had less to celebrate in the expanded competitions of the professional era despite possessing players of the quality of John Eales, Tim Horan, Chris Latham, Quade Cooper and David Wilson over the years. Latham, who later moved to England, had the distinction of being named Australian Super 12 player of the year for four years on the trot up to 2005. They were beaten semi-finalists three times between 1996 and 2001 and more recently finished just outside the top four in 2010 when Cooper broke Eales' record for most points in a season by racking up 171.

Queensland played matches at Ballymore, a 24,000-capacity stadium in Herston, Brisbane, that hosted games in the 1987 World Cup, from 1966 to 2006. The Reds then moved to Lang Park which has more than twice the capacity of the old ground. Ballymore was earmarked to host games at the 2003 World Cup but ticket demand saw all Brisbane matches switched to the bigger arena. The QRU is based at Ballymore which remains the spiritual heart of Queensland rugby while an application to develop Ballymore Sports Academy, with a motel and a club on the site was approved in 2010 despite the protests of some locals.

Below: The Reds take on Ulster in a tour match in Ireland.

MATTER OF FACT
Club: QR Queensland Reds
Formed: 1996
Located: Brisbane, Australia
Administrative address: 231 Butterfield Street, Herston, Brisbane, Queensland 4006
Phone: +61 7 3354 9333
Email: rugby@qru.com.au
Website: www.qru.com.au

Super Rugby records
Honours: Winners 1994, 1995 (Super 10)
Best finish: Semi-finals 1996, 1999, 2001
Record: P 178, W 79, L 96, D 3
Most appearances: 148 Sean Hardman (2000–)
Most points: 609 Elton Flatley (1996–2004)
Biggest win: 50-10 v Western Force, 2010
Biggest defeat: 92-3 v Bulls, 2007

Ground: Suncorp Stadium
Address: 40 Castlemaine Street, Milton, Queensland 4064
Capacity: 52,500
To get there: Milton/Roma Street stations then shuttle bus/short walk
Stands: Eastern, Western, Northern, Southern

Bars in ground: See opposite
Bars nearby: See opposite

Legends
John Eales: Goal-kicking second row who won World Cups in 1991 and 1999 when captain. Nicknamed 'Nobody' as in 'Nobody's perfect' he scored over 400 points for the Reds and the John Eales medal is awarded to Australia's Player of the Year.
Stan Pilecki: Queensland hero. Prop who was the first player to play 100 games for Queensland and the first man of Polish descent to play for Australia. He won 18 Wallaby caps between 1978 and 1983 and the Pilecki Medal is awarded to the Reds Player of the Year.

Need to know: The Reds anthem which fans sing on match days was recorded in 2007 and written with the help of Chocolate Starfish front man Adam Thompson. It includes lyrics such as 'With thunder in our hearts we'll rip this game apart'.

MELBOURNE

Above: *Melbourne has built a reputation as a youthful and vibrant city.*

Art on the Yarra

Melbourne is known as Australia's arts and cultural city. It's been the location for hundreds of films, including the first *Mad Max* (1979), the Baz Luhrmann-directed *Strictly Ballroom* (1992), the TV miniseries *Salem's Lot* (2004), *Charlotte's Web* (2006). It has a heritage stretching back to 1906 when *The Story of Ned Kelly* was filmed in the city, said to be the world's first feature-length film. The city also gave us Cate Blanchett, Eric Bana and Olivia Newton-John (born in England but grew up in Melbourne).

The earliest Australian television broadcast was from the city in 1929 and it has continued to play an important role in that industry in Australia. The city's station GTV-9 broadcast the moon landing in 1969 and later *Neighbours*, the soap in which Kylie Minogue started her climb to fame, was produced in the city.

Sport is also central to life in Melbourne; it was the host of the 1956 Summer Olympics and the 2006 Commonwealth Games and is considered the home of Australian Rules Football, with the rules drawn up by the Melbourne Football Club in 1859 and the bulk of the teams forming the national league from this area. The city is also an important centre for music, dance and education.

The city winds itself around the Yarra River on the south coast of the country and looks across the Bass Strait towards Tasmania, which is some 290 km (181 miles) away. The main street for nightlife is King Street, which runs from North Melbourne through the CBD and across the Yarra to the Southbank, while the St Kilda district is the area for beach life and the place to enjoy a laid-back beer or snack.

3 THINGS YOU MUST DO...

1 KING STREET

Nothing arty about King Street; this is where you will find clubs and strippers till your heart (and other body parts) are content. Try Spearmint Rhino (14 King St, tel: +61 3 9629 2300). When: 19.00–late. Price: from free (to 20.30) to $20. Dances: $20–$100.

2 CROWN CASINO

Food, drink, dancing, shopping and gambling – all in one place (8 Whiteman St, tel: +61 3 9292 8888). To get there: trams 96, 109, 112 to Casino Exhibition Centre or 55 to Casino East.

3 THE ARTS CENTRE

Art, opera, performance, exhibitions and shopping can be found at the Arts Centre (100 St Kilda Rd, tel: +61 03 9281 8350). For what's on: the artscentre.com.au. To get there: any tram (except 1) along the St Kilda Road to Arts Centre or the free Melbourne City Tourist Shuttle stops at the Arts Centre.

Above: Melbourne, situated on the south coast of Australia, is built around the Yarra River.

Weather	Low (°C)	High (°C)	Rain (mm)	Sunset
January	13	26	50	20.45
February	13	26	49	20.35
March	13	24	56	20.00
April	11	19	58	19.14
May	8	17	53	17.35
June	6	14	53	17.09
July	6	14	49	17.11
August	6	15	48	17.33
September	9	18	58	18.00
October	9	19	66	18.24
November	11	22	58	19.54
December	12	24	58	20.26

DOCKLANDS STADIUM

The roof comes off

The Docklands Stadium was completed in 2000 and has been no stranger to sponsor name changes, being at times the Colonial Stadium, Telstra Dome and now Etihad Stadium. It hosted seven matches in the 2003 Rugby World Cup, including two quarter-finals plus the second Test of the 2001 Lions tour to Australia. It also hosted Australia against England in the 2008 Rugby League World Cup and has staged one-day international cricket – indoors.

The ground has a retractable roof that can open or close in eight minutes, is surrounded by bars and restaurants and can squeeze in up to 74,000 fans for events such as concerts.

Costing AUS$460 million (€333 million) to construct, the stadium is found in Docklands, an area around the Yarra River that was notorious for its rave party scene in the 1990s, and is home to five AFL teams.

The quality of the playing surface has been criticized, due to the north-south layout of the ground that reduces the amount of sunlight the pitch receives. But officials seem to have conquered this problem after taking advice from, among others, people who run and worked on the Emirates Stadium in London.

Below: Rugby must battle for attention in the heartland of Aussie Rules.

MATTER OF FACT
Stadium: Etihad Stadium
Located: Melbourne, Australia
Address: 74 Docklands, 740 Bourke Street, Docklands, Victoria 3008
Phone: +61 3 8625 7700
Email: enquiries@etihadstadium.com.au
Website: www.etihadstadium.com.au
Capacity: 53,359
To get there: Southern Cross Station (rail) and five-minute walk across Bourke Street footbridge
Stands: Not named (Coventry End, Lockett End)

Stadium tours
Open: Mon– Fri 11.00, 13.00, 15.00 (take 60 mins approx) weekends/evenings by arrangement; $14 adults, $11 concessions, $7 under-14s, $37 family ticket, groups (10 or more) $11 adults, $9 concessions, $6 under-14s
Tel: +61 3 8625 7277,
Email: tours@eithadstadium.com.au

First match: Australia 44 South Africa 23, 2000
First Test: Australia 44 South Africa 23, 2000
Tests hosted: 17
Australia record: P 11, W 9, L 2, D 0

Bars in ground: Axcess One, EJ Whitten, Captain's Bar & Bistro, Beer Garden, Locker Room, Legends
Bars nearby: Watermark Bar (800 Bourke Street, The Promenade, Victoria Harbour, Docklands, Melbourne 3008, +61 3 9642 1880, www.watermarkbar.com.au); **James Squire Brewhouse & Restaurant** (439 Docklands Drive, Waterfront City, Docklands, Melbourne 3008, +61 3 9600 0700, www.jamessquirebrewhouse.net); **Yarra's Edge Bar & Cafe** (70 Lorimer Street, Docklands, Melbourne 3207, +61 3 9681 8289); **The Nixon Hotel** (757 Bourke Street, Docklands, Melbourne 3008, +61 3 9642 3272, www.nixonhotel.com.au)

Finally . . . Shocked by the number of Lions fans travelling to Australia in 2001, the ARU handed out gold scarves, hats and placards to Aussie fans ahead of the second Test in Melbourne. The ruse helped with the Wallabies winning 35-14.

REBELS

New kids on the block

After failing with bids for a Super Rugby franchise for the start of the 2006 season, Victoria was made Australia's sole candidate for the 15th Super Rugby franchise and beat off South Africa's Southern Kings to take their place in the 2011 competition. Rod Macqueen, the World Cup-winning Australia coach, was installed, the likes of Danny Cipriani, Stirling Mortlock, Michael Lipman and Sam Cordingley were recruited and the Melbourne Rebels were born.

The Rebels share AAMI Park, with Melbourne Storm, the rugby league side, and soccer sides Melbourne Victory and Melbourne Heart. The ground hosted its first match – a rugby league Test between Australia and New Zealand – in May 2010 and seats over 30,000 spectators under a distinctive domed roof. It is called the 'Bubble Dome' by locals because of its space-age design but unfortunately on the opening night the roof leaked and fans were soaked. The stadium cost AUS$268 million (€194 million) to build and the architects claim that no seat in the arena is more than 30 metres (98 feet) from the action while front-row seats are just five metres (16 feet) away from the pitch.

The stadium is surrounded by some of Melbourne's most famous landmarks such as the Botanical Gardens, Rod Laver Arena and the Melbourne Cricket Ground but most fans will hit the pubs and bars around Flinders Street Station before matches

Below: The newly formed Rebels chose to play home matches at the futuristic AAMI Park.

MATTER OF FACT
Club: The RaboDirect Rebels
Formed: 2010
Located: Melbourne, Australia
Administrative address: Visy Park Gate 3, Royal Parade, Carlton North, Victoria 3054
Phone: +61 3 9221 0700
Email: info@melbournerebels.com.au
Website: www.melbournerebels.com.au

Super Rugby records (First season 2011)

Ground: AAMI Park
Address: Melbourne & Olympic Parks Trust, Batman Ave, Melbourne 3001
Capacity: 30,500
To get there: 10-minute walk from Flinders Street Station (train) or tram no 70
Stands: Western, Southern, Eastern, Northern

Bars in ground: Not named
Bars nearby: Transport Hotel (Federation Square, cnr Flinders and Swanston Streets, Melbourne VIC 3000, +61 3 9654 8808, www.transporthotel.com.au); **PJ O'Brien's Irish Pub** (Ground Floor, Southgate Arts & Leisure Precinct, Southgate, Melbourne VIC 3000, +61 3 9686 5011, www.pjobriens.com.au); **The Sherlock Holmes Inn** (415 Collins Street, Melbourne VIC 3000, +61 3 9629 1146, www.thesherlockholmes.com.au); **The European Bier Cafe** (120 Exhibition Street, Melbourne VIC 3000, +61 3 9663 1222, www.europeanbiercafe.com.au)

Legends (Melbourne)
Sir Edward 'Weary' Dunlop: Surgeon and war hero, imprisoned by the Japanese in World War II, he was the first Victorian to play for the Wallabies, in 1932. A second row or number 8, there is a statue of Dunlop in Melbourne's Royal Botanic Gardens.
Ewen McKenzie: Melbourne-born prop who debuted for Australia in 1990, playing his last Test in 1997. Played for Queensland Reds and coached the Waratahs and Stade Français before returning to take charge of the Reds.

Need to know: AAMI Park is built on Edwin Flack Field, named after Australia's first Olympian. English-born Flack moved to Australia, aged five, and in 1896 won two athletics gold medals at the Athens Olympics and, as a social tennis player, a bronze in the men's double events, thanks to a kind draw.

PERTH

Above: *Central Park (centre of photo) is Perth's tallest building at 249 metres (817 feet) while the second tallest, BankWest Tower is to its right.*

Far, far away

The capital of Western Australia is one the world's most remote cities, being more than 2,700 km (1,690 miles) away from Adelaide by road to the east and almost 4,000 km (2,500 miles) from Darwin to the north and the nation's inland capital Canberra. Indonesia's capital Jakarta is only 3,000 km away (1,875 miles) albeit as 'the crow flies'. Thank goodness for planes then.

Yet, in many ways, the city of just around 1.5 million people can be said to be excellently located, being built around the Swan River as its urban area winds its way to the Indian Ocean, and with Australia's Coral Coast and the legendary Outback both within close proximity.

And if the residents can pull themselves away from the beautiful beaches they'll happily be in Europe drinking a beer and enjoying the sights a good few hours before Sydneysiders, thanks to their location in the far west of the country.

Although this laid-back city is spread out (no shortage of space here), if you don't fancy venturing far most of your entertainment needs can be found in the small area around Wellington Street, Hay Street and Barrack Street (where you will see the modern-looking Swan Bell Tower).

For shopping, King Street is well known for its range of international designer outlets and top-notch locally run boutiques, while nearby Northbridge offers a more eclectic range of shops for those who prefer to root around looking for bargains.

Northbridge also offers a good selection of restaurants and boasts the Perth Cultural Centre with its art gallery, museum and library. Other popular areas for food and drink are Subiaco, a short distance to the west, and Mount Lawley and Highgate to the north.

3 THINGS YOU MUST DO...

1 COTTESLOE BEACH

Swim, surf, snorkel, or just relax by the Indian Ocean and take in the sights of the beach. Cottesloe Beach is one of the city's favourite sand and sea spots. To get there: a 15-minute drive southwest from the city centre on the Stirling Highway, Transperth bus to Cottesloe or train to Cottesloe Station.

2 OCEAN BEACH HOTEL

The hotel (Cnr Marine Parade and Eric St, Cottesloe, tel: +61 8 9384 2555) is the place to rub shoulders with AFL players (West Coast Eagles and Fremantle Dockers). When: Mon–Sat 10.00–midnight, Sun 10.00–22.00. To get there: a 15-minute drive southwest, bus to Cottesloe or train to Cottesloe Station.

3 FREMANTLE

Perth's port town. Head here for great architecture, markets, shops and the famed Cappuccino Strip with its many bars and cafés. To get there: trains runs regularly to Fremantle Station (30 mins). Night buses run back to Como and Bull Creek until 04.00.

Above: King's Park War Memorial commemorates fallen Western Australians.

Weather	Low (°C)	High (°C)	Rain (mm)	Sunset
January	17	29	8	19.26
February	17	29	10	19.20
March	16	27	22	18.52
April	15	24	48	18.13
May	13	22	126	17.40
June	10	19	180	17.20
July	9	17	169	17.24
August	10	19	145	17.40
September	10	19	86	18.00
October	12	20	56	18.19
November	14	24	20	18.41
December	16	27	13	19.08

SUBIACO OVAL

Super Subiaco

First used for Australian Rules football in 1908, the Subiaco Oval was one of the few grounds in Australia not named after a faceless corporate sponsor, taking its name from the Subiaco suburb of Perth in which it is situated. However, this changed in October 2010 when it finally succumbed to the sponsorship dollar and was renamed Patersons Stadium.

It was home to the Western Force Super Rugby outfit, but they have moved to the smaller nib Stadium, and the Oval is now only used for international rugby union matches – the Wallabies hosted England here on their 2010 tour.

It is home to Perth's two AFL teams, the West Coast Eagles and the Fremantle Dockers and was renovated in 2000, ahead of the Rugby World Cup in 2003, to its current capacity. England played two pool matches at the ground that year, beating South Africa and Georgia on their way to winning the title. However, the ground was scheduled to be demolished in 2014 to make way for a 60,000-seater WA Stadium at the nearby Kitchener Park.

There are some bars around the ground but because of it location most of the pre- and post-match drinking action takes place in the Northbridge area of the city. Travel to and from the stadium is included with tickets for all big events. It is not, however, the best viewing arena for rugby union as it is an oval and fans are a long way from the action when it is set up for union.

Below: *With a new stadium planned for Perth in 2014, these could be the final years at the Subiaco.*

MATTER OF FACT
Stadium: Paterson Stadium
Located: Perth, Australia
Address: Subiaco Road, Subiaco, Perth, WA 6901
Phone: +61 8 9381 2187
Email: subi.reception@wafc.com.au
Website: www.subiacooval.com.au
or www.wafootball.com.au
Capacity: 43,500
To get there: West Leederville Station (train)
or Subiaco Station (train)
Stands: NAB, 2-tier, 3-tier, Eastern

Stadium tours
Open: By arrangement only. Tuesdays & Thursdays, Feb–Nov, 10.00, 14.00; $10 adults, $7 concessions, free children (accompanied by adult). Groups of 10 and over only.
Tel: +61 8 9381 2187

First Test: Australia 13 South Africa 14, 1998
Tests hosted: 15
Australia record: P 11, W 7, L 3, D 1

Bars in ground: Not named
Bars nearby: Pure Bar (331 Hay Street, Subiaco, Perth 6008, +61 8 9382 3330, www.purebar.com.au);
JB O'Reilly's (99 Cambridge Street, West Leederville, Perth 6007, +61 8 9382 4555, www.jboreillys.com.au); **Paddy Maguire's** (328 Barker Road, Subiaco, Perth 6008, +61 8 9381 8400, www.paddymaguries.com);
Ess Bar (531 Hay Street, Subiaco, Perth 6008, +61 8 9381 5099, www.essbar.com.au)

Finally… The history Aussie Rules football in Western Australian is commemorated by various rooms and entrances which are named after legendary figures of the game in the region. These include John Todd, Merv McIntosh, Steve Marsh, Polly Farmer and Merv Cowan.

WESTERN FORCE

May the Force be with you

Eyebrows were raised in 2004 when Perth beat off Melbourne for the right to host Australia's newest Super 14 team but Western Force were in place for the 2006 season, with former New Zealand coach John Mitchell at the helm. Big signings were made, including lock Nathan Sharpe and hooker Brendan Cannon, and within days of being made available Western Force had more memberships, 13,000, than any other Australian franchise.

Then reality kicked in. Force played their first match, a warm-up game at the Subiaco Oval, against Central Cheetahs, the other newcomer to Super Rugby that year, and lost 29-19. The seasons since have been difficult with a mid-table position of 7th, in 2007, their best effort in their first five campaigns.

Force originally played their home games at Subiaco Oval but for the 2010 campaign shifted to the smaller ME Bank Stadium, which was renamed the nib Stadium in July of that year after a change of sponsor.

The ground, built on land known as Loton's Paddock (named after a former mayor of Perth) is dominated by the heritage-listed Mediterranean-style white gates at the northwest corner on Bulwer Street. The stadium, built on the site of the old Perth Oval, was redeveloped in 2003 and more expansion was approved in 2010. There are bars all around the ground that open an hour before kick-off, but many local fans meet in the famous Oxford Hotel in Leederville, which has been open since 1906, and take a shuttle bus to the ground.

The Perth Glory football team share the stadium, with English striker Robbie Fowler making his first appearance at the ground for the club in July 2010.

Below: After a rocky start, Western Force are still fighting to establish themselves in Super Rugby.

MATTER OF FACT
Club: Emirates Western Force
Formed: 2005
Located: Perth, Australia
Administrative address: Meagher Drive, Floreat WA 6014
Phone: +61 8 9383 7714
Email: info@rugbywa.com.au
Website: www.westernforce.com.au

Super Rugby records
Honours: None
Best finish: 7th 2007
Record: P 65, W 24, L 37, D 4
Most appearances: 62 Nathan Sharpe (2006–)
Most points: 337 Cameron Shepherd (2006–)
Biggest win: 55-14 v Lions, 2009
Biggest defeat: 53-0 v Crusaders, 2007

Ground: nib Stadium (formerly ME Bank Stadium)
Address: 310 Pier Street, Perth WA 6000
Capacity: 20,500 (25,000 after proposed redevelopment)
To get there: Two-minute walk from Claisebrook Station (train) or 10 minutes from East Perth Station (train)
Stands: The Shed, Eastern, Grandstand, Western, Southern, Family

Bars in ground: Western Brick Bar, Southern Brick Bar, Northern Marquee Bar, Eastern Marquee Bar
Bars nearby: The Brisbane Hotel (292 Beaufort Street, Highgate, Perth WA 6003, +61 8 9227 2300, www.thebrisbanehotel.com.au); **The Shed** (69–71 Aberdeen Street, Northbridge, Perth WA 6003, +61 8 9228 2200, www.the-shed.com.au); **The Oxford Hotel** (368 Oxford Street, Leederville, Perth WA 6007, +61 8 9444 2193, www.theoxford.com.au)

Legends
Nathan Sharpe: Western Force's first captain after moving from the Reds. Over 80 Wallaby caps and on the bench (behind John Eales and David Giffin) in Australia's team of the decade announced in 2005.
David Pocock: Would have played for Force earlier but was not allowed to until he was 18. Flanker who ousted 100-capper George Smith from the Australian Test side in 2009. Dislocated his thumb against Wales in 2009, put it back in himself and kept playing.

Need to know: Matt Giteau was thought to be the highest paid player in Australia when he joined Force in 2007 for a rumoured AUS$1.5 million (€1.1 million).

NEW ZEALAND

<table>
<tr>
<td>

THE

3

**MINUTE
GUIDE**

</td>
<td>

</td>
<td>

Capital: *Wellington.* **Language:** *English.* **Beers:** *Tui, Speight's.* **Food:** *Roast lamb and mutton, Hokey pokey ice cream, ANZAC biscuits.* **National Anthem:** *God Defend New Zealand.*
Population: *4.3 million.* **Time zone:** *GMT +12.* **Emergency number:** *111.*
Did you know? *New Zealand is the first major country to celebrate New Year every year. Bong.*
Rugby body: *New Zealand Rugby Union, PO Box 2172, Wellington, 6140 New Zealand.*
Tel: 64 4 499 4995. Web: ww.allblacks.com

</td>
</tr>
</table>

Below: Stop us if you can. All Blacks rugby is renowned for its strength and power.

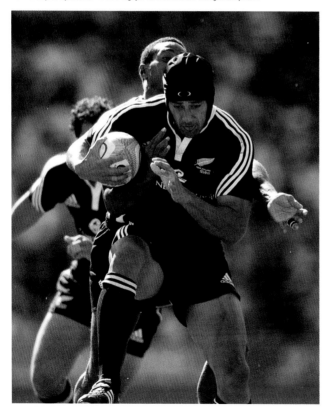

Home of the Haka

Any trip to New Zealand will be enlivened by a taxi driver telling you who should be playing at first five-eighth for Auckland or your hotel maid informing you what her all-time All Black front row would be. In the 'Land of the Long White Cloud' everyone wants to play rugby for New Zealand or at least have an opinion on the side.

If you want to gauge the passion for the sport in the country, walk into a bar and ask someone about the 1905 'Originals', a touring team led by Dave Gallaher who played 35 matches around Europe, including five Tests, and lost only once. The sole defeat of the tour came at the hands of Wales and New Zealanders claim wing Bob Deans should have had a try allowed that would have staved off a 3-0 loss. All Black fans still insist Deans grounded the ball over the line – and the tour took place over a century ago!

Since then New Zealand has provided rugby with colossal players such as Colin Meads, Sean Fitzpatrick, Graham Mourie and the awe-inspiring Jonah Lomu, who burst on to into the world's consciousness in South Africa in 1995.

But one thing that has been missing since 1987, when the side led by David Kirk won the inaugural tournament, is a World Cup. For most of the time since then New Zealand has been the best side in the world only to fail at the global jamboree when it really matters.

New Zealand sides traditionally perform the 'haka' before matches, a Maori dance that challenges the opposition and, for many, is worth the entrance fee alone.

Above: *The capital's Westpac Stadium, one of the many venues for the 2011 World Cup.*

TEST RECORD (capped internationals only)

Versus	First Test	Played	Won	Lost	Drawn
Argentina	Oct 1985	13	12	0	1
Australia	Aug 1903	139	95	39	5
England	Dec 1905	33	26	6	1
France	Jan 1906	49	36	12	1
Ireland	Nov 1905	23	22	0	1
Italy	May 1987	11	11	0	0
Scotland	Nov 1905	27	25	0	2
South Africa	Aug 1921	81	45	33	3
Wales	Dec 1905	27	24	3	0
British & Irish Lions	Aug 1904	38	29	6	3

Most international caps: Sean Fitzpatrick (1986–1997) 92 Tests
Most international points: Dan Carter (2003–2010) 1,118 pts, 74 Tests
(28t, 192c, 196p, 2d)
Most international tries: Doug Howlett (2000–2007) 49 tries, 62 Tests

WORLD CUP RECORD

Year	Venue	Finished
1987	Australia & NZ	Winners
1991	England	Semi-finals
1995	South Africa	Runners-up
1999	Wales	Semi-finals
2003	Australia	Semi-finals
2007	France	Quarter-finals

Most World Cup appearances: Sean Fitzpatrick, 17 matches (1987, 1991, 1995)
Most World Cup points: Grant Fox, 170 points (1987, 1991)
Most World Cup tries: Jonah Lomu (1995, 1999) 15 tries, 11 matches
Record World Cup win: 145-17 v Japan, Bloemfontein, 1995
World Cup coaches: 1987 Brian Lochore; 1991 Alex Wyllie; 1995 Laurie Mains; 1999 John Hart; 2003 John Mitchell; 2007 Graham Henry

WELLINGTON

Above: *A bronze sculpture by Henry Moore, in the Botanic Gardens.*

The windy city

Famous for its weather (not good; it's known as the Windy Wellington), the capital of New Zealand is located at the bottom of the North Island, looking out across the Cook Strait towards the South Island. It is from here that Interislander ferries run south to Picton.

The small city centre area supports a population of about 400,000 and is home to many of the nation's important buildings – political and legal landmarks such as Parliament House and the Beehive (the executive wing), Government House, the official home of the Governor-General, and the Supreme Court of New Zealand,

The city supports a busy arts and cultural scene with the Museum of New Zealand Te Papa Tongarewa, Museum of Wellington City & Sea, the National Library of New Zealand, as well as being home to the Royal New Zealand Ballet and the New Zealand Symphony Orchestra. The film industry is an important one for the city and its profile has risen in recent years thanks to the work of producer and director Peter Jackson, a local man who operates from the eastern suburb of Miramar. Jackson is well known for his work on the Lord of the Rings trilogy, the 2005 version of *King Kong* and sci-fi movie *District 9*.

Wellington has lively nightlife, with most revellers heading to the central Courtenay Place, especially on the weekends, which has no shortage of bars, live-music venues and clubs. Cuba Street and Cuba Mall is another popular area among the city partygoers. There are also some great bars to be found on the Wellington Waterfront. But Wellington really comes into its own with its range of restaurants, with Malaysian, Japanese and Indian cuisine particularly popular. Check out Oriental Bay, Cuba Street and the Newtown suburb and enjoy.

3 THINGS YOU MUST DO...

1 CUBA STREET
Cafés, bars and restaurants line this popular street along with its bohemian shops and it attracts Wellington's hip crowd. Try the superbly kitsch Mighty Mighty (Level 1, 104 Cuba St, tel: +64 4 385 2890). When: Wed–Sat 16.00–late. To get there: centrally located.

2 CABLE CAR
A gentle 600-metre ride with great views. The Cable Car (tel: +64 4 472 2199) runs from Lambton Quay. When: cars run every 10 mins, Mon–Fri 07.00–22.00, Sat 08.30–22.00, Sun and holidays 09.00–22.00. Price: $5 return adults, $2 child 5–15. To get there: most buses pass through Lambton Quay.

3 MUSEUM OF NEW ZEALAND TE PAPA TONGAREWA
The national museum (55 Cable St, tel: +64 4 381 7000) for everything you ever wanted to know about New Zealand. When: daily 10.00–18.00 (21.00 Thur). Price: free, but some special exhibitions have charges. To get there: a short walk from the centre or bus 24 to Te Papa Museum.

Above: *For great views across the city, take Wellington's cable car.*

Weather	Low (°C)	High (°C)	Rain (mm)	Sunset
January	14	21	80	20.57
February	14	21	81	20.42
March	12	19	85	20.07
April	11	18	97	19.13
May	9	13	119	17.29
June	7	13	117	17.00
July	6	12	139	17.02
August	6	12	122	17.28
September	9	14	97	17.56
October	9	15	102	19.27
November	10	17	87	20.01
December	12	19	89	20.37

WESTPAC STADIUM

The Cake Tin

Built in 2000, and better known as the Cake Tin for its round, metallic appearance, Westpac Stadium is home to the Hurricanes Super Rugby franchise, the Wellington Lions rugby union provincial outfit and Wellington Phoenix football club. As well as rugby and football, the ground also stages one-day international cricket.

The Westpac replaced the rickety old Athletic Park as Wellington's premier rugby venue when Australia, thanks to a last-minute kick from John Eales, won the first Test match at the ground by a single point in 2000.

In happier times for the All Blacks, fly-half Dan Carter scored 33 points here in 2005, including two tries, as the Lions were crushed 48-18 in the second Test.

Found just over a kilometre (about a mile) from the central business district of Wellington, the stadium is used for around 50 events a year and has hosted concerts by the Rolling Stones, Kiss and AC/DC. In 2000 it became the first venue to host the Edinburgh Military Tattoo outside of the Scottish capital.

The stadium staged the New Zealand v England match in rugby league's Four Nations tournament in 2010 and for the 2011 Rugby World Cup Westpac Stadium was rostered to host seven matches including the group match between South Africa and Wales and two quarter-finals. During Rugby World Cup 2011 it had to switch its name to Wellington Regional Stadium because of the tournament's sponsorship policy.

MATER OF FACT
Stadium: Westpac Stadium
Located: Wellington, New Zealand
Address: 147 Waterloo Quay, Wellington 6011, New Zealand
Tel: +64 4 473 3881
Email: info@westpacstadium.co.nz
Website: www.westpacstadium.co.nz
Capacity: 34,500
To get there: Five-minute walk from Wellington Station (rail) or shuttle from bus terminus
Stands: Not named due to its circular shape

Stadium tours
Open: Weekdays by arrangement only. NZ$5 adult, NZ$3 child. Minimum group charge NZ$45.
Tel: +64 4 472 3881
Email: email@wrfu.co.nz

First match: Hurricanes 40 Sharks 23, 2000
First Test: New Zealand 23 Australia 24, 2000
Tests hosted: 15

New Zealand record: P 14, W 12, L 2, D 0

Bars in ground: Pavilion Bar
Bars nearby: Magills Bar & Restaurant, 182 Thorndon Quay, Pipitea, Wellington 6011, +64 4 472 7528, magillsbar@hotmail.com);
Bodega (101 Ghuznee Street, Te Aro, Wellington 6011, + 64 4 384 8212, www.bodega.co.nz);
The Waterloo (27 Waterloo Quay, Wellington 6011, +64 4 499 4485, www.waterloo.co.nz);
The Backbencher (34 Molesworth, Wellington 6011, +64 4 472 3065, www.backbencher.co.nz);

Finally... Tana Umaga is one of the city's favourite sons and played his last game for the Hurricanes in August 2007. His career, which included 74 All Black caps, is celebrated with a tribute at Aisle 13 (his number) of the Westpac.

Below: *Is it a flan? Is it a biscuit? Is it a blancmange? No it's a Cake Tin. Or says its nickname.*

HURRICANES

Expect the unexpected

The Wellington-based Hurricanes claim to be the largest Super Rugby franchise in New Zealand, with a catchment area taking in half of the North Island and a population of 920,000. To the delight of their countrymen from Auckland and Christchurch, however, this numerical advantage has not been capitalized on as the Hurricanes managed to reach just one final in the first 14 years of the competition. In five seasons from 2003 onwards they reached two semi-finals and a final but were beaten by the Crusaders on each occasion.

The Hurricanes actually hosted the first Super 12 match, in 1996, losing 28-36 to the Blues, but with the likes of Tana Umaga and Christian Cullen started to play an exciting brand of running rugby which led to them adopting the motto 'Expect the Unexpected'. In 2000 the Wellington Hurricanes were re-branded as the Hurricanes, moved from Athletic Park to the newly-built Westpac Stadium, near the city's waterfront, and signed the megastar Jonah Lomu. However, they could still only finish eighth.

Umaga's influence grew and in 2005 they reached the semi-finals, and a year later made it to the final under a new captain, Rodney So'oialo. The final was played in a pea-souper of a fog in Christchurch, with the Hurricanes losing out 19-12. The game marked the last appearance of fly-half David Holwell, who scored 676 points in 76 games from 1998 to 2006.

In 2010 the Hurricanes finally got one over the Crusaders when they persuaded former All Blacks hooker Mark Hammett to join them as coach for the 2011 season from his post at Canterbury in an attempt rid themselves of their reputation as under-achievers.

Below: Tensions boil over between Hurricanes' Tamati Ellison (left) and Adam Thomson of Highlanders.

MATTER OF FACT
Club: The Hurricanes
Formed: 1996
Located: Wellington, New Zealand
Administrative address: Level 1, 113 Adelaide Road, Newtown, Wellington 6021, New Zealand
Tel: +64 4 389 0020
Email: mail@wrfu.co.nz
Website: www.hurricanes.co.nz

Super Rugby records
Honours: None
Best finish: Runners-up 2006
Record: P 171, W 89, L 78, D 4
Most appearances: 122 Tana Umaga (1996–2007)
Most points: 676 David Holwell (1998–2004 and 2006)
Biggest win: 56-7 The Brumbies, 2009
Biggest defeat: 60-7 The Blues, 2002

Ground: Westpac Stadium
Address: 147 Waterloo Quay, Wellington 6011, New Zealand
Capacity: 34,500
To get there: Five-minute walk from Wellington Station (rail) or shuttle from bus terminus
Stands: Not named due to its circular shape

Bars in ground: See opposite
Bars nearby: See opposite

Legends
Christian Cullen: Full-back who won 85 caps for the Hurricanes and 58 for the All Blacks. A brilliant runner, he was dubbed the 'Paekakariki Express' and should have won double the number of international caps he did.
Jerry Collins: Former Wellington dustman turned Hurricanes and All Black flanker. Renowned for his tough tackling on the pitch and generosity off it. He once turned out for Barnstaple seconds as a favour for a friend and stood his round in the bar afterwards. Had stints in France and went on to the Ospreys.

Need to know: Hurricanes' mascot, Captain Hurricane, made the headlines when his hurriplane was stolen in 2007. It was taken from a trailer in Paraparaumu but found nearby shortly afterwards. A man was charged and the person who tipped off police received two passes to the Westpac Stadium.

AUCKLAND

Above: *Auckland Harbour Bridge at sunset.*

City of sails

Auckland is commonly known as the 'city of sails' and it is sometimes said that there are more boats per head of population here than anywhere else in the world (it beats the more-sheep-than-people joke, at least).

A quick visit to the Westhaven Marina, the largest in the city, and you'll see the sailing passion of the city at first hand. To emphasize this sailing backdrop, Auckland was the centre of the international yachting world when it hosted the prestigious America's Cup regatta in 2000 and again in 2003.

Auckland is a very multi-cultural city and is, in fact, the largest Polynesian city in the world, as well as being home to many people with an Asian background, a group whose numbers have grown rapidly in recent years. The hills in and around Auckland are mostly extinct volcanoes, including Mount Eden, which itself looks over Eden Park. The

stadium is 4 km (2.5 miles) southwest of the city centre.

The relatively low-level nightlife scene is spread around the city but the Viaduct Harbour, naturally close to the water's edge, is a great place to hang out, with a wide range of bars, restaurants and cafés. This is one of the liveliest parts of Auckland after dark. The Sky City entertainment complex, off Federal Street, also boasts a numbers of bars and lively restaurants, including the revolving Orbit if you are looking for ever-changing views to go with your food.

The city is situated to the north of the North Island and is the dominant city in New Zealand with a population of over 1.3 million in the greater urban area, giving it significant clout in a country that has just over four million people in total.

3 THINGS YOU MUST DO...

1 SKY TOWER

You can enjoy 360-degree views from the tower (Cnr Victoria and Federal Sts, tel: +64 9 363 6000). When: Sun–Thur 08.30–22.00, Fri–Sat 08.30–23.30. Price: for observation, sky deck and café, $28 adult, $18 concessions, $11 child 5–14. To get there: 10-min walk from train and bus stations.

2 HARBOUR FERRY TO DEVONPORT

Take a 15-min harbour cruise over to historical Devonport, a small village full of restaurants, cafés, galleries, boutiques and some pretty beaches. When: departures every 15 mins from 06.15–23.00 (Mon–Thur), every 30 mins from 06.15–01.00 (Fri–Sat), 07.15–10.00 (Sun). Price: $10 adult.

3 KELLY TARLTON'S ANTARCTIC ENCOUNTER AND UNDERWATER WORLD

Antarctica exhibition (23 Tamaki Dr, tel: +64 9 531 5065) with penguins, piranhas, sharks. When: daily 09.30–17.30. Price: $31.50 adult, $15.80 child 4–14. To get there: free shuttle bus from opposite the ferry terminal (172 Quay St).

Above: *Looking out towards New Zealand's largest city.*

Weather	Low (°C)	High (°C)	Rain (mm)	Sunset
January	16	23	79	20.44
February	15	23	94	20.33
March	15	22	81	20.01
April	13	18	97	19.18
May	11	17	131	17.36
June	9	13	137	17.13
July	8	13	145	17.14
August	9	14	122	17.35
September	9	16	102	18.00
October	12	17	101	19.23
November	12	20	89	19.54
December	14	21	79	20.26

EDEN PARK

Where big finals are won

Eden Park, 4 km (2.5 miles) from the centre of Auckland, has hosted Test rugby union since 1921 and Test cricket since 1930. It is the biggest sporting arena in New Zealand and the first ground to be awarded the right to host two Rugby World Cup finals when it was booked for the 2011 showpiece match. It was the venue for the first Rugby World Cup final in 1987, won by New Zealand, hosted the 1988 Rugby League World Cup final and is home of the Blues rugby union franchise.

Auckland have played rugby at Eden Park since 1925, and the All Blacks have built up a fearsome record at the ground although they were nearly beaten by anti-apartheid protestors who disrupted the 1981 Test against South Africa by dropping flour bombs on the stadium (and some fans) from a light aircraft.

The ground underwent extensive redevelopment, costing NZ$240 million (€136 million), ahead of the 2011 World Cup, with the capacity increased to 60,000. The South Stand was transformed into a 22,000-seat structure with 50 corporate boxes and a new unroofed East Stand, with a capacity of 8,600, replaced the old terraces.

The area of Kingsland is full of lively bars to sink a few beers before the game so take advantage of the free shuttle buses.

Below: Eden Park, the first ground to be awarded two Rugby World Cup finals.

MATTER OF FACT
Stadium: Eden Park
Located: Auckland, New Zealand
Address: Reimers Ave, Kingsland, Auckland, New Zealand 1024
Tel: +64 9 815 5551
Email: mdixon@edenpark.co.nz (or via website)
Website: www.edenpark.co.nz
Capacity: 60,000 (by 2011 Rugby World Cup)
To get there: Kingsland Station (rail). Regular free shuttle buses run round Sandringham, Balmoral, Mt Eden and New North Roads.
Stands: ASB, West, South, North East, Terraces

Stadium tours
Open: On request (not match days or public holidays); $15 adult, $5 senior citizen, student and sports teams, free under-5s
Tel: +64 9 815 5551, cmartin@edenpark.co.nz

First Test: New Zealand 5 South Africa 9, 1921
Tests hosted: 69
New Zealand record: P 65, W 53, L 10, D 2

Bars in ground: Not named
Bars nearby: The Kingslander (470 New North Road, Kingsland, Auckland 1002, +64 9 849 5777, www.thekingslander.co.nz); **Neighbourhood** (498 New North Road, Kingsland, Auckland 1021, +64 9 522 4004, www.neighbourhood.co.nz); **Tabou Bar & Bistro** (462 New North Road, Kingsland, Auckland 1021, +64 9 846 3474, www.tabou.co.nz); **The Clare Inn** (274–278 Dominion Road, Mt Eden, Auckland, +64 9 23 8233, www.theclareinn.com)

Finally... The Eden Park Hall of Legends is a history of New Zealand rugby and cricket. Opened in 2001 it has more than 2,000 items of sporting memorabilia on display.

BLUES

Stronghold of New Zealand rugby

The phrase 'When Auckland rugby is strong, New Zealand rugby is strong', which was reportedly first heard in the 1920s, has had to be revised since 2003 when the Canterbury franchise have held sway and bragging rights over their rivals from the North Island.

Auckland were founder members of the New Zealand Rugby Football Union in 1883 and the city has had a huge say in the fate of the national side ever since. Auckland Grammar School alone has provided more than 50 All Blacks to the Silver Fern cause.

The-then Auckland Blues, with the legendary figure of Sean Fitzpatrick at hooker, a young Carlos Spencer at fly-half and greats such as Michael Jones and Zinzan Brooke in the pack, won the inaugural Super 12 tournament in 1996 and backed it up the following year. They were coached then by Graham Henry, a former schoolmaster at Auckland Grammar School, although a native of Christchurch, who later took charge of Wales and the All Blacks.

Retirements hit the Blues badly until, in 2003, Doug Howlett, Mils Muliaina and Joe Rokocoko helped them to a third Super Rugby title which was made more satisfying as they defeated their South Island cousins, the Crusaders, 21-17 in the final. Post-2003 the Blues' form dipped alarmingly, despite keeping up their quota of All Black representation, although they did make the semi-finals of the Super 14 in 2007. In 2008, the Samoan Pat Lam, who has a huge reputation in the northern hemisphere after playing stints with Newcastle and Northampton, took over as coach having guided Auckland's provincial outfit to the Air New Zealand Cup and the Ranfurly Shield. The Auckland-born former flanker oversaw a mini-revival with the Blues just missing out on a semi-final spot in the 2010 Super 14 tournament but they were still struggling to live up to Henry's legacy.

Below: Joe Rokocoko, Fijian-born wing, has been a Blues hero since joining them in 2003.

MATTER OF FACT
Club: The Blues
Formed: 1996
Located: Auckland, New Zealand
Administrative address: Level 6, ASB Bank Stand, enter off Gate 5, Walters Road, Eden Park, Auckland 1024
Tel: +64 9 815 4850 (office)
or +64 9 815 4828 (info line)
Email: francie.stacey@aucklandrugby.co.nz
Website: www.theblues.co.nz

Super Rugby records
Honours: Winners 1996, 1997, 2003
Best finish: First 1996, 1997, 2003
Record: P 184, W 111, L 70, D 3
Most appearances: 106 Keven Mealamu (2000–)
Most points: 619 Adrian Cashmore (1996–2000)
Biggest win: 60-7 v Hurricanes, 2002
Biggest defeat: 51-13 v Reds, 1996

Ground: Eden Park
Address: Reimers Ave, Kingsland, Auckland, New Zealand 1024
Capacity: 60,000 (for 2011 World Cup)
To get there: Kingsland Station (rail)
Stands: ASB, West, South, North East, Terraces

Bars in ground: See opposite
Bars nearby: See opposite

Legends
Sean Fitzpatrick: Hooker who was a World Cup winner in 1987 under David Kirk, long-time captain of the All Blacks and Auckland and long-time hard-nut who enjoyed telling referees their job. Ninety-two New Zealand caps, he is now a TV commentator in England.
Michael Jones: The greatest flanker ever, 'The Iceman' was described by former All Black coach John Hart as 'almost the perfect rugby player'. Refused to play on Sundays because of religious beliefs, and has 55 caps despite savage injury problems. Later coached Samoa.

Need to know: The Shakespeare Brewery & Hotel in central Auckland is an English-style pub that brews all its beers on site. These include Falstaff's Real Ale, Puck's Pixillation – that weighs in at over 11 per cent ABV – and Willpower Stout. Established in 1898, it is a short cab ride, or longer stagger, from Eden Park.

CHRISTCHURCH

photonewzealand/Ralph Tait

Above: The region's players have dominated All Blacks teams in recent years, peaking in 2002 in game against Ireland, when 14 of the team came from the Crusaders.

Southern charm

Christchurch, the main city on New Zealand's South Island, was left devastated after an earthquake hit the city on 22 February 2011. Dozens of people were killed and hundreds were injured.
The city lies on the east coast by the Pacific Ocean. To the north is the Waimakariri River and to the southeast the volcanic slopes of Port Hills, a popular recreation area and a great place for views across the city.

The 19th century ChristChurch Cathedral, at the heart of the city in Cathedral Square, was severely damaged during the 2011 quake. A few streets to the west are the city's Art Gallery and Arts Centre, the Canterbury Museum and the Botanic Gardens.

For culture of a completely different sort the 24/7 Christchurch Casino is also nearby, as is the main shopping street, the pedestrianized Cashel Street, and the popular Regent Street, with its selection of small shops and brightly coloured façades. The quaint tram, which originally started running in 1905 (although it had to be resurrected in 1995), runs around a small city loop and is a popular and easy way for visitors to get around the central sights.

Christchurch is generally a gentle, sedate place, known as the Garden City, and is the launch pad for those looking to explore the rugged South Island. It is also known as the gateway to the Antarctic, with explorers Ernest Shackleton and Robert Scott both having set off from the port for expeditions into the iceland to the south.

If you're looking for a different kind of adventure then the main area for nightlife in Christchurch is by the river along Oxford Terrace. Known simply as 'The Strip' to the locals, this is where you will find a good selection of bars and clubs. Another popular hang-out is SOL Square, the hub of the area known as South of Lichfield Lane and which is only a short distance from the city centre.

3 THINGS YOU MUST DO...

1 ADDINGTON RACEWAY

Get hooked on the strange but addictive sport of Trotting Racing at the raceway (75 Jack Hinton Dr, tel: +64 3 338 9094). When: usually Fri at 17.30 but some Thurs. Price: free except big race days. To get there: nearest train station is Addington or short taxi ride from the centre.

2 CHRISTCHURCH CASINO

Win your fortune. Or lose your shirt. This is your author reminding you to bet responsibly boys and girls (34 Victoria St, tel: +64 3 365 9999). Open: 24/7. Price: free entry. To get there: centrally located.

3 CHRISTCHURCH GONDOLA

Take the 500 metre ride up in the gondola for views across the Pacific Ocean, the city and towards the snowy Southern Alps (10 Bridle Path Rd, Heathcote Valley, tel: +64 3 384 0700). When: daily 10.00–21.00. Price: $24 adult, $10 child 5–15. To get there: buses 28, 35 run from outside the City Exchange.

Above: A boatmen makes his way down the city's Avon River.

Weather	Low (°C)	High (°C)	Rain (mm)	Sunset
January	12	22	56	21.05
February	12	21	45	20.47
March	10	19	48	20.09
April	8	17	48	19.11
May	4	12	66	17.27
June	3	11	70	16.52
July	2	10	66	16.57
August	2	12	48	17.25
September	5	14	44	17.55
October	7	17	44	19.28
November	8	19	48	20.03
December	12	21	56	20.41

LANCASTER PARK

Where a dynasty reigns

The use of Christchurch as a World Cup venue was thrown into doubt after an earthquake hit the city in 2011. The redeveloped AMI Stadium was officially opened in January 2010 following a NZ$60 million (€34 million) upgrade to what is historically and commonly known as Lancaster Park. The renovations included the building of the 13,000-seater Deans Stand, commemorating Canterbury's most famous rugby dynasty, that started with the 1905 All Black Bob Deans, and the first European settlers in the area.

The new ground was awarded five pool matches and two quarter-finals for the 2011 Rugby World Cup and its new capacity of 38,628 was boosted to 45,000 for the tournament by the addition of temporary seating despite a damaging earthquake in October 2010. But during the tournament the ground was due to be tagged Stadium Christchurch because of advertising restrictions.

Called Jade Stadium from 1998 to 2007, the venue which also hosts international cricket, was the scene of Don 'The Boot' Clarke's famous 60-metre goal that gave the All Blacks a last-gasp 9-6 win over Mike Weston's English tourists in 1963. Prior to that Lancaster Park had staged the first All Blacks game in New Zealand when they took on New South Wales in 1894.

Below: An upgrade on the stadium was completed in 2010 before an earthquake devastated the city.

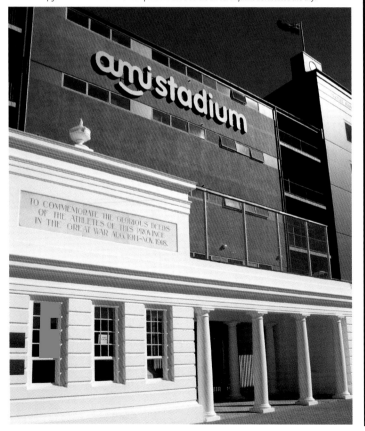

MATTER OF FACT
Stadium: AMI Stadium
Located: Christchurch, New Zealand
Address: 30 Stevens Street, Phillipstown, Christchurch 8011
Tel: +64 3 379 1765/0800 4 AMI STADIUM (free)
Email: enquiries@amistadium.co.nz
or info@vbase.co.nz
Website: www.amistadium.co.nz
Capacity: 38,628 (45,000 for RWC 2011)
To get there: Route 31/32 (bus)
Stands: Deans, Tui, Hadlee, PKMC

Stadium tours
Open: By arrangement only, no tours a week before an event. Community tours free (schools etc, max 25) Corporate tours NZ$60 (1–25), NZ$120 (25–50)
Tel: +64 3 379 1765
Email: joanne.mcmaster@amistadium.co.nz

First match: England v Colonies 1882
First Test: New Zealand 5 Australia 16, 1913
Tests hosted: 50
New Zealand record: P 48, W 39, L 9, D 0

Bars in ground: Not named
Bars nearby: Stadium Sports Bar & Bistro (77–79 Stevens Street, Phillipstown, Christchurch 8011, +64 3 374 4142); **The Embankment Tavern** (181 Ferry Road, Phillipstown, Christchurch 8011, +64 3 379 3760); **The Twisted Hop** (6 Poplar Street, Poplar Lanes, Christchurch 8011, +64 3 962 3688, www.thetwistedhop.co.nz); **Fitzgerald Arms Tavern** (333 Cashel Street, Linwood, Christchurch 8011, +64 3 963 1766, www.thefitztuiclubrooms.co.nz)

Finally... The old Lancaster Park faced financial problems in World War I. The solution was to plough up the pitch and use it as a potato field to raise revenue.

CRUSADERS

Leading the Crusade

Speak to any taxi driver in Christchurch and you will hear at first hand the resentment the locals felt when Auckland was awarded the 2011 Rugby World Cup final (and to make matters worse both semi-finals). The Crusaders, the local Super Rugby franchise who incorporate seven provinces at the top of the South Island, have recently helped the area get its own back on it rivals from the north.

Canterbury rugby was at its lowest ebb when professionalism arrived in 1996 – they had supplied just one player for the All Blacks touring squad to France and Italy the previous year – and it was no surprise when they finished bottom in first Super 12 with just two wins.

A root-and-branch review and some aggressive player recruitment saw the side, based at the old Lancaster Park, now the AMI Stadium, come sixth the next year before winning the Super 12 in 1998. That win set up a period of unprecedented dominance based on players such as Andrew Mehrtens, Reuben Thorne, Justin Marshall and Caleb Ralph.

The smooth emergence of global superstars such as Dan Carter and Richie McCaw ensured their prominence continued into the Super 14 with Carter and McCaw establishing themselves as the two leading figures in All Black rugby. Wayne Smith, who went on to coach Northampton and the All Blacks, kick-started the upturn in fortunes when he took over from Vance Stewart in September 1996. Robbie Deans carried on his work when he took over in 2000 to become the most successful coach in Super Rugby history.

The revolution, or 'The Crusade' as the locals term it, peaked when the franchise supplied 14 players in the New Zealand side who took on Ireland in 2002. Auckland's Doug Howlett was the odd man out in the starting XV.

Below: *North Island v South Island clash as the Crusaders (in red) take on the Hurricanes.*

MATTER OF FACT

Club: The Crusaders
Formed: 1996
Located: Christchurch, New Zealand
Administrative address: Level One, 5 Durham Street, Christchurch 8013
Tel: +64 3 379 8300
Email: info@crfu.co.nz
Website: www.crusaders.co.nz

Super Rugby records

Honours: Winners 1998, 1999, 2000, 2002, 2005, 2006, 2008
Best finish: First 1998, 1999, 2000, 2002, 2005, 2006, 2008
Record: P 196, W 131, L 59, D 6
Most appearances: 129 Reuben Thorne (1997–2008)
Most points: 1,078 Dan Carter (2003–)
Biggest win: 96-19 v Waratahs, 2002
Biggest defeat: 52-16 v Reds, 1996

Ground: AMI Stadium
Address: 30 Stevens Street, Phillipstown, Christchurch 8011
Capacity: 38,628 (45,000 for World Cup 2011)
To get there: Route 31/32 (bus)
Stands: Deans, Tui, Hadlee, PKMC

Bars in ground: See opposite
Bars nearby: See opposite

Legends

Todd Blackadder: Became the first player to lift the Super Rugby trophy three times as captain when captaining the Crusaders in 1998, 1999 and 2000. Left for Edinburgh in 2001, and was forwards coach with Scotland. Appointed Crusaders coach in 2008.
Richie McCaw: All Black captain and flanker who led the Crusaders to Super 14 titles in 2005, 2006 and 2008. Regarded as the finest flanker of his generation, he was the first player to be named IRB Player of the Year twice when taking the honour in 2006 and 2009.

Need to know: The stadium is a short walk from the bars of Cashel Street, most notably the Stock X Change, made famous by cricketer Jesse Ryder who injured his hand when breaking a window trying to get into the toilet. Also a favourite post-match hang-out for Crusaders players.

DUNEDIN

Above: *The rugged South Island. Dunedin is on the southeast coast of New Zealand by the Pacific Ocean.*

Students, sports and Scots

This is the city of 'S' – students and sport. Both dominate this small southeast coast city of less than 250,000 people (as well as the cold winters). The well-regarded University of Otago provides more than a tenth of that population and its students and those of other educational institutions have built a reputation for heavy partying. You'll find no shortage of students (except in the summer) or partying wherever you look. A lot of the action is focussed around the central Octagon and the various streets that run off it, especially the main George Street.

But most sports fans instantly think of Dunedin as the beating heart of New Zealand rugby because of Carisbrook, the city's legendary sporting arena (now replaced by Forsyth Barr) that visiting teams always feared seeing on the fixture list. And while there are many other sports in what is the second-largest city on the South Island – cricket, football, basketball, ice hockey – it is rugby that this city lives and breathes.

The city has strong Scottish roots (Dunedin is sometimes referred to as the Edinburgh of the South) and when scouring the bars around the Octagon you won't fail to see the statue of poet Robbie Burns, which is over 100 years old. Nearby the statue is the Otago Settlers Museum, which was founded in 1898 to commemorate the 50th anniversary of the planned Scottish settlement of Dunedin. The social history museum celebrates the various peoples – Scottish, Maori, Chinese – that have settled in the region.

Within easy walking distance of this small central area you will also find many other sites of interest including St Paul's Cathedral, the Fortune Theatre, the Regent Theatre, Dunedin Public Art Gallery, as well as Speight's Brewery (which offers tours), Cadbury's World (also offers tours) and the city's casino.

3 THINGS YOU MUST DO...

1 BALDWIN STREET

This is the steepest street in the world according to the *Guinness Book of Records*, with a slope of 1 to 2:9. Run up it, cycle up it or walk up it for great views. To get there: 4 km (2.5 miles) to the north of the city off the North Road.

2 BREWERY TOUR

Speight's is the beer brewed in Dunedin. Take a 90-minute tour, with tasting (200 Rattray St, tel: + 64 3 4777 697). When: Mon–Thur 10.00, 12.00, 14.00, 18.00, 19.00, Fri–Sun 10.00, 12.00, 14.00, 16.00, 18.00. Price: $20 adult, $8 child 5-18. To get there: a five-minute walk from the Octagon.

3 WILDLIFE

Otago is home to a diversity of wildlife including the Royal Albatross, fur seal, sea lion and Yellow-Eyed penguin. Tour companies offer a chance to get up close. Try Back to Nature Tours (tel: + 64 3 479 2009) who offer a six-hour Discover the Peninsula Tour. Price: $89 adult, $45 child under 14.

Above: Dunedin is the second biggest city on the South Island with a population of around 250,000.

Weather	Low (°C)	High (°C)	Rain (mm)	Sunset
January	10	18	86	21.11
February	10	19	75	20.51
March	9	17	76	20.13
April	7	15	70	19.08
May	5	12	81	17.21
June	3	9	81	16.47
July	3	10	79	16.50
August	3	11	78	17.21
September	5	13	69	17.52
October	7	15	78	19.31
November	7	17	81	20.08
December	9	18	89	20.48

FORSYTH BARR STADIUM

New House of Pain?

When Carisbrook, in Dunedin, staged its last All Blacks match, against Wales in June 2010, there was plenty of sorrow as the bulldozers prepared to move into the well-nicknamed 'House of Pain'. That 42-9 win over the Welsh was typical of the agony inflicted on visiting teams as New Zealand won 31 times from 37 games there between 1908 and 2010. But the ground itself was dilapidated and the Forsyth Barr Stadium, a short walk from the centre of Dunedin at University Park at the southern end of Logan Park was scheduled to be finished in time for the 2011 World Cup with Scotland, England, Italy and Ireland all playing games in the city.

Construction started on the new ground in June 2009 and the stadium, housing just 30,000 fans, is also the home of the Otago Highlanders. The University of Otago is the only university in New Zealand with a stadium on its campus.

There was opposition to the project, because of the cost, NZ$200 million (€113 million), but legal action to prevent the funding of the stadium from the public purse was defeated.

Below: Artist's impression of the new Forsyth Barr Stadium.

MATTER OF FACT
Stadium: Forsyth Barr Stadium
Located: Dunedin, New Zealand
Address: Cnr of Anzac Ave and Awatea Street, Dunedin 9016
Tel: +64 3 479 2823
Email: info@forsythbarrstadium.co.nz
Website: www.forsythbarrstadium.co.nz
Capacity: 30,500
To get there: 15-minute walk from CBD. Dunedin Station (train) is 1.5 km (1 mile)
Stands: South, North, East, West

First match: n/a
First Test: n/a
Tests hosted: n/a
New Zealand record: n/a

Bars nearby: The Original Robert Burns Pub (374 George Street, Dunedin 9016, +643 479 2701); **The Baaa Sports Café & Bar** (746 Great King Street, North Dunedin 9016, +64 3 477 7718, www.thebaaa.co.nz); **Starters Bar** (157 Frederick Street, Dunedin 9016, +64 (0)3 477 8988, www.startersbar.co.nz); **Inch Bar** (8 Bank Street, Opoho, Dunedin 9010, +64 3 473 6496)

Finally... The Forsyth Barr Stadium has a clear plastic roof and is New Zealand's biggest indoor arena (it is second only to Melbourne's Etihad Stadium in the southern hemisphere). The roof is 37 metres (121 feet) high, four metres (13 feet) higher than that at the Millennium Stadium in Cardiff.

HIGHLANDERS

Highland fling

The three provincial rugby unions south of the Waitaki River – North Otago, Otago and Southland – combined to form the Otago Highlanders for the initial Super 12 season in 1996 and made the semi-finals three years on the spin from 1998, making the final in 1999. They were beaten 24-19 by the Crusaders in that final and although they made the semi-finals again in 2002, with a side including Taine Randell and Anton Oliver, the rest of the decade was a disappointment and summed up when Laurie Mains resigned as coach in 2003 after falling out with senior players. Mains said Oliver was the ringleader, while Oliver responded by accusing the former All Black coach of being 'poorly organized, a Jekyll and Hyde' and unwilling to learn to use a computer. Ouch.

An overhaul of the squad in 2004 did little to arrest the decline and the Highlanders spent the next few years in the doldrums under coach Greg Cooper, who left for the Blues in 2007. Glenn Moore's stint ended in 2010 after a 12th-place finish and the former All Black flanker Jamie Joseph was handed the poisoned chalice.

'The name and image of the Highlander conjure up visions of fierce independence, pride in one's roots, loyalty, strength, kinship, honesty, and hard work.' says the Highlanders' website. These attributes were not shown in their results in the late 2000s despite having All Blacks such as Jimmy Cowan, Israel Dagg and Tom Donnelly in the squad.

The Highlanders were due to move to the Forsyth Barr Stadium from Carisbrook, aka 'The House of Pain', for the start of the 2011 Super 15 season.

Below: Scrum-half Jimmy Cowan has been with the Highlanders since 2003.

MATTER OF FACT
Club: The Highlanders
Formed: 1996
Located. Dunedin, New Zealand
Administrative address: Forsyth Barr Stadium, Anzac Drive, Dunedin 9016
Tel: +64 3 466 4010
Email: highlanders@highlanders-rugby.co.nz
Website: www.highlanders-rugby.co.nz

Super Rugby records
Honours: None
Best finish: Runners-up 1999
Record: P 180, W 85, L 93, D 2
Most appearances: 127 Anton Oliver (1997–2010)
Most points: 817 Tony Brown (1997–2004)
Biggest win: 65-23 v Bulls, 1999
Biggest defeat: 70-26 v Brumbies, 1996

Ground: Forsyth Barr Stadium
Address: Anzac Drive, Dunedin 9016
Capacity: 30,500
To get there: 15-minute walk from CBD. Dunedin Station (train) is 1.5 km (1 mile)
Stands: South, North, West, East

Bars nearby: See opposite

Legends
Anton Oliver: Outspoken All Black hooker who played 127 Super Rugby matches for the Highlanders. Went to Oxford University on retirement, played in the Varsity Match and has been wooed by political parties.
Josh Kronfeld: Outstanding flanker who helped New Zealand to 1995 World Cup final. Moved to Leicester in 2001 before retiring in 2003. As a player he daubed anti-nuclear testing slogans on his scrum-cap.

Need to know: The Highlanders are so named because of the huge Scottish influence in the Otago area. Scottish immigrants arriving in New Zealand in the 1840s founded Dunedin, which is the old Gaelic name for Edinburgh.

HAMILTON

Above: *Hamilton is situated in the middle of the Waikato region in the North Island and is the largest inland city in the country.*

Coffee time

Although built on a site of former Maori villages, Hamilton, some 135 km (80 miles) south of Auckland, is a relatively new city having achieved its status only in 1945. Today the urban area is home to around 200,000 people.

Built along both sides of the Waikato River, Hamilton has been nurturing its reputation for its coffee culture, and in the area along, and off, Hood Street and Victoria Street in particular you will find any number of places for your espresso, machiato or cappuchino fix, as well as a number of bars and restaurants should coffee not be your thing.

A large student population, thanks to the University of Waikato, which is situated on the east side of the river, ensures things can get pretty lively. Close by is Hamilton Lake, and although the city is an inland one, it has a strong culture of sailing.

Being so close to Auckland, the city is often overlooked by visitors to the country. However, the city does boast a number of attractions.

Hamilton Gardens remains a major draw card for the Waikato region and hosts a number of annual events such as the Hamilton Gardens Summer Festival. The collection of gardens includes an American Modernist Garden, a Japanese Garden of Contemplation and an Italian Renaissance Garden.

Other places of interest include Hamilton Zoo, St Peter's Cathedral, the Riff Raff statue (in honour of former resident Richard O'Brien, creator of the *Rocky Horror Show*) and the Waikato Museum. Established in 1987, the museum is spread over five levels and features thousands of exhibits, including a 200 year old Waka taua (a Maori war canoe)

3 THINGS YOU MUST DO...

1 WATERWORLD

Get wet and have fun, with pools, slides, plus spa, sauna and steam rooms (Garnett Ave, tel: +63 7 958 5860). When: Mon–Fri 06.00–21.00, Sat 07.00–21.00. Sun and holidays 09.00–21.00. Price: $5 adult, $2.50 child 2–15. To get there: bus Te Rapa 18.

2 RIFF RAFF

Richard O'Brien, creator of the *Rocky Horror Show*, used to live in Hamilton and this statue (Victoria St) stands as celebration to the show. To get there: centrally located.

3 BALLOON

Enjoy some peace and quiet and beautiful scenery with a four-hour balloon trip (Kiwi Balloon Company, 29a Corrin St, tel: +63 7 843 8538). When: daily, weather permitting. Price: $290 per person.

Above: The annual Balloons Over Waikato Festival. The five-day event takes place in March/April.

Weather	Low (°C)	High (°C)	Rain (mm)	Sunset
January	16	23	72	20.44
February	15	23	90	20.33
March	15	22	79	20.01
April	14	18	92	19.18
May	11	18	125	17.36
June	10	14	130	17.13
July	9	14	142	17.14
August	9	14	112	17.35
September	9	16	98	18.00
October	12	18	98	19.23
November	12	20	83	19.54
December	14	21	75	20.26

WAIKATO STADIUM

Rugby Park reborn

Waikato Stadium, which opened in 2002 with a game between the Chiefs and the Crusaders, replaced the old Rugby Park which did not host any more international rugby after the 1987 World Cup, when Argentina played Fiji. Located in the heart of Hamilton it is now host to the Chiefs in Super Rugby and Waikato in New Zealand's domestic competition and was awarded three pool games in the 2011 Rugby World Cup.

Rugby Park had a chequered past. In 1934 the grandstand roof collapsed, although there were no casualties, and in 1981 a match involving South Africa was abandoned when anti-apartheid protestors invaded the pitch.

International rugby returned to the ground in 2002, when New Zealand thrashed Italy 64-10, and has been on the roster ever since with Wales playing their first international there in the summer of 2010.

The Greenzone Embankment, a standing area, is renowned as the party area of the ground, while the five-floor Brian Perry Stand houses the changing rooms, shops, media and corporate lounges. The capacity can be increased to over 30,000 for big events with temporary seating.

Below: Looking down on the New Zealand Maoris as they take on the Lions.

MATTER OF FACT
Stadium: Waikato Stadium
Located: Hamilton, New Zealand
Address: 128 Seddon Road, Whitiora 3204
Tel: +64 7 958 5800
Email: admin@waikatostadium.co.nz
Website: www.waikatostadium.co.nz
Capacity: 25,800
To get there: Free shuttle bus from Hood Street on match days.
Stands: WEL Network, Brian Perry, Goal Line Terrace, Greenzone.

Stadium tours
Open: By arrangement only. $2 per person.
Tel: +64 7 958 5800
Email: admin@waikatostadium.co.nz

First Test: New Zealand Maori 4 Fiji 14, 1939
Tests hosted: 10
New Zealand record: P 7, W 6, L 1, D 0

Bars in ground: Not named
Bars nearby: Speight's Ale House Hamilton
(30 Liverpool Street, Hamilton 3204, +64 7 834 3442, www.speights-hamilton.co.nz), **The Londoner** (596 Victoria Street, Hamilton 3204, +64 7 839 9441), **The Bank Bar & Brasserie** (117 Victoria Street, Hamilton 3204, +64 7 839 4740, www.thebank.co.nz), **Biddy Mulligan's Irish Pub** (742 Victoria Street, Hamilton 3204, +64 7 834 0306)

Finally… Unveiled in February 2004, the Whatanoa Gateway commemorates the ancient Ngati Wairere Pa and the burial ground near the stadium. Maori carvings also dominate the players' tunnel at the venue.

CHIEFS

Chiefs attraction

Based at Waikato Stadium in Hamilton, the Chiefs were the only New Zealand side not to have made the last four of the Super 12 competition until their breakthrough season in 2004. They lost out to the Brumbies that time but made the final in 2009, only to be thrashed by the Bulls.

The franchise, which has seen players such as Walter Little, Jonah Lomu and Ian Jones don the black strip, represents the unions of Waikato, Bay of Plenty, Counties Manukau, King Country and Thames Valley. At the start of the Super 12 they also represented North Harbour and Northland who were 'given' to the franchise to dilute the number of All Blacks who could play for the Auckland-based Blues. This position was reversed in 1999 when North Harbour and Northland returned to the Blues and Counties Manukau and Thames Valley went to the Chiefs.

Waikato is traditionally a strong rugby area. They provided 14 of the starting team who lost 40-16 to Great Britain in 1930 and became the first provincial union to beat a touring South African team when the Springboks were seen off 14-10 in 1956. France were also defeated in 1961, as were Australia, Fiji, Wales, Argentina in later years and the Lions midweek side, captained by Will Carling in 1993.

Waikato fans ring cowbells at matches, and the fashion has spread to Chiefs games. The Waikato mascot is a cow, known as Mooloo, and the Waikato side are known as the Mooloo Men, with New Zealanders referring to anyone who comes from the area as a 'Mooloo'.

Below: Chiefs legend Mils Muliaina was born in Samoa but moved to New Zealand at the age of two.

MATTER OF FACT
Club: The Chiefs
Formed: 1996
Located: Hamilton, New Zealand
Administrative address: Cnr Tristram and Abbotsford Streets, PO Box 9507, Hamilton
Tel: +64 7 839 5675
Email: admin@chiefs.co.nz
Website: www.chiefs.co.nz

Super Rugby records
Honours: None
Best finish: Runners-up 2009
Record: P 178, W 83, L 91, D 4
Most appearances: 82 Michael Collins (1997–2005)
Most points: 738 Stephen Donald (2005–)
Biggest win: 47-9 v Lions, 1997
Biggest defeat: 61-17 v Bulls, 2009

Ground: Waikato Stadium
Address: 128 Seddon Road, Whitiora 3204, New Zealand
Capacity: 25,800
To get there: Free shuttle bus from Hood Street on match days.
Stands: WEL Network, Brian Perry, Goal Line Terrace, Greenzone.

Bars in ground: Not named
Bars nearby: CBD Corner Pub (26 Hood Street, Hamilton 3204, +64 7 834 3400, www.cbdpub.co.nz); **Shenanigans Pub** (127 Victoria Street, Hamilton 3204, +64 7 839 2310); **The Helm Bar & Kitchen** (22 Ulster Street, Whitoria 3200, +64 7 839 2545, www.thehelm. co.nz); **The Outback Inn** (141 Victoria Street, Hamilton 3204, +64 7 839 6354, www.outback.co.nz)

Legends
Mils Muliaina: New Zealand full-back who joined the Chiefs in 2005 from the Blues. Only player to play every All Black Test in 2004, and accomplished Sevens player who won gold at the 2002 Commonwealth Games.
Walter Little: Powerful centre who formed a legendary midfield partnership for the All Blacks with Frank Bunce. Made 50 Test appearances and would have made more but for injuries and selection vagaries.

Need to know: The Chiefs rewrote the record books when they beat the Lions (South Africa) 72-65 in Johannesburg in February 2010. The 137 points beat the previous highest match total set by Natal's 75-43 win over the Highlanders in 1997 with the match containing 18 tries.

SOUTH AFRICA

<table>
<tr><td>

THE

3

MINUTE GUIDE

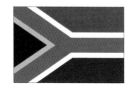

</td><td>

Capitals: *Cape Town (Legislative), Pretoria (Administrative), Bloemfontein (Judicial).*
Languages: *11 official languages.* **Beers:** *Castle, Carling Black Label, Bosun's Bitter.*
Food: *Boerewors (sausage), pap and vleis (porridge and meat), Biltong (cured meat).*
National Anthem: *Nkosi Sikilel' iAfrica (God Bless Africa).* **Population:** *49 million.*
Time zone: *GMT +2.* **Emergency numbers:** *1011 (police and fire), 10177 (medical).*
Did you know? *The largest diamond in the world was found near Pretoria in 1905. It was 3,106 carat.* **Rugby body:** *South African Rugby Union, SA Sport Science Institute, Boundary Road, Newlands, Cape Town 7725. Tel: +27 21 659 6700 . Web: www.sarugby.co.za*

</td></tr>
</table>

Below: Watch rugby then see the wildlife of Africa.

Rainbow rugby

South Africa may have welcomed the round-ball fraternity to their country in 2010 but among the white population rugby union is far and away the more popular game. South Africa's sporting isolation, before their return in 1992 (although the Lions had toured in 1980) cut the country's rugby fans to the quick. When they were awarded the hosting rights for the 1995 Rugby World Cup, there was only one fairy-tale outcome, and the Springboks delivered a 15-12 win over the All Blacks in the final. They added a second World Cup in France in 2007, this time beating England in the final, under coach Jake White, who, in the typically politicized world of South African rugby, was out of a job as soon as the trophy was lifted.

Like New Zealanders, South Africans are fanatical about rugby. There are even programmes covering school games on television including Craven Week, named after the most influential figure in the game in the country. Danie Craven played for the mighty Springboks of the 1930s, selected, managed and coached the national side and was president of the South African Rugby Board before his death in 1993.

The term 'The Springboks' was first used on the 1906–07 tour of Great Britain and France, led by captain Paul Roos, and has remained, although the ANC government tried to force South African sports teams to name themselves the Proteas after the national flower. Nelson Mandela's intervention, as a gesture to Afrikaner rugby fans, prevented this although the title still occasionally causes controversy.

Above: *Take a cable car ride up Table Mountain and see views of one the world's most beautiful cities – if the mountain's 'tablecloth' of cloud is not on top.*

TEST RECORD (capped internationals only)

Versus	First Test	Played	Won	Lost	Drawn
Argentina	Nov 1993	13	13	0	0
Australia	Jul 1993	71	41	29	1
England	Dec 1906	31	18	12	1
France	Jan 1913	38	21	11	6
Ireland	Nov 1906	19	14	4	1
Italy	Nov 1995	10	10	0	0
New Zealand	Aug 1921	81	33	45	3
Scotland	Nov 1906	20	16	4	0
Wales	Dec 1906	25	23	1	1
British & Irish Lions	Jul 1891	46	23	17	6

Most international caps: Percy Montgomery (1997–2008)102 Tests
Most international points: Percy Montgomery (1997–2008) 893 points, 102 Tests (25t, 153c, 148p, 6d)
Most international tries: Joost van der Westhuizen (1993–2003) 38 tries, 89 Tests, Bryan Habana (2004–) 38 tries, 66 Tests

WORLD CUP RECORD

Year	Venue	Finished
1987	Australia & NZ	Did not play
1991	England	Did not play
1995	South Africa	Winners
1999	Wales	Third
2003	Australia	Quarter-finals
2007	France	Winners

Most World Cup appearances: Os du Randt, 16 appearances (1995, 1999, 2007)
Most World Cup points: Percy Montgomery 111 points, 12 matches (1999, 2007)
Most World Cup tries: Bryan Habana 8 tries, 7 matches (2007)
Record World Cup win: 72-6 v Uruguay, Perth, 2003
World Cup coaches: 1995: Kitch Christie; 1999: Nick Mallett; 2003 Rudolf Straeuli; 2007: Jake White

PRETORIA

Above: *Every spring the blossom of the jacaranda trees light up the streets of Pretoria.*

Jacaranda City

Lying some 70 km (44 miles) to the north of Johannesburg, the city of Pretoria is South Africa's administrative capital (there are three capitals, Cape Town and Bloemfontein being the other two).

Known as the Jacaranda City for the explosion of pink the city enjoys when the thousands of jacaranda trees lining the streets bloom in the springtime, Pretoria is a more relaxed place than its larger neighbour to the south.

The seat of the South African government is found at the Union Buildings, famously the place where Nelson Mandela was inaugurated as the country's first democratically elected president in 1994. The large, semi-circular shaped buildings, and indeed the city itself (which is sometimes referred to as Tshwane, although this is the metropolitan area) are increasing becoming symbols of democracy in the country.

However, Pretoria has fierce Afrikaner roots. It was founded by Marthinus Pretorius, one of the leaders of the Voortrekkers who sought out a homeland of their own, and it was named after his father Andries, who led his people to victory over the Zulus in the Battle of Blood River (1838). The city is home to the monolithic Voortrekker Monument, which pays tribute to the pioneers who migrated to the area from the Cape from the 1830s. Today you are certainly more likely to hear Afrikaans spoken among the white population in Pretoria than English.

With a large student population, Hatfield is a popular area for nightlife, especially those wanting to party late into the night. For a slightly more upmarket night out head to Menlyn Square, another busy area for bars. Just off here is Menlyn Park, one of several retail centres in this shopping-mall-mad country. Simply mention Menlyn (or Brooklyn Mall) to see the excitement on the faces of the locals.

3 THINGS YOU MUST DO...

1 ELEPHANT SANCTUARY
Get up close with African elephants (Hartbeespoort Dam, tel: +27 12 258 0423). When: educational programmes at 08.00, 10,00, 14,00 (and 12.00 from June–Oct). Price: R325–R525 adults, R165–R215 child 3–14. Rides: R350 adult, R250 child (must be 8). To get there: 32 km (20 miles) west of Pretoria.

2 THE ANN VAN DYK CHEETAH CENTRE
See cheetah, wild dog, hyena, vultures and more (De Wildt, tel: +27 12 504 9906). When: cheetahs run Tues, Thur, Sat, Sun 08.00, three-hour tours Tues, Wed, Thur, Sat, Sun, 13.30 (plus 08.30 Wed). Price: R220. To get there: De Wildt is 37 km (23 miles) northwest of Pretoria on the R566.

3 HATFIELD
Boosted by the large student population (the university is nearby) Hatfield is the area to head to for bars, restaurants and clubs. Try the Drop Zone (Hatfield Sq, tel: +27 12 362 6528). To get there: Hatfield is to the east of the city centre.

Above: The Voortrekker Monument honours the Afrikaners who sought out a homeland in the north in the 1800s.

Weather	Low (°C)	High (°C)	Rain (mm)	Sunset
January	19	28	130	19.02
February	18	27	101	18.49
March	18	26	80	18.37
April	14	24	45	18.07
May	10	22	21	17.38
June	8	18	6	17.25
July	7	19	7	17.28
August	9	21	7	17.42
September	14	24	20	17.56
October	15	25	71	18.07
November	17	26	110	18.23
December	18	27	111	18.45

LOFTUS VERSFELD

Legend of Loftus

One of the oldest and most intimidating, grounds in South Africa, Loftus Versfeld was built in 1906, when it was known as the Eastern Sports Ground and lies about 3 km (2 miles) from the centre of Pretoria.

Renamed in 1933, after Robert Owen Loftus Versfeld, who founded organized rugby in the area, died in the eastern stand from a heart attack, the ground was significantly upgraded ahead of the 2010 soccer World Cup when it hosted six games, one in the round of 16. The first upgrade, when changing rooms and toilets were added came only after the profitable All Blacks tour of 1928.

It is rugby union for which the ground is famous and the locals are fanatical about the game. Home to the Vodacom Bulls, the Super Rugby giants, and the Blue Bulls Currie Cup outfit, the stadium hosted games in the 1995 Rugby World Cup, including one quarter-final, when New Zealand beat Scotland, and the third-place play-off, when France saw off England.

In 2009 it was the scene of Morné Steyn's last-minute, 52-metre penalty that clinched the series for South Africa against Paul O'Connell's Lions, avenging the 1997 defeat at the hands of Martin Johnson's tourists.

That same year Loftus hosted the Super 14 final when the Bulls ran in eight tries to hammer the Chiefs 61-17 to the delight of their raucous fans. If it was not an epic on the scale of the Test match against the Lions, the locals were not complaining.

Loftus, as it is known locally despite several different sponsors, is a 10-minute walk from Rissik Station or a grubber kick from Loftus Versfeld Park Stadium. Once inside the ground, carry cash as none of the food and drink outlets accept cards.

Below: Loftus, one of the most intimidating stadiums in the country for visiting teams.

MATTER OF FACT
Stadium: Loftus Versfeld Stadium
Located: Pretoria, South Africa
Address: Kirkness Street, Pretoria 0002
Tel: +27 12 344 4011
or ticket office +27 12 420 0700
Email: tracey-lee@bluebull.co.za
Website: www.thebulls.co.za
Capacity: 51,762
To get there: Rissik Station or Loftus Versfeld Park Station (train)
Stands: Grandstand, Northern, South Pavilion, Eastern

Stadium tours
Not currently available but being considered

First match: 1908
First Test: British & Irish Lions 9 South Africa 6, 1955
Tests hosted: 35
South Africa record: P 30, W 22, L 8, D 0

Bars in ground: The Trophy Room, Matchday beer garden
Bars nearby: Eastwood's Tavern (391 Eastwood Street, Pretoria 0083, +27 12 344 0243, www. eastwoods.co.za); **Trademarx Sports Cafe** (Cnr Lynnwood Road & Kirkness Street Arcadia, Pretoria 0007, +27 12 344 5000, www.trademarx.co.za); **The Oxford Olde English Pub** (1114 Burnett Street, Pretoria 0083, +27 12 362 7177); **Hillside Tavern** (Rynlal Building, 320 The Hillside Road, Pretoria 0081, +27 12 348 1402)

Finally... Loftus Versfeld is one of the most intimidating places in world rugby for opponents and the altitude does not help. The stadium is 1,350 metres (4,500 feet) above sea level, making it as uncomfortable as Johannesburg for visitors who arrive in the city unprepared.

BULLS

Hitting the bull

Mostly drawn from Pretoria and Limpopo Province, formerly Northern Transvaal, the Bulls Super 15 franchise has a lot to live up to. Northern Transvaal were a formidable side with players such as Naas Botha, lock Frik du Preez, wing Tom van Vollenhoven and scrum-half Joost van der Westhuizen taking them to 31 Currie Cup finals up to 2009.

In Super Rugby it was a different story with the franchise winning only seven games in the competition from 1998 to 2002, and being whitewashed in that final campaign. But coach Heyneke Meyer managed to inspire them and signed off his stint as coach when the Bulls became the first South African side to win the Super 14 — beating the Sharks 20-19 in the final, in Durban, in 2007. The next year was a flop with a 10th place finish but they won the title in 2009 and 2010 beating the Chiefs and the Stormers respectively in the final. The fact that South Africa were world champions during this period is probably no coincidence and players such as Bakkies Botha, Bryan Habana, Victor Matfield, Morné Steyn and Bryan Habana were all highly regarded internationals with second row Botha, an on-field terminator, reinforcing the stereotype of the hard-man Afrikaner.

Bulls fans are a colourful, noisy lot, with painted faces and horned hats and their image was enhanced in 2010 when the blue army invaded Soweto. With Loftus Versfeld out of action ahead of the soccer World Cup, the Bulls elected to hold their Super 14 semi-final and final at Orlando Stadium in the township. The sight of Afrikaners drinking beer with locals in Soweto was dubbed one of South Africa's greatest moments of racial reconciliation.

Below: Bulls legend Victor Matfield (here in Toulon colours) is one of many Boks who's been attracted by Europe's rich leagues.

MATTER OF FACT

Club: Vodacom Bulls
Formed: 1997
Located: Pretoria, South Africa
Administrative address: Loftus Versfeld, Kirkness Street, Pretoria 0002
Tel: +27 12 420 0700
Email: tracy-lee@bluebull.co.za
Website: www.bluebulls.co.za

Super Rugby records

Honours: Winners 2007, 2009, 2010
Best finish: Winners 2007, 2009, 2010
Record: P 182, W 88, L 88, D 6
Most appearances: 114 Pedrie Wannenburg (2002–2010)
Most points: 757 Morné Steyn (2005–)
Biggest win: 92-3 v Reds, 2007
Biggest defeat: 73-9 v Brumbies, 1999

Ground: Loftus Versfeld
Address: Kirkness Street, Pretoria 0002
Capacity: 51,762
To get there: Rissik Station or Loftus Versfeld Park Station (train)
Stands: Grandstand, Northern, South Pavilion, Eastern

Bars in ground: See opposite
Bars nearby: See opposite

Legends

Victor Matfield: Lock who was a World Cup winner in 2007, when he was named man of the match in the final, and Super 14 champion in 2007, 2009 and 2010. Considered the best line-out forward of his generation.

Bryan Habana: Wing who scored eight tries in the 2007 World Cup and once raced a cheetah. His 82nd-minute try gave the Bulls a 20-19 win over the Sharks in the 2007 Super 14 final and probably earned Habana free drinks in Pretoria for life.

Need to know: Naas Botha, who played fly-half for Northern Transvaal is still revered in the area but regarded with less affection by rival fans. Four times South African Player of the Year and 11-time Currie Cup finalist, he was tagged 'Nasty Booter' for his kicking by journalists covering the 1980 Lions tour.

CAPE TOWN

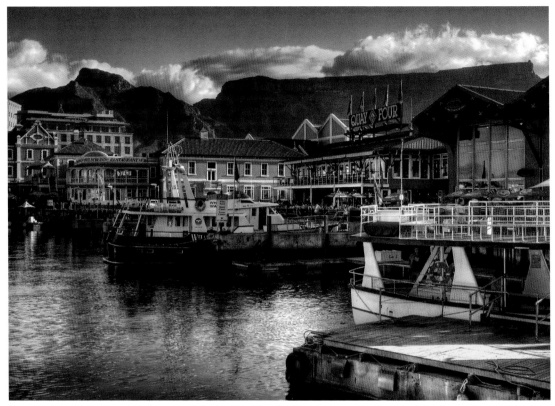

Above: Cape Town's Waterfront is one of Africa's biggest tourist attractions. The pub Quay Four (pictured centre) is said to sell more draught beer than any other pub in the country.

A beautiful life

Life's pretty good for Capetonians. Nestled against the imposing Table Mountain and flanked by the Atlantic Ocean and Indian Ocean, visitors very quickly declare that this is a city that has it all.

Beautiful warm summers, plentiful rains, an abundance of wine farms nearby, good-quality restaurants, a vibrant nightlife, sandy beaches and beautiful scenery, international sporting events, excellent shopping, affordable prices, and it has to be said, very beautiful people. It's not a bad list is it?

The locals even put a positive spin on the wind that can whistle down the streets with ferocity sometimes, dubbing it the Cape Doctor because it blows away all the germs and keeps the city healthy. It's no wonder that so many visitors end up staying or buying holiday homes in the city.

The V&A Waterfront, an ever-growing complex of shops, offices, restaurants and bars, is a magnet for tourists who enjoy the waterside location, the working harbour and the relaxed, cosmopolitan atmosphere. This is said to be the busiest tourist attraction in the country and it's easy to see why. It is from here that you can get ferries to Robben Island, where Nelson Mandela and other leaders of today's South Africa were imprisoned as they fought to free the country from apartheid.

Heading away from the city, you will find wine farms till your vino heart's content in the Stellenbosch, Constantia, Paarl, Robertson and Worcester areas.

Popular city beaches are Camp's Bay and Clifton, while Bloubergstrand, Noordhoek and Boulder's Beach (where you can sometimes swim with penguins) can be found further out.

3 THINGS YOU MUST DO...

1 CABLE CAR

Take the revolving car to the top of Table Mountain for great walks and views (Tafelberg Rd, tel: +27 21 424 2121). When: varies depending on light but approx 08.30–18.00 (winter) and 08.00–21.30 (summer). Price R160 return adult, R80 child 4-17. To get there: try Rikki Taxis (tel: +27 21 418 6713).

2 LA MED

Simply the best place to drink cocktails while looking at beautiful views and beautiful people (off Victoria Rd, tel: +27 21 438 5600). When: Mon–Fri noon–late, Sat–Sun 09.00–late. To get there: Camps Bay buses stop nearby or try Rikki Taxis (tel: +27 21 418 6713).

3 WINE FARM

If you like wine you'll love the Stellenbosch wine route. Try Morgenhof Estate (Klapmuts Rd, R44, tel +27 21 889 5510) for a tasting and lunch. When: daily for tastings. Lunch, Jun–Sept, Tues–Sun 12.00–14.30, Oct–May, daily 12.00–15.00. To get there: 55 km (34 miles) east of Cape Town.

Above: The city bowl of Cape Town nestles against the slopes of Table Mountain.

Weather	Low (°C)	High (°C)	Rain (mm)	Sunset
January	16	26	15	20.01
February	16	26	8	19.53
March	14	24	23	19.23
April	12	22	48	18.41
May	10	19	79	18.06
June	8	18	78	17.45
July	7	17	89	17.48
August	8	18	66	18.06
September	10	19	41	18.29
October	11	22	31	18.49
November	13	23	19	19.14
December	14	24	10	19.43

NEWLANDS

Storm the Castle

Home of the Stormers, Western Province and Ajax Cape Town football team, Newlands Rugby Stadium is one of the most historic in South Africa, with rugby first played there in 1890. Permanent stands were not erected until 1919 and the ground has undergone a serious of developments leading up to the 1995 Rugby World Cup in which it hosted four games including the tournament opener, England's last gasp quarter-final win over Australia and their semi-final capitulation to a Jonah Lomu-inspired New Zealand. It has also hosted many matches against the Lions with the tourists winning the first Test there in 1997, 25-16. However, controversially, Paul O'Connell's 2009 touring party did not play a Test match there with sports-mad Capetonians having to settle for matches involving the Emerging Springboks and Western Province.

The third-oldest rugby ground in the world, Newlands is also in one of the best settings, in the shadow of Table Mountain and offers some of the best viewing facilities for spectators, with the seating close to the pitch compared to many major stadiums.

Match day is party time at Newlands with the bars on the Castle Lawns at the ground keeping fans well lubricated with products from the nearby brewery (which offers tours).

Below: Built beside the Castle Brewery, Newlands is situated in the plush suburb of the same name.

MATTER OF FACT
Stadium: Newlands Rugby Stadium
Located: Cape Town, South Africa
Address: Boundary Road, Newlands, 7700, Cape Town
Tel: +27 21 659 4600
Email: lrayner@wprugby.co.za
Website: www.thestormers.co.za
Capacity: 51,900
To get there: Newlands Station (train)
Stands: Grandstand, Railway, Danie Craven, Jan Pickard

Stadium tours
Open: By arrangement Mon–Fri 09.00–16.00; groups only Sat and holidays. Various tours from R46-R68 adults, R12-R25 children; R17-R55 OAPs
Tel: +27 21 686 2150
Email: gatenew@mweb.co.za
Web: www.newlandstours.co.za

First match: Villager try Stellenbosch goal, 1890
First Test: South Africa 0 Great Britain 4, 1891
Tests hosted: 50
South Africa record: P 48, W 32, L 14, D 2

Bars in ground: Not named. Match days: Castle Lawns beer garden open on Boundary Road
Bars nearby: O'Hagans Pub & Grill (Boundary Road, Newlands, Cape Town, +27 21 689 1177, www.ohagans.co.za); **Springbok Pub** (1 Sport Pienaar Road, Newlands, Cape Town 7945, +27 21 671 4251, www.springbokpub.com); **Foresters Arms** (52 Newlands Avenue, Southern Suburbs 7700, +27 21 689 5949); Pig & Swizzles (24A Main Road, Cape Town 7700, +27 21 689 1915)

Finally . . . Newlands staged the first Lions game in South Africa against Western Province on 9 July 1891 and has hosted more Lions matches than any other South African venue. The province beat the tourists in 1910 and 1938 and the teams fought out a 0-0 draw in 1896. One for the purists.

STORMERS

Whipping up a storm

Western Province Rugby Football Union was formed in 1883 and their side, known as *Die Streeptruie*, dominated the Currie Cup, South Africa's domestic competition, to such an extent that their title in 2001 was the 32nd time they had lifted the trophy. They competed as Western Province in the 1995 Super 10 and the 1996 Super 12 although they failed to qualify for the next year's competition. In 1998 the Stormers, or Western Stormers as they were known then, first competed in the Super 12 making the semi-finals in 1999 and 2004 before finally getting to the final, led by Schalk Burger, in 2010. History records that Burger complained about the referee, Craig Joubert, in the aftermath of a 25-17 defeat but more historically that the match was played at Orlando Stadium in Soweto.

Although the Stormers have Western Province as their main pool of players they also draw talent from the Boland Cavaliers. They are a magnet for big crowds thanks to the enthusiasm of the locals and numerous advertising campaigns over the years ranging from 'Storm Warning' to 'Men-in-Black' and 'Commandos' after the team went on a boot camp in Saldanha in the Western Cape.

The franchise have also used iconic players such as Bobby Skinstad, Percy Montgomery, Corné Krige, Burger and Conrad Jantjes in their drive to attract bigger crowds and in June 2000 supplied 11 players to the South African side who played England. It was the biggest representation from one team in a Springbok outfit for 72 years. In 2008 Rassie Erasmus was appointed coach and caught the attention of the rugby world by reportedly planning to stage a Twenty20 version of rugby.

Below: Stormers (playing in white) in line-out action against the Blues of Auckland.

MATTER OF FACT
Club: Vodacom Stormers
Formed: 1997 (as Super Rugby franchise)
Located: Cape Town, South Africa
Administrative address: 5th floor Newlands Terraces, 8 Boundary Road, Newlands 7700 Cape Town
Tel: +27 21 659 4600
Email: lrayner@wprugby.co.za
or enquires@wprugby.co.za
Website: www.thestormers.co.za

Super Rugby records
Honours: None
Best finish: Runners-up 2010
Record: P 157, W 75, L 78, D 4
Most appearances: 79 Breyton Paulse (1998–2007)
Most points: 528 Peter Grant (2006–2010)
Biggest win: 56-18 v Lions, 2009
Biggest defeat: 75-14 v Bulls, 2005

Ground: Newlands Rugby Stadium
Address: Boundary Road, Newlands, 7700 Cape Town
Capacity: 51,900
To get there: Newlands Station (train)
Stands: Grandstand, Railway, Danie Craven, Jan Pickard

Bars in ground: See opposite
Bars nearby: See opposite

Legends
Schalk Burger: Tough flanker who was IRB International Player of the Year in 2004 but blotted his copybook with a notorious gouging incident against the Lions in 2009 when he was winning his 50th cap. World Cup winner in 2007.
Corné Krige: Flanker revered in South Africa, less so in England where he led a violent attack on English players during a 53-3 defeat in the 2002 Test at Twickenham. His Super Rugby career ended prematurely after ban for head-butting and he finished his playing days at Northampton.

Need to know: No matter how well the Stormers are performing they are always one of the best supported franchises in Super Rugby. In 2010 they attracted an average of around 43,000 fans to Newlands, double the Super 14 average that season.

BLOEMFONTEIN

Above: *Bloemfontein City Hall.*

The land of cheetahs

The heart of Afrikanerdom (and also where the ruling party, the African National Congress was founded) Bloemfontein is one of the three capitals of the country, being the judicial capital and seat of the Supreme Court of Appeal, the highest court in the country.

Located in the centre of the country, it is 400 km (250 miles) south of Johannesburg, 160 km (100 miles) east of mining town Kimberley, and 140 km (88 miles) west of Maseru, the capital of Lesotho.

You may sometimes hear the city called Manguang, which is the Sesotho name, meaning place of the cheetahs, the speedster from where the Super Rugby side take their name.

The city also supports the Eagles cricket team and Bloemfontein Celtic, who play in football's Premier League. All the teams play in the centrally located Free State sports complex.

Near here is the popular Waterfront shopping centre, called Loch Logan, with its many retail outlets and restaurants. Close by the Waterfront is Second Street where you will find plenty of bars and more eating places.

Late drinking places do exist if you ask around and there are always the hotels, of course, but by and large the city is a sleepy one and at times it can feel like it has shut down early.

By day Bloemfontein becomes museum central. One of the most popular is the Anglo Boer War Museum, but there are no shortage of other choices, including the Fire Station Museum, the National Museum, the SA Armour Museum, the Presidency Museum, Oliewenhuis Art Museum, and Choet Visser Rugby Museum, a privately owned collection of jerseys, photographs, ties and other interesting items of rugby memorabilia, that can be visited by appointment.

3 THINGS YOU MUST DO...

1 SKYDIVING

You've always fancied jumping out of a plane and hanging by a thread, haven't you? Now's your chance thanks to Bloemfontein Skydiving Centre (Tempe Airfield, tel: +27 51 451 1143 or +27 76 394 6059). When: Sat and holidays but other days can be booked.

2 ANGLO BOER WAR MUSEUM

The museum (Monument Road, tel: +27 51 447 0079) gives an insight into the war of 1899–1902 including the concentration camps. When: Mon–Fri 08.30–16.30, Sat 10.00–17.00, Sun 11.00–17.00, holidays 09.00–17.00. To get there: south of the centre, nearest train station is Showground.

3 GAME

Beef or chicken sir? Fed up with the usual? Then taste game: springbok, ostrich, gemsbok and more. Try the Famous Butcher's Grill (Holiday Inn Garden Court, cnr Nelson Mandela and Melrose Drive, tel: +27 51 444 4980). When: 12.00–23.00 (12.00–01.00 bar). To get there: west of the centre.

Above: The often sleepy city of Bloemfontein comes alive for rugby.

Weather	Low (°C)	High (°C)	Rain (mm)	Sunset
January	16	26	15	19.18
February	16	26	7	19.12
March	13	25	18	18.48
April	12	22	51	18.12
May	9	18	79	17.42
June	8	18	84	17.26
July	7	17	89	17.28
August	8	18	64	17.45
September	10	19	43	18.01
October	11	21	31	18.17
November	13	23	16	18.36
December	14	24	10	19.00

FREE STATE STADIUM

State of the Nation

More popularly known as Free State Stadium, Vodacom Park is home to the Super 15 side the Cheetahs, Currie Cup outfit the Free State Cheetahs and Bloemfontein Celtic, a soccer team who play in green-and-white hoops like their more famous counterparts from Glasgow.

Developed for the 1995 Rugby World Cup, the ground holds unhappy memories for the Japanese rugby team who played three pool matches in Bloemfontein that year. After conceding 57 points to Wales and 50 to Ireland they were beaten 145-17 by New Zealand as the All Blacks ran in 21 tries although Simon Culhane blotted his copybook by missing one conversion out of 21.

Vodacom Park was further improved for football's World Cup in 2010 when it hosted six games including England's infamous 4-1 defeat by Germany. This R241 million (€25 million) refit included the addition of a second tier to the western pavilion grandstand, installation of new turnstiles, floodlights, a new sound system and electronic scoreboards.

The ground is close to Loch Logan Waterfront, the biggest shopping centre in central South Africa and the entertainment capital of Bloemfontein, which houses over 100 shops and 20 restaurants and there are plenty of pubs nearby including the eccentrically decorated Die Mystic Boer.

Below: Improved for use in football's World Cup 2010, Free State Stadium has a capacity of 48,000.

MATTER OF FACT
Stadium: Vodacom Park
Located: Bloemfontein, South Africa
Address: Att Horak Street, Bloemfontein, Free State 9300
Tel: +27 51 407 1700/ 01 (tickets)
Email: tickets@fsrugby.co.za
Website: www.vodacomcheetahs.co.za
Capacity: 48,000
To get there: Bloemfontein Station (train) 2 km (1.5 miles)
Stands: Main, Open

First match: Junior Springboks 12 British & Irish Lions 15, 1955
First Test: South Africa 11 New Zealand 11, 1960
Tests hosted: 21
South Africa record: P 18, W 13, L 4, D 1

Bars in ground: Castle Deck
Bars nearby: Die Mystic Boer (84 Kellner St, Bloemfontein 9300, +27 51 430 2206 www.diemysticboer.co.za); **Barba's Café** (16 2nd Avenue, Westdene, Bloemfontein; +27 51 430 2542); **Stones** (Cedar House Building, 150 Zastron Street, Corner of 2nd Avenue, Bloemfontein 9301, +27 51 448 6484, www.stones.co.za); **Warehouse Pub and Grill** (Cnr Marula Street & McKenzie Street, Ooseinde, Bloemfontein 1901, +27 832 823 323)

Finally… Bloemfontein's bikers parade on the pitch on game day on their Harley-Davidsons adding to the atmosphere. Clad in Cheetahs shirts, around 30 of them rev their engines up to full throttle as the players run on to the pitch.

CHEETAHS

Free State's finest

The Central Cheetahs, or Vodacom Cheetahs as they are formally known, entered the newly-expanded Super 14 in 2006, along with Western Force, drawing players from Free State Cheetahs, Griquas and Northern Free State Griffins. The Cheetahs surprised many when they were not the whipping boys of the new-look competition, finishing 10th in their first season. The Cheetahs gained the fifth South African franchise spot ahead of the Southern Spears, who they beat 48-0 in a friendly game ahead of their first season in Super Rugby, which proved the point that they deserved their spot in the big time.

The area has always provided plenty of players who represent the Springboks and that was a major plank in their argument for inclusion in the Super 14. Players such as Juan Smith, CJ van der Linde, Ashley Johnson and Heinrich Brussow have all donned the green national jersey since the formation of the franchise. Further back, Brendan Venter and Ruben Kruger both came out of Free State while Popeye Strydom and Basie Vivier were also notable Springboks who played for the province.

In 2007 the former South African hooker Naka Drotske took over as coach but the Cheetahs struggled in the Super 14 and had not managed to better their first season's finishing position by the end of the 2010 campaign. They also had a desperate record on their travels to Australia and New Zealand.

The Cheetahs play their home games at Vodacom Park, although in 2010 they played a match at North West Stadium in Welkom and have also played games at GWK Park, an 18,000-capacity venue in Kimberley.

Below: Prop CJ van der Linde has represented South Africa numerous times while at the Cheetahs.

MATTER OF FACT
Club: Vodacom Cheetahs
Formed: 2005
Located: Bloemfontein, South Africa
Administrative address: Vodacom Park, Att Horak Street, Bloemfontein, Free State 9301
Tel: +27 51 407 1700
Email: tickets@fsrugby.co.za
Website: www.cheetahsrugby.co.za

Super Rugby records
Honours: None
Best finish: 7th 1997
Record: P 76, W 22, L 52, D 2
Most appearances: 61 Meyer Bosman (2006–)
Most points: 139 Naas Olivier (2009–)
Biggest win: 59-10 v Lions, 2010
Biggest defeat: 55-7 v Crusaders, 2008

Ground: Vodacom Park
Address: Att Horak Street, Bloemfontein, Free State 9301
Capacity: 48,000
To get there: Bloemfontein Station (train) 1.5 miles (2 km)
Stands: Main, Open

Bars in ground: See opposite
Bars nearby: See opposite

Legends:
Juan Smith: Back rower who was key member of South Africa's 2007 Rugby World Cup winning squad. Topped 70 caps in Super Rugby in 2010 and rated one of the best flankers in the world when fit.
Kabamba Floors: Great name and a decent flanker who was Player of the Year in the Currie Cup in 2006. Twice suspended, once for missing a flight home, by the Cheetahs in 2008. He has also played on the wing.

Need to know: Although the Cheetahs were not formed until 2005 and only entered the Super 14 in 2006, the Orange Free State qualified to play in the competition in 1997 before South Africa adopted the idea of franchises.

DURBAN

Above: *Durban's beachfront. It's long and it's sandy.*

Where East meets West

Durban is a vibrant city in the province of KwaZulu-Natal, and is often referred to as a place where East meets West. There are prominent Zulu and Asian populations which makes for an interesting mix of cultures. The city has one of the busiest ports in Africa and is a magnet for tourists, although like the rest of the South Africa the division between poverty and wealth is huge, with many Zulus living in shanty towns out of the city.

Durban has sunshine for approximately 320 days a year and 100 km (62 miles) of coastline with superb beaches, some of which are protected by shark nets. Away from the sun and sea visitors flock to the Durban North Japanese Gardens, Mitchell Park Zoo, Umgeni River Bird Park and the Durban Botanic Gardens. uShaka Marine Park on Bell Street is the largest attraction of its type in Africa and many tour operators offer helicopter trips over the stunning Drakensberg Mountains, with a glass of champagne when you land on top of the range to top it off.

Like all South Africans, Durban people love their sport. The ABSA Stadium is home to the Sharks rugby team, and the impressive Moses Mabhiba Stadium was built to host games in the 2010 soccer World Cup. Golf is also popular with Durban Country Club, Zimbali and Selbourne being among the leading courses in the area.

By night the city is full of busy bars, restaurants and clubs with one of the most popular being Joe Cools on North Beach which is open from the morning until late.

Like any part of South Africa travellers have to exercise common sense about which areas in Durban they go to and are warned not to venture onto the beaches in the dark.

3 THINGS YOU MUST DO...

1 ZULU BATTLEFIELDS

Visit Fugitive's Drift (tel: +27 34 642 1843 or +27 34 271 8051) and take in the battlefields of Rorke's Drift, where 11 Victoria Crosses were won in 1879, and take a tour of Isandlwana where the British were routed a day earlier. To get there: 3.5 hour drive from Durban (N3 and R33).

2 THE GOLDEN MILE

The most popular tourist spot in Durban (tel: Tourism KwaZulu-Natal, +27 86 010 1099) running from South Beach to the Suncoast Casino and Entertainment World. Features the Blue Lagoon, Mini Town (a replica of Durban) and many vendors selling Zulu art, plus bars and restaurants.

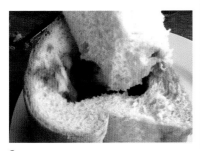

3 BUNNY CHOW

Durban speciality made of curried meat or vegetable cased in a hollowed out loaf of bread. Served with carrot, onion and chilli salad, they come in quarter, half and full loaves. Use your fingers and enjoy the mess. Stalls and Bunny Chow shops are all over Durban.

Above: Rickshaw drivers can be found touting for business along the beachfront.

Weather	Low (°C)	High (°C)	Rain (mm)	Sunset
January	21	27	109	19.00
February	22	27	121	18.54
March	20	27	124	18.30
April	18	26	76	17.53
May	14	24	51	17.22
June	13	24	32	17.04
July	11	22	28	17.08
August	13	23	38	17.24
September	15	23	69	17.42
October	17	24	109	17.57
November	18	25	122	18.18
December	19	26	119	18.43

KING'S PARK

Fit for Kings

Historically known as King's Park, but Absa Stadium from 1999, this ground is situated close to Durban's 'Golden Mile', in the King's Park Sporting Precinct, is home to the Sharks and is next door to Moses Mabhida Stadium, constructed for the 2010 football World Cup.

Sport has been played on the site since 1891, with the stadium undergoing extensive renovations in the 1980s and further upgrades ahead of the 1995 Rugby World Cup.

It staged five games including the semi-final between South Africa and France which was memorable for a torrential downpour that flooded the pitch so an army of helpers had to sweep water from the playing area. Ruben Kruger's try helped South Africa to a 19-15 win on their way to their first Webb Ellis Cup.

Durban has also been the scene of epic Test matches involving the Lions, who clinched the series with a Jeremy Guscott drop goal there in 1997. That was the first Lions tour with a huge travelling support and their fans turned the beach bars of Durban into a sea of red.

Doubts were cast over the ground's future when the nearby football ground was built but the Sharks remained determined to stay put. Match day in Durban is a unique experience. There are not too many cities where you can have a paddle on the beach in the sun and stroll to the ground in time for kick-off.

Below: A swim just before the match anyone? Durban's rugby stadium is close to the beachfront.

MATTER OF FACT
Stadium: Absa Stadium
Located: Durban, South Africa
Address: 12 Jacko Jackson Drive, Durban 4001
Tel: +27 31 308 8400
Email: sandy@thesharks.co.za
Website: www.sharksrugby.co.za
Capacity: 52,000
To get there: Umgeni Station (train) 1 km (0.6 miles)
Stands: North, South, East, West

Stadium tours
Open: By arrangement only
Tel: Marketing dept, +27 31 308 8484

First Test: South Africa 3 British & Irish Lions 0, 1962
Tests hosted: 30
South Africa record: P 26, W 16, L 7, D 3

Bars in ground: Trinity, Left Wing, Right Wing, Wildebeest, Bale & Barrel, Crate & Barrel, Zwanathi, Ithefeni, Tighthead, Loosehead, Jawlers, Umgeni Lounge, Tewkweni Lounge, Beer Huts
Bars nearby: Billy the Bums (504 Windermere Road, Morningside, Durban 3610, +27 31 303 1988, www.billythebums.co.za); **The Keg & Spear** (44 Isaiah Ntshangase Road, Moses Mabhida Stadium, Durban 4001, +27 31 582 8232, www.atthekeg.co.za); **Harvey Wallbangers,** (Corner of Broadway and Kensington Drive, Durban North, +27 31 563 4887, www.harveys. co.za); **Joe Cool's** (137 Lower Marine Parade, North Beach, Durban, +27 31 332 9697, www.joecools.co.za)

Finally... Jacko Jackson Drive, where Absa Stadium stands, is named after the former mayor of Durban, HW Jackson, who served between 1957 and 1958. Earlier in his life he was regarded as one of Natal's finest full-backs, although he was not recognized at international level.

SHARKS

Shark bite

The Sharks, previously Natal, the Natal Sharks and Coastal Sharks in Super Rugby, are based at Durban's Absa Stadium. Drawing players from the province of KwaZulu-Natal they reached three finals without success in 1996, 2001 and 2007. The failure in 2007 was particularly galling as they lost out to the Bulls at Absa Stadium, with the visitors scoring an 83rd-minute try to clinch victory. That year, led by John Smit, they had topped the regular-season table only to see the honour of becoming the first South African side to win the tournament fall to their rivals from Pretoria.

KwaZulu-Natal Rugby Union was formed back in 1890 and it was similar story in the Currie Cup for the Natal side, who had to wait until their centenary season for their first success in the competition.

Despite the lack of silverware, the Natal academy continues to pump out players of international quality with JP Pietersen, François Steyn and Tendai Mtawarira among recent graduates. Big games at Absa Stadium are often prefaced by age-group contests involving young Sharks players and act as a warm-up event for the main event. There are also signing sessions ahead of games and events as diverse as dog shows or members of the Sharks medical team offering advice to amateur players. It is a complete day out.

Match day is also enlivened by the presence of the Sharks mascots, the Flasher Girls, who do almost exactly what their name suggests. Most fans claim they are there to watch the rugby... yeah right.

Below: Not many players get past John Smit. The Sharks and South African captain has more than 100 caps.

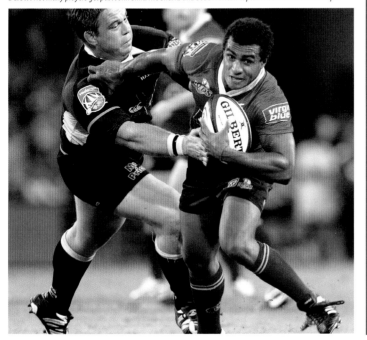

MATTER OF FACT
Club: The Sharks
Formed: 1997
Located: Durban, South Africa
Administrative address: Absa Stadium, PO Box 307, Durban 4000
Tel: +27 31 308 8400
Email: sandy@thesharks.co.za
Website: www.sharksrugby.co.za

Super Rugby records
Honours: None
Best finish: Runners-up 1996, 2001, 2007
Record: P 184, W 89, L 89, D 6
Most appearances: 111 John Smit (1998–)
Most points: 390 Butch James (2001–2007)
Biggest win: 59-16 v Reds, 2007
Biggest defeat: 77-34 v Crusaders, 2005

Ground: Absa Stadium
Address: 12 Jacko Jackson Drive, Durban 4001
Capacity: 52,000
To get there: Umgeni Station (train) 1 km (0.6 miles)
Stands: North, South, East, West

Bars in ground: See opposite
Bars nearby: See opposite

Legends
John Smit: Hooker, but able to play prop as well, who captained South Africa to victory in the 2007 Rugby World Cup. Passed 100 caps in 2010 and was in charge of the Springboks during their 2009 series win over the Lions.
Tendai Mtawarira: Zimbabwean-born prop and crowd favourite known as 'The Beast'. Sharks fans roar 'Beeeeeeeast' every time he gets the ball. He got the better of Phil Vickery in the first Test of the 2009 Lions series and Vickery was dropped, although he beasted 'The Beast' when recalled for the final match.

Need to know: When the franchise became known as the Sharks in 1995 there was a lot of opposition to the name change. Now a world-recognized brand, they were previously known as the Banana Boys.

JOHANNESBURG

Above: Johannesburg attracts people from across Africa and the rest of the world, all in search of their share of the golden life.

The city of gold and hopes

Welcome to the city of gold. Egoli, meaning the place of gold, is a popular name for Johannesburg (as is Jo'burg and Jozi) and it lives up to its name having built a reputation as the place to do serious business. Although not one of South Africa's three capital cities, Johannesburg is the driving force behind the real action and anyone who is anyone in this country has to do business with this place.

Jo'burg also attracts migrants from across Africa and the rest of the world attracted by the hope and opportunities offered by South Africa's biggest city. The hills around Jo'burg are rich with gold and diamonds, driving the wealth and allure of the city. It's hard not to get caught up in the energy of Jo'burg because this is the type of city where the phone starts ringing with opportunities as soon as you have landed.

With the urban decline of the city centre (with its skyline dominated by the high-rise Carlton Tower, Hillbrow Tower and Ponte City) in the late 1980s and early 1990s, the de facto centre shifted north to Sandton where you will find gleaming office blocks, huge shopping centres, hotels, and many restaurants and bars. This is also the home to the Johannesburg Stock Exchange, Africa's largest exchange, which moved here in 2000 from the city centre.

To the east are the areas of Benoni, Brakpan and Boksburg in an area known collectively as the East Rand, and dominated by the giant slag heaps of earth that have been emptied from the ground as generations have dug in search of riches.

To the southwest is Soweto, the famous township that is home to well over a million people. Another well-known but smaller township area, Alexandra, is to the northeast.

3 THINGS YOU MUST DO...

1 BALLOON SAFARI

Watch game while drifting along in a balloon. Book at Mabula Lodge in the Northern Province with Bill Harrop's Balloon Safaris (tel: +27 11 705 3201). Includes accommodation, meals, game drives and balloon safari. Price: R5,040–R6,520 each. To get there: a 2.5-hour drive from Jo'burg.

2 THE CRADLE OF HUMANKIND

Visit the birthplace of mankind and discover the history of humanity at Maropeng (Sterkfontein, tel: +27 14 577 9000). When: daily 09.00–17.00. Price: R105 adults, R60 child 4–14. To get there: 40 km (25 miles) northwest of Jo'burg.

3 STEAK

Jo'burg has some great restaurants and steak is juicy, tender and affordable. Try Turn 'n Tender (Cnr 3rd and 7th Ave, tel: +27 11 788 7933) which has been cooking steaks since 1977. When: daily from 11.30. Price: a 300g is R98. To get there: in Parktown North, between the city centre and Sandton.

Above: Painted wooden statues can be found in markets across South Africa.

Weather	Low (°C)	High (°C)	Rain (mm)	Sunset
January	14	26	114	19.04
February	14	25	116	19.00
March	13	24	87	18.38
April	10	22	38	18.07
May	7	19	28	17.38
June	5	17	7	17.24
July	4	17	8	17.28
August	6	21	8	17.43
September	9	23	23	17.57
October	12	25	62	18.06
November	14	25	107	18.24
December	14	26	125	18.46

ELLIS PARK

Scene of Springbok glory

It might now be known as Coca-Cola Park officially but for rugby fans the world over it is simply Ellis Park, the stronghold of South African rugby, and scene of some of the most historic matches in rugby history.

These include the 1995 Rugby World Cup final when Nelson Mandela appeared on the pitch wearing a Springbok jersey to present François Pienaar with the trophy. During the tournament the ground staged six matches and was one of the few rugby grounds used during the 2010 FIFA World Cup when it hosted seven matches including one quarter-final.

Built on the site of a rubbish dump and opened in 1928, Ellis Park was revamped for the 1995 event and in 2005 became the first black-owned stadium in South Africa.

Located at the centre of Johannesburg, and named after JD Ellis, the councillor who gave permission to construct it, the stadium was upgraded again ahead of the 2010 football World Cup with a new tier being built on the north stand to bring its capacity to over 62,000, a VIP area installed and better facilities for disabled fans incorporated.

The stadium is also home to the Lions Super 15 franchise and stages matches for Orlando Pirates football team.

Below: Ellis Park, where the Boks lifted the World Cup in 1995.

MATTER OF FACT
Stadium: Coca-Cola Park
Located: Johannesburg, South Africa
Address: 44 Staib Street, Johannesburg 2028
Tel: +27 11 402 8644
Email: info@ellispark.co.za
Website: www.ellispark.co.za
Capacity: 62,567
To get there: Ellis Park Station (train) next door, Doornfontein Station (train) 600 metres
Stands: East, South, North, West

Stadium tours
Open: Mon and Thur, 08.00–15.30, tours last 45 mins; R50 adults, R20 children
Tel: +27 11 402 8644
Email: Susan@ellispark.co.za

First match: Transvaal v Natal, 1928
First Test: South Africa 6 New Zealand 7, 1928
Tests hosted: 46
South Africa record: P 43, W 30, L 11, D 2

Bars in ground: Pete's Pub, East Bars, NW Bar
Bars nearby: The Guildhall (88 Market Street, Johannesburg 2001, +27 11 833 1770); **California Pub & Restaurant** (178 Sivewright Street, Doornfontein, Johannesburg); **Ellis Park Hotel** (19 Derby Road, Johannesburg 2094, +27 11 614 7896, www.ellisparkhotel.co.za); **Paddy's Sports Bar** (Canterbury Crossing, Corner of Bram Fischer and Hunter Street, Johannesburg 2198, +27 11 781 3826, www.paddyscorner.co.za); **Cotton Pub And Grill** (1 Cotto Twist Street, Johannesburg 2001, +27 12 334 5059)

Finally . . . It is not rugby at Ellis Park without a *braai*, (barbecue) to soak up the beers. The stadium has a *braai* area on the north side of the ground and you don't even have to bring your own meat. Packs with chops, steaks and boerewors can be bought at the stadium. Reserve your *braai* early though.

LIONS

Lions lost pride

The Lions Super 15 franchise originally played as Transvaal in the tournament. They were then the Gauteng Lions and after that known as the Cats between 1996 and 2006. But they played more like pussy cats in the 2010 season when they managed to concede 585 points and lose every single match when finishing bottom of the table for the fifth time. That helped contribute to an unwanted record – a losing run of 14 matches in Super 14, spread over two seasons.

They did reach the semi-finals in 2000 and 2001 but the lack of success nearly spelled the end for them as a franchise in 2006. Then, the Southern Spears won a legal ruling that they could replace the lowest-ranked South African team in that year's Super 14 but the cash-strapped Spears eventually abandoned their proposals and let the Lions off the hook.

The spike in the fortunes of the franchise coincided with the arrival of former All Black coach Laurie Mains, although even the renowned New Zealander could not get them beyond the last four of the tournament. Later, the coaching skills of Springbok legend Chester Williams could not raise them out of their stupor and John Mitchell, another Kiwi, was appointed head coach in 2010 after a spell with Western Force in Australia and a period helping out the Xerox Lions, the Currie Cup team.

Based in Johannesburg, they have a pool of players drawn from the Lions, Leopards and Pumas unions and play at the cathedral of South African rugby, Ellis Park, a ground every rugby fan in the world must visit.

Below: *Centre Walter Venter scores against Waratahs.*

MATTER OF FACT
Club: Auto & General Lions
Formed: 1996
Located: Johannesburg, South Africa
Administrative address: Johannesburg Stadium, 124 Van Beek Street, Doornfontein Johannesburg 2028
Tel: +27 11 402 2960
Email: olgav@glru.co.za or via website
Website: www.lionsrugby.co.za

Super Rugby records
Honours: None
Best finish: Semi-finals 2000, 2001
Record: P 177, W 46, L 127, D 4
Most appearances: 69 Cobus Grobbelaar (2004–) and André Pretorius (2002–2009)
Most points: 645 André Pretorius (2002–2009)
Biggest win: 53-3 v the Chiefs, 2000
Biggest defeat: 64-0 v the Brumbies, 2000

Ground: Coca-Cola Park
Address: 44 Staib Street, Johannesburg 2028
Capacity: 62,567
To get there: Ellis Park Station (train) next door, Doornfontein Station (train) 600 metres
Stands: East, South, North, West

Bars in ground: See opposite
Bars nearby: See opposite

Legends
André Pretorius: Fly-half who spent a decade at the franchise before moving to Western Force in 2009. Back-up to Butch James in South Africa's World Cup winning side of 2007 and went on as a replacement in the 15-6 win over England in the final.
Cobus Grobbelaar: Flanker who had the dubious distinction of captaining the Lions in 2010 when they lost every game of the Super 14 campaign. Virtually ignored by the national selectors, and known as 'Baywatch', Grobbelaar managed to retain his sense of humour in a car crash of a season.

Need to know: Despondent Lions fans have at least had the sight of the pre-match dancers – lengthily known as the Auto & General Vox Datapro FeLions dancers – who entertain the crowd before games. In 2010 many followers must have felt like watching their routines, then leaving the ground.

CANADA

Rocky roads

Canada can lay claim to being the dominant rugby nation in North America, are probably only second to Argentina in the whole of the Americas and they have played in every World Cup to date, reaching the quarter-finals in 1991. Then, their team containing some legends of the Canadian game, such as Al Charron and Gareth Rees lost out 29-13 to the All Blacks in the last-eight match in Lille. Rees, fly-half or full-back, was one of a small group of players to play in all of the first four World Cups. He went on to play for Wasps and Harlequins and he and Rod Snow were suspended for 30 days for their part in the infamous Battle of Boet Erasmus in a match against South Africa in the 1995 World Cup.

In 2003 the Churchill Cup was set up in a bid to raise the standard of the game in Canada and the United States. England send their Saxons team every year to compete in the tournament and Ireland, the New Zealand Maori and France A have also appeared. In 2008 Canada appointed Kieran Crowley, a World Cup winner in 1987 with New Zealand, as coach, who guided them through qualifying to their seventh successive World Cup.

Above: Downtown Vancouver.

Governing body: Rugby Canada
Address: 40 Vogell Road, Suite 26, Richmond Hill, ON L4B 3N6 Canada
Tel: +1 905 780 8998
Website: www.rugbycanada.ca
Email: info@rugbycanada.ca

Main Test venues: Ellerslie Park (Edmonton), Commonwealth Stadium (Edmonton), York Stadium (Toronto), Swanguard Stadium (Vancouver), Thunderbird Stadium (Vancouver), Swilers Rugby Park (St John's, Newfoundland), Twin Elm Rugby Park (Ottawa)

Most international caps: 78 Al Charron (1990-2003)
Most international points: 491 Gareth Rees, 55 Tests (1986-1999)
Most international tries: 24 Winston Stanley, 63 Tests (1994-2003)
First Test match: v Japan, Osaka, 1932 (lost 9-8)

WORLD CUP RECORD

Year	Venue	Finished
1987	Australia & NZ	Pool (3rd)
1991	England	Quarter-finals
1995	South Africa	Pool (3rd)
1999	Wales	Pool (3rd)
2003	Australia	Pool (4th)
2007	France	Pool (5th)

Most World Cup appearances: 14 Rod Snow (1995, 1999, 2003, 2007)
Most World Cup points: 120 Gareth Rees, 13 matches (1987, 1991, 1995, 1999)

FIJI

Paradise lost

Any country that regards rugby union as its national sport and can produce players like the extraordinary Rupeni Caucaunibuca and Waisale Serevi is deserving of complete support but the fact is, like the other South Sea islands, Fiji is virtually ignored by the major nations when it comes to touring. They make it to New Zealand and Australia often enough so the big boys should be ashamed they can't extend the odd trip to this beautiful, rugby-mad island. Fijian-born players such as Joe Rokocoko have represented New Zealand so the All Black attitude to playing full-blown Test matches on the island is bemusing.

The shame is that matches in Suva are magnificent occasions with fans walking miles to get a glimpse of their heroes. The stadium, which has also hosted the South Pacific Games, is bang next door to the Pacific Ocean which gives you one of the most spectacular views in world sport. It is just a pity more fans have not experienced it.

On the field Fiji reached the quarter-finals of the Rugby World Cup in 1987 and 2007, when they beat Wales 38-34 in one of the matches of the tournament on their way to the last eight. The Fijians also excel at the seven-a-side game, winning a record ninth Hong Kong Sevens title in 2009.

Above: *What rugby? Taking it easy on Nanuya Lailai Island, Yasawa.*

Governing body: Fiji Rugby Union
Address: 35 Gordon Street, Suva, Fiji
Telephone: +679 330 2787
Website: www.fijirugby.com
Email: frfu@connect.com.fj

Test venues: National Stadium (Suva), Churchill Park (Lautoka), Prince Charles Park (Nadi)

Most international caps: 65 Nicky Little (1996–)
Most international points: 652 Nicky Little, 63 Tests (1996–)
Most international tries: 20 Sanivalati Laulau, 32 Tests (1980–1985)
First Test match: v Samoa, Apia 1924 (won 6-3)

WORLD CUP RECORD

Year	Venue	Finished
1987	Australia & NZ	Quarter-finals
1991	England	Pool (4th)
1995	South Africa	DNQ
1999	Wales	Lost Quarter-final play-off
2003	Australia	Pool (3rd)
2007	France	Quarter-finals

Most World Cup appearances: 11 Mosese Rauluni and Nicky Little (both 1999, 2003, 2007)
Most World Cup points: 125 Nicky Little, 11 matches (1999, 2003, 2007)

GEORGIA

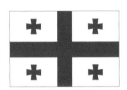

On my mind

Nicknamed the Lelos, a term from a national sport with similarities to rugby, the Georgian national side qualified for the Rugby World Cups in 2003, 2007 and 2011. In the latter they came close to causing the upset of the tournament when they almost beat Ireland. They were camped on the Irish line when the full-time whistle went with Ireland just 14-10 ahead. The side also play in the European Nations Cup, a second-tier competition and their win in 2010, clinched after beating Russia 36-8 in neutral Trabzon, Turkey, gave them their third title.

Georgia have struggled financially, with players using old Soviet tractors to make scrummaging machines, but many of their top stars are now based in France. This migration was encouraged by Claude Saurel, a Frenchman who coached the national side.

The Georgian Rugby Union was founded in 1964 and they gained membership of the IRB in 1992 with Saurel's appointment as coach in 1999 raising the profile of a side who narrowly missed out on qualifying for the 1999 Rugby World Cup.

The Boris Paichadze National Stadium in Tbilisi, named after a local footballing hero, is one of the best facilities in Eastern Europe, home to FC Dinamo Tbilisi and holds an all-seated crowd of over 55,000.

Above: *Sioni Cathedral, Tbilisi.*

Governing body: Georgian Rugby Union
Address: 9A Cholokashvili Avenue, Tbilisi 0162 Georgia
Telephone: +995 32 204535
Website: www.rugby.ge
Email: office@rugby.ge

Test venue: Boris Paichadze National Stadium (Tbilisi)

Most international caps: 63 Malkhaz Urjukashvili (1997–)
Most international points: 320 Pavle Jimsheladze, 57 games (1995–2007)
Most international tries. 18 Mamuka Gorgodze, 33 games (2003–2009)
First Test match: v Zimbabwe, Kutaisi, 1989 (won 16-3)

WORLD CUP RECORD

Year	Venue	Finished
1987	Australia & NZ	Not invited
1991	England	DNQ
1995	South Africa	DNQ
1999	Wales	DNQ
2003	Australia	Pool (5th)
2007	France	Pool (4th)

Most World Cup appearances: 8 Akvsenti Giorgadze & Merab Kvirikashvili (both 2003, 2007)
Most World Cup points: 35 Merab Kvirikashvili, 8 matches (2003, 2007)

JAPAN

Japan blossoming

British sailors introduced rugby to Japan in the 1870s and since then more clichés have been written about the relative size of their national side and how they compensate for it than you can shake a stick at. A small stick, obviously. However, in 1968 they beat the Junior All Blacks, ran England close in 1971 and beat Scotland in Tokyo in 1989.

In 2007 the Brave Blossoms appointed the former All Black wing John Kirwan as coach and he proclaimed he wanted to harness the 'Samurai Spirit' of the Japanese nation. They held their first ever training camp ahead of the 2007 Rugby World Cup and went on to draw with Canada and narrowly lose 35-31 to Fiji, who themselves made the last eight.

The authorities missed a trick when they passed over Japan's bid, in favour of New Zealand, to host the 2011 Rugby World Cup. The infrastructure was all in place following Japan's part in staging the 2002 FIFA World Cup but the IRB went with the New Zealanders and Japan will host the tournament in 2019. However, Japan can boast the most prolific try scorer in international rugby in Daisuke Ohata, who passed David Campese's record of 64 Test touchdowns when he scored a hat-trick against Georgia in 2006. Aussies will say only a quarter of his scores came against tier-one nations but it is still in the record books.

Above: *Mount Chureito peace pagoda in Sengen Park, Yamanashi*

Governing body: Japan Rugby Football Union
Address: 2-8-35 Kitaaoyama Minato-ku, Tokyo 1070061 Japan
Telephone: +81 3 5771 1332
Website: www.jrfu.org
Email: jrfu@rugby-japan.or.jp

Test venues: Chichibunomiya Rugby Stadium (Tokyo), Sendai Stadium (Miyagi), Kintestsu Hanazon Rugby Stadium (Osaka), Mizuho Rugby Stadium (Nagoya), Yurtec Stadium (Sendai), Niigata Stadium (Niigata)

Most international caps: 79 Yukio Motoki (1991–2005)
Most international points: 422 Keiji Hirose, 40 Tests (1994–2005)
Most international tries. 69 Daisuke Ohata, 58 Tests (1996–2006)
First Test match: v British Colombia, Vancouver, 1930 (drew 3-3)

WORLD CUP RECORD

Year	Venue	Finished
1987	Australia & NZ	Pool (4th)
1991	England	Pool (3rd)
1995	South Africa	Pool (4th)
1999	Wales	Pool (4th)
2003	Australia	Pool (5th)
2007	France	Pool (4th)

Most World Cup appearances: 9 Yukio Motoki (1995, 1999, 2003) & Masahiro Kunda (1991, 1995, 1999)
Most World Cup points: 40 Toru Kurihara, 4 matches (2003)

TONGA

Going green

Rugby is the national sport in Tonga and if this beautiful island could have persuaded players of Tongan descent such as Jonah Lomu and Willie Ofahengaue to turn out in their red shirts they would be an even more fearsome prospect. As it is, the sight of their players performing the Sipi Tau, a war dance, before matches is enough to send shivers down the spine. Memorably during the 2003 World Cup, the Tongans faced up to the Haka, by marching towards the All Blacks – it was one of the abiding images of the tournament.

The Ikale Tahi beat Australia in Brisbane in 1973, levelling the Test series, and competed in five of the first six Rugby World Cups. Their best effort was in 2007 when they beat USA and Samoa and narrowly lost, 30-25, to eventual champions South Africa. Their pre-tournament camp had been sponsored by an Irish bookmaker but the IRB banned the players from dying their hair green ahead of the pool match against England. Prior to that the colourful characters Inoke Afeaki and Epi Taione had sported green tattoos to thank their benefactor but their results ensured qualification for 2011.

The national side play matches at Teufaiva Stadium in Nuku'alofa, which has been their home since 1924, and hosted matches in the 2008 Pacific Nations Cup.

Above: *Rugby is the national sport on this beautiful island.*

Governing body: Tonga Rugby Union
Address: PO Box 369, Fasi moe A Nuku'alofa, Tonga
Telephone: +676 26045/26044
Website: www.tongarugbyunion.com
Email: tupou.pone@gmail.com

Test venue: Teufaiva Stadium (Nuku'alofa)

Most international caps: 41 Elisi Vunipola (1990–2005)
Most international points: 281 Pierre Hola, 37 Tests (1998–)
Most international tries. 13 Josh Taumalolo, 24 Tests (1998–)
First Test match: v Fiji, Nuku'alofa, 1924 (won 9-3)

WORLD CUP RECORD

Year	Venue	Finished
1987	Australia & NZ	Pool (4th)
1991	England	DNQ
1995	South Africa	Pool (3rd)
1999	Wales	Pool (3rd)
2003	Australia	Pool (5th)
2007	France	Pool (3rd)

Most World Cup appearances: 8 Inoke Afeaki (1995, 2003, 2007), Pierre Hola (2003, 2007) & Ephraim Taukafa (2003, 2007)
Most World Cup points: 61 Pierre Hola, 8 matches (2003, 2007)

RUSSIA

The invasion is coming

Rugby was widely disapproved of in Russia until the downfall of communism and the Rugby Union of Russia became affiliated to the IRB in 1990. Any thoughts of world domination on the rugby field were swiftly quashed and they did not qualify for their first Rugby World Cup until a 21-21 draw with Romania secured their place at the 2011 tournament in New Zealand.

The Russian Revolution led to some players leaving the country and the most famous Russian rugby export is Prince Alexander Obolensky who scored two tries on his debut for England against the All Blacks in 1936 and played for Oxford University. His family had emigrated when he was aged one.

When the Soviet Union was disbanded many players headed for rugby league, one explanation for their failure to qualify for the World Cup. Determined to qualify for the 2003 Rugby World Cup the Russians fielded several South African imports but were disqualified for picking ineligible players.

In 2010 Russia took part in the Churchill Cup, winning the Bowl competition, under the guidance of the Englishman and former Saracens coach Steve Diamond. The Russians also have a Sevens team who play in the IRB World Series and beat Australia in the London Sevens in 2006.

Above: *A street-level view from Moscow's Red Square.*

Governing body: Rugby Union of Russia
Address: 8-428, Luzhnetskaya nab, Moscow, 119992, Russia
Telephone: +7 495 725 4680
Website: www.rugby.ru
Email: rugbyunion@roc.ru

Test venues: Sparta Stadium (Moscow), Stadium Junost (Krasnodor), Sochi Stadium, Central Stadium (Krasnoyarsk)

Most international caps: 38 Alexander Khrokin (2002–)
Most international points: 235 Yuriy Kushnarev, 30 Tests (2006–)
Most international tries. 15 Alexander Gvozdovsky, 26 Tests (2005–2010)
First Test match: v Barbarians, 1992 (won 27-23)

WORLD CUP RECORD

Year	Venue	Finished
1987	Australia & NZ	Not IRB member
1991	England	DNQ
1995	South Africa	DNQ
1999	Wales	DNQ
2003	Australia	DNQ (disqualified)
2007	France	DNQ

Most World Cup appearances: N/A (first appearance 2011)
Most World Cup points: N/A (first appearance 2011)

UNITED STATES

Still holding Olympic gold

Here is a quiz question. Who are the reigning Olympic champions at rugby union? Answer… the United States, who won the 1924 gold medal in France, the last time 15-a-side rugby was held at the Games. The attractions of American Football to prospective rugby players has held the Eagles back ever since and they have never made it into the top 10 in the IRB World Rankings despite playing in five of the first six Rugby World Cups. However, players such as Mike Hercus, Dave Hodges, Dan Lyle and Tom Billups have all made an impression playing professionally in Europe and by 2010 around half of the national squad were employed abroad.

The United States Rugby Football Union (now USA Rugby) was formed in 1975 on the back of a revival in the game, the Eagles played Australia in a Test match a year later and by 1987 they were deemed powerful enough to be invited to the first Rugby World Cup. In 2006 they signalled their ambitions by luring Nigel Melville, a former England international and club coach, to be their chief executive, and in 2010 former Ireland coach Eddie O'Sullivan returned for a second stint with the Eagles. The Eagles have no official home ground but play many matches at Infinity Park in Glendale, Colorado.

Above: Capitol Hill, Washington, DC, home of the United States Congress.

Governing body: USA Rugby
Address: 2500 Arapahoe Avenue, Suite 200 Boulder, CO 80302, USA
Telephone: +1 303 539 0300
Website: www.usarugby.org
Email: info@usarugby.org (directs you back to website)

Test venues: Infinity Park (Glendale), Broward County Park (Lauderhill), Blackbaud Stadium (Charleston), Dick's Sporting Goods Park (Commerce City), Toyota Park (Chicago), Buck Shaw Stadium (Santa Clara), Rio Tinto Stadium (Utah), Rentschler Stadium (Hartford), Boxer Stadium (San Francisco)

Most international caps: 62 Luke Gross (1996–2003)
Most international points: 465 Mike Hercus, 48 Tests (2002–)
Most international tries. 26 Vaea Anitoni, 46 Tests (1992–2000)
First Test match: v Australia, Berkeley, 1912 (lost 8-3)

WORLD CUP RECORD

Year	Venue	Finished
1987	Australia & NZ	Pool (3rd)
1991	England	Pool (4th)
1995	South Africa	DNQ
1999	Wales	Pool (4th)
2003	Australia	Pool (4th)
2007	France	Pool (5th)

Most World Cup appearances: 10 Alec Parker (1999, 2003, 2007)
Most World Cup points: 77 Mike Hercus, 8 matches (2003, 2007)

SAMOA

You're the Manu

Manu Samoa, as they are called in their own country, competed as Western Samoa from 1924 to 1997 and when they beat Wales in the 1991 Rugby World Cup one Welshman reportedly said 'Thank goodness we weren't playing the whole of Samoa'. They very nearly upset the England applecart in Melbourne in 2003 – the eventual champions led by only a single point with 10 minutes left until accelerating away to win 35-22.

Many of that Samoan side have played with distinction in Europe, notably Brian Lima, Sailosi Tagicakibau, Steve So'oialo and Terry Fanolua with the remarkable Lima, known as 'The Chiropractor' for his harsh tackling, playing in five World Cups. He was the youngest player, at 19, in the 1991 tournament.

The islanders are renowned for relishing the physical side of the game but many players of Samoan descent have been lured away to play for New Zealand. One notable exception was the great Pat Lam, who famously led Northampton to their Heineken Cup win in 2000 carrying a painful shoulder injury.

Home games, of which there are too few against major nations, have been played at Apia Park since 1924. The ground holds 15,000 and staged the 2007 Pacific Games.

Above: Many Samoan players have left views like this to go and play in Europe...

Governing body: Samoa Rugby Union
Address: Cross Island Road, Malifa, Apia, Samoa PO Box 618
Telephone: +685 24 986
Website: www.samoarugbyunion.ws
Email: sruoffice@srfu.ws

Test venue: Apia Park (Apia)

Most international caps: 65 Brian Lima (1991–2007)
Most international points: 184 Earl Va'a, 28 Tests (1996–2003)
Most international tries. 31 Brian Lima (1991–2007)
First Test match: v Fiji, Apia, 1924 (lost 6-0)

WORLD CUP RECORD

Year	Venue	Finished
1987	Australia & NZ	Not invited
1991	England	Quarter-finals (as Western Samoa)
1995	South Africa	Quarter-finals (as Western Samoa)
1999	Wales	Lost Quarter-final play-off
2003	Australia	Pool (3rd)
2007	France	Pool (4th)

Most World Cup appearances: 18 Brian Lima (1991, 1995, 1999, 2003, 2007)
Most World Cup points: 62 Silao Leaegailesolo, 4 matches (1999)

SEVENS

Above: The Hong Kong Sevens is renowned for its festival atmosphere and its success paved the way for the creation of the IRB World Series.

Running rugby

If you have ever been to a sevens festival and woken up with the mother of all hangovers after a day drinking you can blame Ned Haig. He is personally responsible for every splitting sevens morning-after headache in history.

Haig was a butcher from Melrose in Scotland who turned out for his local team and went onto the committee when he hung up his boots. When the club needed an injection of cash, in April 1883, Haig came up with the bright idea of hosting a day-long tournament for teams in the area and a day of drinking for the spectators.

He later wrote: "Want of money made us rack our brains. As it was hopeless to think of having several games in one afternoon with 15 players on each side, the teams were reduced to seven". He has a lot of lost afternoons and nights to answer for.

More than 2,000 people turned up on the day and the ladies, obviously

early-day WAGs, donated a trophy, the Melrose Cup. Sevens was up and running. Winners of the Rugby World Cup Sevens, which are held once every four years, now receive a trophy called the Melrose Cup and it has been lifted by giants of the 15-a-side game such as Jonah Lomu, Lawrence Dallaglio and Mils Muliaina.

Nowadays teams of highly trained and motivated athletes play sevens in the IRB World Series and the Commonwealth Games. At the 2009 IOC Congress, the Olympic bigwigs voted to stage sevens at the 2016 games in Rio de Janeiro.

These events are of the pinnacle of the game but, thankfully, many tournaments retain the old amateur ethos of sevens where they are a pre-season or end-of-campaign excuse for an almighty drink-up for players and fans alike.

Get-togethers such as the Bournemouth Sevens attract hundreds of

SEVENS   WORLD SERIES

EDINBURGH · · LONDON   · HONG KONG   DUBAI ·   · USA   ADELAIDE · WELLINGTON ·   SOUTH AFRICA ·

teams, with many participants and supporters camping out in fields for three days of beers mixed up with a bit of fun rugby.

The Rosslyn Park Sevens sees more than 3,000 children playing the game, although with slightly less booze, has involved teams from Romania, Ukraine and Calcutta in recent times and given many stars of the future such as Dallaglio, Will Carling and Rob Andrew an early taste of tournament rugby.

The great Gareth Edwards turned out for the winners, Millfield, in the event in 1966 after turning down the chance to play for Wales Schools at Twickenham and says playing in the final is one of his best rugby memories.

Years before thousands of fans went on Lions tours or to Rugby World Cups they flocked to the Hong Kong Sevens for three days of general debauchery. Tokkie Smith, a South African and the chairman of the Hong Kong Rugby Football Union, and Ian Gow, an executive with a tobacco company, had the brainwave for the festival and on 28 March 1976 their dream was realized when 12 teams and 3,000 fans turned up for the event that was won by a team called Cantabrians who represented New Zealand. Nowadays the stadium is rocking with 40,000 fans every day.

The first Rugby World Cup Sevens was, appropriately, held at Murrayfield and won by the unfancied England side who in the true traditions of the game had only met up the week before and had only one practice match. Dallaglio recalls that they started the week by celebrating Damien Hopley's birthday where they 'well and truly

smashed the ice', were given the run around by Hawick in a training session the next day but went on to beat the Australia of Michael Lynagh and David Campese in the final.

The popularity of the shortened game snowballed in the 1990s and by the end of the decade the IRB decided to get involved in the lucrative sevens circuit by sanctioning the IRB World Series. This series now stretches to eight tournaments around the globe and has spawned a number of sevens specialists who never get to play in an 80-minute game.

There are compensations... Playing for seven minutes each way, getting plenty of ball and representing your country in locations such as Australia, South Africa, Hong Kong and Las Vegas takes some beating. Especially when your club mates are having their backsides royally kicked on a frosty Saturday afternoon at Bath or in a quagmire at Llanelli.

The IRB World Series Sevens is big business now. The London Sevens in 2010 drew over 78,000 spectators, with more than 1,000 dressed up as super heroes – another world record for the RFU – and the same year Premiership clubs participated in a pre-season sevens series in a bid to get fans into their grounds during the summer. If only Ned Haig knew what he was starting all those years ago in Melrose.

157

USA SEVENS

Tournament: USA Sevens
Stadium: Sam Boyd Stadium
Located: Las Vegas, United States
Address: 7000 E. Russell Road, Las Vegas, NV 89122
Phone: +1 702 895 4978 (stadium) or +1 888 784 2977 (ticket line)
Capacity: 36,800
To get there: 11 km (7 miles) from McCarran International Airport,
12 km (8 miles) from Las Vegas Strip
Tournament website: www.usasevens.com
Tournament email: sevens@usasevens.com
Past winners: 2004 Argentina; 2005 New Zealand; 2006 England; 2007 Fiji;
2008 New Zealand; 2009 Argentina; 2010 Samoa

ADELAIDE SEVENS

Tournament: Adelaide Sevens
Stadium: Adelaide Oval
Located: Adelaide, Australia
Address: War Memorial Drive, North Adelaide, SA 5006
Phone: +61 8 8300 3800 (stadium) or +61 8 7224 8150
(tournament enquiries)
Capacity: 32,000
To get there: Adelaide Station (train) 1.5 km (1 mile)
Tournament website: www.adelaidesevens.com.au
Tournament email: info@sarugby.com.au
Past winners: 2007 Fiji; 2008 South Africa; 2009 South Africa; 2010 Samoa

HONG KONG SEVENS

Tournament: Cathay Pacific/Credit Suisse Hong Kong Sevens
Stadium: Hong Kong Stadium
Located: Hong Kong
Address: 55 Eastern Hospital Road, So Kon Po, Causeway Bay, Hong Kong
Phone: +852 2 504 8311 (enquiries) or +852 3 128 8288 (tickets)
Capacity: 40,000
To get there: Causeway Bay Station (metro)
Tournament website: www.hksevens.com
Tournament email: info@hksevens.com or warrick.dent@hkrugby.com
Past winners: 2002 England; 2003 England; 2004 England; 2005 Fiji; 2006
England; 2007 Samoa; 2008 New Zealand; 2009 Fiji; 2010 Samoa

DUBAI SEVENS

Tournament: Emirates Airline Dubai Rugby Sevens
Stadium: The Sevens
Located: Dubai, UAE
Address: Al Ain Road, Dubai, UAE
Phone: +971 4 321 0008 (enquiries) or +971 4 4443459 (tickets)
Capacity: 50,000
To get there: Free buses from five Dubai locations (see website)
Tournament website: www.dubairugby7s.com
Tournament email: donal@promoseven.com
Past winners: (from 1999); 1999 New Zealand; 2000 New Zealand; 2001 No
winner; 2002 New Zealand; 2003 South Africa; 2004 England; 2005 England;
2006 South Africa; 2007 South Africa; 2008 South Africa; 2009 New Zealand

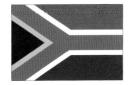

SOUTH AFRICA SEVENS

Tournament: Emirates Airline South Africa Sevens
Stadium: Outeniqua Park Stadium
Located: George, South Africa
Address: CJ Langenhoven Street, George 6529
Phone: +27 21 659 6720 (enquiries) or +27 83 915 8000 (tickets)
Capacity: 10,000
To get there: George Station (train)
Tournament website: www.sarugby.net/www.irb.com
Tournament email: steven@sarugby.co.za
Past winners: 1999 Fiji; 2000 New Zealand; 2001 New Zealand; 2002 Fiji; 2003 England; 2004 New Zealand; 2005 Fiji; 2006 New Zealand; 2007 New Zealand; 2008 South Africa; 2009 New Zealand

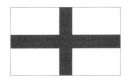

LONDON SEVENS

Tournament: Emirates Airline London Sevens
Stadium: Twickenham
Located: Twickenham, London
Address: Twickenham Stadium, Rugby Road, Twickenham TW1 1DZ
Phone: +44 208 831 6641 (enquiries) or +44 871 222 2017 (tickets)
Capacity: 82,000
To get there: 10-minute walk from Twickenham Station (train) or bus 267/281/H22 or free shuttle from Richmond (match days)
Tournament website: www.rfu.com/londonsevens
Tournament email: ChrisBurns@RFU.com
Past winners: 2001 New Zealand; 2002 New Zealand; 2003 England; 2004 England; 2005 South Africa; 2006 Fiji; 2007 New Zealand; 2008: Samoa; 2009 England; 2010 Australia

EDINBURGH SEVENS

Tournament: Emirates Airline Edinburgh Sevens
Stadium: Murrayfield Stadium
Located: Murrayfield, Edinburgh
Address: Roseburn Street, Edinburgh EH12 5PJ
Phone: +44 131 346 5078 (enquiries) or +44 131 346 5100 (tickets)
Capacity: 67,500
To get there: 15-minute walk from Haymarket Station (train) or buses 12, 16, 22, 26, 30, 31, 38
Tournament website: www.edinburgh7s.com
Tournament email: marianne.lee@sru.org.uk
Past winners: 2007 New Zealand; 2008 New Zealand; 2009 Fiji; 2010 Samoa

NEW ZEALAND SEVENS

Tournament: New Zealand International Sevens
Stadium: Westpac Stadium
Located: Wellington, New Zealand
Address: 147 Waterloo Quay, Wellington 6011, New Zealand
Phone: +64 4 389 0020 ext 704 (enquiries)
Capacity: 34,500
To get there: Five minute walk from Wellington Station (train) or shuttle from bus terminus
Tournament website: www.nzisevens.co.nz
Tournament email: steve.walters@WRFU.CO.NZ
Past winners: 2000 Fiji; 2001 Australia; 2002 South Africa; 2003 New Zealand; 2004 New Zealand; 2005 New Zealand; 2006 Fiji; 2007 Samoa; 2008 New Zealand; 2009 England

OTHER RUGBY COUNTRIES

Arabian Gulf
Arabian Golf RFU, The Players' Club, The
Sevens Rugby Ground, Al Ain Road, Dubai
PO Box 65785
Tel: +971 4 809 6652
Email: info@agrfu.com
Web: www.agrfu.com

Belgium
Federation Belge de Rugby, Avenue de
Marathon Laan 135c, Bte 5, 1020 Brussels
Tel: +32 2 479 93 32
E-mail: fbrb@rugby.be
Web: www.rugby.be

Brazil
Brasil Rugby, Escritório Administrativo, Rua
João Lourenço, 683 – Conjunto 21, Vila Nova
Conceição, Sao Paulo CEP 04508-031 Brazil
Tel: +55 11 2985 0008
Email: office@brasilrugby.com.br
Web: www.brasilrugby.com.br

Chile
Av Larrain 11.095, Interior Parque Mahuida,
La Reina, Santiago de Chile, Chile
Tel: +56 2784 0925
Email: feruchi@feruchi.cl
Web: www.feruchi.cl

Croatia
Trg Krešimira Cosica 11, Zagreb 10000 Croatia
Tel: +385 1 365 0250
Email: cro.rugby@rugby.hr
Web: www.rugby.hr

Czech Republic
Zátopkova 100/2, Praha 6-Strahov, Prague
16017 Czech Republic
Tel: +42 0 23335 1341
Email: rugby@cstv.cz
Web: www.rugbyunion.cz

Germany
Postfach 1566, Hanover D 30015, Germany
Tel: +49 5111 4763
Email: office@rugby-verband.de
Web: www.rugby.de

Hong Kong
Room 2001 Olympic House, 1 Stadium Path,
So Kon Po, Causeway Bay, Hong Kong
Tel: +852 2504 8311
Email: info@hkrugby.com
Web: www.hkrugby.com

Ivory Coast
Stade Félix Houphouët-Boigny, Plateau
Abidjan, 01 BP 2357 Ivory Coast
Tel: +225 2021 2083
Email: z_marcellin@yahoo.fr

Kazakhstan
Office 305, 85 A Dostyk Street, Almaty,
050010 Kazakhstan
Tel: +772 7261 0511
Email: kaz-rugby@mail.ru

Kenya
RFUEA Grounds, Ngong Road, PO Box 48322,
Nairobi 00100 Kenya
Tel: +254 20 325 8000
Email: inf@kenyarfu.com
Web: www.kenyarfu.com

Korea
Room 506 88 Oryn-Dong, Songpa-Gu Seoul
137-749, Korea
Tel: +822 420 4244
Email: rugby@sports.or.kr
Web: www.rugbysports.or.kr

Lithuania
Žemaites rue 6, Vilnius LT-3117 Lithuania
Tel: +370 5233 5474
Email: litrugby@takas.it
Web: www.litrugby.lt

Madagascar
Lot III M 39 Ambohijanahary ouest,
Antananarivo 101 Madagascar
Tel: +261 20222 5760
Email: fmr-rugby@moov.mg

Malta
Club House, Marsa Sports Complex, Aldo
Moro Road, Marsa, MRS 9064 Malta
Tel: +356 2122 1492
Email: secretary@mrfu.org
Web: www.maltarugby.com

Moldova
Str Columna 106, Chisinau 2012 Moldova
Tel: +373 2222 2674
Email: rugbymold@yahoo.com
Web: www.rugby.md

Morocco
Porte n°9 Complexe Sportif Mohamed V,
Maàrif - Casablanca, 20100 Morocco
Tel: +212 5229 48247
Email: frmr@menara.ma
Web: www.rugbymaroc.ma

Namibia
Lichtenstein Street, Olympia, Windhoek,
Namibia
Tel: +264 6125 1717
Email: nru@iway.na

Netherlands
PO Box 8811, Amsterdam 1006 JA
Netherlands
Tel: +312 0 480 8100
Email: info@rugby.nl
Web: www.rugby.nl

Papua New Guinea
PO Box 864, Port Moresby, National Capital
District 111 Papua New Guinea
Tel: +675 323 4212
Email: rugbypng@datec.net.pg

Above: *Papua New Guinea Chief Prime Minister Sir Michael Somare after the PNG*
Pukpuk's won the Oceania Cup in 2009 by beating the Cook Islands to reach the World
Cup qualifiers against Samoa.

Paraguay
Independencia Nacional, 250 casi Pdte.
Franco, Asuncion, Paraguay
Tel: +595 2149 6200
Email: info@urp.org
Web: www.urp.org.py

Poland
Ul. Marymoncka 34, Warsaw 01-813 Poland
Tel: +482 2835 3587
Email: poczta@pzrugby.pl
Web: www.pzrugby.pl

Portugal
Rua Julieta Ferrão no. 12 - 3o, Sala 303 Lisbon
1600-131 Portugal
Tel: +351 2179 91690
Email: geral@fpr.pt
Web: www.fpr.pt

Romania
B-dul Marasti 18-20, Sector 1 Bucharest
011468 Romania
Tel: +40 2 1224 5482
Email: frr@frr.ro
Web: www.frr.ro

Spain
C/ Ferraz, 16 – Cuarto Derecha, Madrid
28008 Spain
Tel: +349 1541 4978
Email: secretaria@ferugby.com
Web: www.ferugby.com

Sri Lanka
7c Reid Avenue, Colombo 00700 Sri Lanka
Tel: +94 11266 7321
Email: slrfuadmin@sltnet.lk
Web: www.srilankarugby.com

Sweden
Idrottens Hus, Stockholm 11473 Sweden
Tel: +468 996524/5
Email: info@rugby.se
Web: www.rugby.se

Trinidad & Tobago
PO Box 5090, Tragarete Road, Port of Spain,
Trinidad & Tobago
Tel: +868 628 9048
Email: contact@ttrfu.com
Web: www.ttrfu.com

Tunisia
BP 318, El Menzah, Tunis 1004 Tunisia
Tel: +2167 123 6088
Email: ftr.nbougattaya@gnet.tn

Uganda
PO Box 22108, Kampala, Uganda
Tel: +2567 1455 5702
Email: info@ugandarugby.com
Web: www.ugandarugby.com

Ukraine
11-B Ivana Mazepy Street, Kiev 01010
Ukraine
Tel: +380 4449 1413
Email: rugbyorggua@gmail.com
Web: www.rugby.org.ua

Uruguay
Ana Monterroso de Lavalleja 2045,
Montevideo 11200 Uruguay
Tel: +598 2 408 0048
Email: uru@uru
Web: www.uru.org.uy

Zimbabwe
PO Box 1129, Harare, Zimbabwe
Tel: +263 470 0283
Email: rugby2@mweb.co.zw
Web: www.zimbabwerugby.com